THREE YEARS WITH
GRANT

As Recalled by War Correspondent
SYLVANUS CADWALLADER

EDITED, AND WITH
AN INTRODUCTION AND NOTES, BY
BENJAMIN P. THOMAS

INTRODUCTION TO THE BISON BOOKS EDITION BY
BROOKS D. SIMPSON

University of Nebraska Press • Lincoln

© 1955 by Benjamin P. Thomas. © renewed 1983 by Salome K. Thomas. Published by arrangement with Alfred A. Knopf, Inc. Introduction to the Bison Books Edition © 1996 by the University of Nebraska Press
All rights reserved
Manufactured in the United States of America

♾ The paper in this book meets the minimum requirements of American National Standard for Information Sciences—Permanence of Paper for Printed Library Materials, ANSI Z39.48-1984.

First Bison Books printing: 1996
Most recent printing indicated by the last digit below:
10   9   8   7   6   5   4   3   2   1

Library of Congress Cataloging-in-Publication Data
Cadwallader, Sylvanus, 1825 or 26
Three years with Grant / as recalled by war correspondent Sylvanus Cadwallader; edited, and with an introduction and notes, by Benjamin P. Thomas; introduction to the Bison Books edition by Brooks D. Simpson.
p.   cm.
Includes bibliographical references and index.
ISBN 0-8032-6369-4 (pa.: alk. paper)
1. United States—History—Civil War, 1861–1865—Campaigns.
2. Grant, Ulysses S. (Ulysses Simpson), 1822–1885.   3. Cadwallader, Sylvanus, 1825 or 26.   4. United States—History—Civil War, 1861–1865—Personal narratives.   5. War correspondents—United States—Biography.   I. Thomas, Benjamin Platt, 1902–1956.   II. Title.
E470.C14   1997
973.7'3'092—dc20
96-30286   CIP

Introduction to the Bison Books Edition

Brooks D. Simpson

Although Ulysses S. Grant and William T. Sherman agreed on many things, they disagreed over the best way to handle the press. Sherman's feuds with reporters became legendary: he termed them "the most contemptible race of men that exist, cowardly, cringing, hanging around and gathering their material out of the most polluted sources." Upon hearing that several correspondents had reportedly perished when a steamboat exploded, he snapped back that there would be news from hell by breakfast. George G. Meade also battled critical correspondents: one aide noted that he "will not even speak to any person connected with the press." Other commanders cultivated reporters. After Shiloh, several generals complained to Henry W. Halleck that their colleagues, as Sherman put it, "kept in their camps paid men of the press, to pick up items to write themselves up and their Rivals down." William S. Rosecrans sought to promote his career at Grant's expense by feeding stories to a Cincinnati scribe.[1]

If Grant despised Rosecrans's activities (indeed, they led to a breach between the two men), he also rejected Sherman's response. He knew that it was better to handle the press than to battle it. The press shaped public perceptions of the progress of the war; in turn political leaders consulted both newspaper editors and public opinion—that always elusive concept—in making their decisions. An American general had to work within these conditions: Grant learned to do so skillfully. "General Grant informs us correspondents that he will willingly facilitate us in obtaining all information," one reporter told his editor; however, Grant was "not very communicative."[2]

This was not to say that Grant did not have his troubles with the press. Like Sherman and Meade, he had been victimized by unfair reporting; he was especially sensitive to attacks on his performance at Shiloh. "I do not look much at the papers now," he told his wife nearly three weeks after the battle, and "consequently save myself much uncomfortable feeling." Although he remarked that the best way to deal with them was to ignore them, he finally admitted: "I have been so shockingly abused that I sometimes think it is almost time to defend myself." The attacks pained him, "for I have a father, mother, wife & children who read them and are distressed by them." Sherman watched as his friend suffered. Once Grant "himself thoughtlessly used the press to give him eclat in Illinois," he observed; now his rivals had come close to "pulling him down" through the press.[3]

It was in the wake of this experience that Sylvanus Cadwallader arrived at Grant's headquarters in the fall of 1862 to secure the release of a reporter for the *Chicago Times* imprisoned for issuing a false report. Cadwallader stayed on as a special correspondent for the *Times*, that city's leading Democratic paper. Suddenly Grant and his staff saw a way to improve the general's standing in the press. The editor of the *Chicago Tribune*, Joseph Medill, had long been a friend of Congressman Elihu B. Washburne, Grant's staunch supporter. Nevertheless, Medill had often expressed reservations about Grant's generalship and politics. It might do some good to secure support elsewhere. Thus when Cadwallader published an account critical of the behavior of one of Grant's regiments, the general did not object, much to the reporter's surprise and relief. Later, Grant rescinded an order banding distribution of the *Times* throughout his command, leading Medill to complain that Grant was a "copperhead" who "openly encourages the dissemination of secession and treason in his army."[4]

In turn, Cadwallader became something more than a reporter. He informed Grant of enemy movements during the battle of

Champion's Hill; once he actually took Confederates prisoner. After joining the *New York Herald* he offered favorable coverage of Grant's campaigns in Virginia; when it looked as if Cadwallader was going to be drafted in September 1864, several staff officers praised his services to *Herald* editor James G. Bennett. Grant told Cadwallader that he had "stuck to the legitimate duties assigned to you, i.e., reported facts without giving political bearing" without playing favorites: "Had your course been pursued by all the profession from the start much of the mortification felt by many would have been avoided and all would have been received as friends and not, as often happens, as something to be dreaded and avoided." However, Cadwallader managed to avoid service by hiring a substitute—a black man. When he boasted of this to Grant, the general replied, "Perhaps the army profited by the exchange."[5]

Cadwallader remained a chief character at headquarters, "a whole souled, affable gentleman who carried with him quite a store of the optimism of life which he shed around him." He did not abuse the privileges he had, and he did not betray confidences. He was present at Appomattox and sketched the McLean house as Grant and Lee met inside (the sketch survives in his papers). The connection between the general and the reporter continued for a year after the war. Cadwallader accompanied the general when he joined Andrew Johnson on the infamous "Swing Around the Circle" in August and September 1866, noting the general's growing disillusionment with Johnson. He also observed the general under the weather, perhaps because of excessive drinking, during the journey from Buffalo to Cleveland—an incident that sparked much rumor. Then the two men drifted apart.[6]

The publication of Grant's *Memoirs* rekindled Cadwallader's interest in his Civil War experiences. Believing that Grant had unjustly slighted John A. Rawlins, his chief of staff, by minimizing his importance as an officer and a friend, Cadwallader—who had christened his own son Rawlins—sought to set things straight. In this crusade he found friends in Charles A. Dana and James H. Wilson. First as a War Department envoy and later as assistant secretary of war, Dana had forged a close relationship with Grant, as had Wilson, who served on his staff (1862–64) before becoming a cavalry commander. In 1868 the two men had collaborated on a campaign biography of Grant, but grew disenchanted with their hero during his presidency. Grant had failed to gratify Dana's ambitions for office; he broke with Wilson when Wilson's brother Bluford proved all too enthusiastic in his efforts to assist Secretary of the Treasury Benjamin Bristow in investigating the Whiskey Ring. One of the targets of Bristow's investigation was Orville Babcock, Grant's private secretary (and a former staff officer and West Point classmate of James Wilson); Wilson himself raised questions about the behavior of another of Grant's former staff officers, Horace Porter (who had also been with Wilson at West Point).

Both Dana and Wilson agreed that Grant had slighted Rawlins; Wilson in particular seemed bent on some sort of personal vendetta against his former chief. "Grant was great enough to have the whole truth known about him," he told Cadwallader, and he was determined to tell the truth. In this endeavor they were joined by two other men: William F. Smith, who claimed that he had seen Grant intoxicated several times, and who attributed his own removal from command in 1864 to Benjamin F. Butler's blackmailing Grant about a reported spree; and Henry Van Ness Boynton, who had made a career out of attacking Grant and other generals associated with the Army of the Tennessee (notably Sherman) in order to boost the reputation of his beloved Army of the Cumberland.[7] Together these five men did a great deal to damage Ulysses S. Grant's reputation. They swapped information and leaked it to others. Wilson wrote biographies of Dana, Smith, and Rawlins in which he inserted anti-Grant material, once citing Cadwallader as a source. Each man had his own purposes to serve and his own axes to grind, especially Wilson, who grew increasingly bitter over the years about his relationship to Grant.[8]

News soon leaked out that Cadwallader was preparing a book about his experiences with Grant. Either because he was ignorant of Cadwallader's sentiments or because he wanted to tell him that he knew what he was up to, Grant's son, Fred, told Cadwallader that he was looking forward to the book; Porter spoke highly of Cadwallader to others. However, Cadwallader chose to share his writings with Wilson, who reviewed the manuscript before drawing upon it.[9]

The major reason Cadwallader sought to write about Grant was to remind people of the role John A. Rawlins played in Grant's life. "Rawlins was the power behind Grant, greater even than Grant himself," he insisted. Nowhere was this more evident than in Rawlins's role in shielding Grant from alcohol: "Later on it was no secret that any staff officer who offered the General a glass of liquor, or drank with him, or in any way whatever connived at his taking so much as a single drink, would be disgracefully dismissed and actually degraded in rank."[10] Thus Cadwallader was more than a little disingenuous when he prefaced his account of perhaps the most famous Grant drinking story by claiming that he did so to counter stories that sought to elevate Rawlins at Grant's expense— for in fact he believed that Rawlins must be restored to his rightful place at Grant's side. He decided to reveal the details of Grant's trip to Satartia, Mississippi, during the Vicksburg campaign in order "to set at rest the conflicting statements which at various times had been published about Gen. Grant's habits." The account also served to explain Cadwallader's privileged status at Grant's headquarters: former correspondent Franc Wilkie alluded to the incident and its aftermath in his memoir of his war experiences.[11]

Cadwallader's manuscript remained unpublished for nearly seventy years. Only a few historians were aware of its existence. When it appeared in print for the first time with the publication of *Three Years with Grant* in 1955 (and an excerpt in the October 1955 issue of *American Heritage*), the story of the Satartia expedition sparked immense controversy. Earl S. Miers and Louis Starr had already incorporated the still-unpublished account in their recently published books; Paul Angle asserted that "the essential truth of Cadwallader's account cannot be argued away." Before his death, Lloyd Lewis examined the Cadwallader manuscript and termed it "highly valuable," especially in its detailed description of a "roaring drunk" Grant. Shelby Foote swallowed the story whole (although he muddled it by trying to reconcile the details with Charles A. Dana's account of the trip to Satartia); so did William McFeely, who concluded that "little about the story, including [Cadwallader's] claim to have been aboard, fails to make sense, unless one is flatly determined to refuse to believe that Ulysses Grant was ever drunk." Both Foote and McFeely claimed that Cadwallader, Dana, and others engaged in a cover-up of the incident, which is particularly amusing in light of the fact that *they* brought it to light after Grant's death.[12]

Grant's grandson, Ulysses S. Grant III, exploded when he heard of Cadwallader's book, especially over the "quite outrageous and imaginary account" of Grant's drinking during the Vicksburg campaign. Several historians rejected the story or questioned essential components. Kenneth P. Williams's denunciation of Cadwallader's entire manuscript erred on the side of excess, for subsequent research has negated a good number of his criticisms. His careful untangling of the accounts of what happened on the Yazoo, however, highlights several contradictions among them and casts doubt upon several historians' renderings of the incident. Bruce Catton, who at first had been inclined to accept stories of Grant's drinking, concluded that Cadwallader's story was "but one more in the dreary Grant-was-drunk garland of myths."[13]

What happened?

Satartia, Mississippi, is on the east bank of the Yazoo River, about fifty miles northeast of Grant's headquarters outside Vicksburg. It became a point of interest to Grant soon after he commenced siege operations against Vicksburg. He knew that Confederate commander Joseph E. Johnston was gathering a force in central Mississippi; he worried that Johnston would use it to attempt to lift the siege by threatening Grant's lines. In late May, he ordered an expedition to devastate the countryside in order to deprive a relief column of forage; at the same time he called for reinforcements to protect his rear. On 2 June he decided to concentrate forces at Mechanicsburg, three miles east of Satartia, to fend off a relief expedition. Two days later he learned that Johnston was indeed advancing toward that area, and had occupied Yazoo City, thirty miles northeast of Satartia.[14]

On 5 June Nathan Kimball, in charge of Union forces around Mechanicsburg, decided to withdraw southward after learning of the Confederate occupation of Yazoo City. Unaware of this, Grant decided to see things for himself. Along with a small escort, he rode to Haynes's Bluff, some fifteen miles north of his headquarters, where he hoped to commandeer a steamer. With him was Charles A. Dana, a special agent of the War Department. Ostensibly sent west by Secretary of War Edwin M. Stanton to inspect the paymaster services in various commands, Dana was really checking out Grant. Aware of Dana's covert purposes, Grant had welcomed him at headquarters and seized the opportunity to improve his standing with the authorities at Washington. In this he had proven highly successful: Dana's telegrams praised his generalship and countered rumors of ineptitude.

Grant was understandably anxious about the security of his lines. He was also under the weather. On 31 May he was sufficiently ill to complain of it to William T. Sherman. Perhaps this was at the root of whatever happened on the Yazoo—if indeed anything happened—for Sherman's medical director, seeing Grant's condition, offered him a glass of wine. The general accepted it; after all, alcohol was a traditional remedy for pain, and Grant had used it before. Whatever relief it offered was temporary: on the evening of 5 June, Rawlins thought that Grant was so ill that he should have been in bed.

But Rawlins was also concerned about the presence of alcohol at headquarters. On 5 June he had come across a box of wine in front of Grant's tent. He wanted to move it, only to learn that Grant was saving it to share with friends when they celebrated the fall of Vicksburg. That night, when Rawlins encountered Grant, the general was "where the wine bottle has just been emptied, in company with those who drink and urge you to do likewise," despite the general's poor health. The chief of staff interpreted Grant's "lack of your usual promptness of decision and clearness in expressing yourself" as signs that perhaps Grant had helped empty the wine bottle. It was just a suspicion, but it was a deeply troubling one, and so Rawlins retired to his tent to compose a letter warning his friend to stay away from alcohol.[15]

It was an ailing general who boarded a steamer at Haynes's Bluff on 6 June. "Grant was ill and went to bed soon after he started," Dana recalled. The steamer made its way along the Yazoo until it encountered a pair of gunboats two miles from Satartia. The gunboat commanders reported Kimball's withdrawal, adding that Satartia was no longer secure and that Grant should turn back. Dana awakened the general. Too ill to digest the news, Grant told Dana to decide what to do; Dana decided to return to Haynes's Bluff. The next morning, Grant "came out to breakfast fresh as a rose, clean shirt and all, quite himself," only to suppose that they were at Satartia. Dana corrected him. Grant, still determined to find out what was going on, ordered cavalry to Mechanicsbug to report on Johnston's movements. At this request, Dana accompanied the detachment.[16]

Cadwallader claimed that he had gone to Satartia on 5 June aboard the steamer *Diligent*, and left it on 6 June. This is entirely possible: perhaps a dispatch for the *Chicago Times* bearing the dateline of Satartia, 6 June, 10 PM, was from Cadwallader. But what comes next cannot be reconciled with Dana's account. Cadwallader asserts that Grant switched boats to the *Diligent*, whereas Dana says nothing of the kind. According to Cadwallader, Grant began drinking on the *Diligent as it continued on its way to Satartia*, and the journalist offers a rather detailed description that had no counterpart in Dana's account. Moreover, he claims that the *Diligent* actually docked at Satartia, and that he (and not Dana) took charge of making sure that Grant returned on the steamer to Haynes's Bluff. Cadwallader's account does not mention Dana; Dana's account does not mention Cadwallader, although, in light of the description Cadwallader gives of the trip, it would have been hard to miss the reporter.[17]

So much for the events of 6 June. On 7 June, Grant sent a cavalry detachment to Mechanicsburg. Dana accompanied it (a fact not mentioned by Cadwallader); one must wonder why Dana would have left Grant's side had the general been in mid-binge. For Grant, according to Cadwallader, secured more liquor and awaited the return of the escort (although, in Dana's account, the expedition headed to Grant's headquarters at Vicksburg, arriving 8 June). Upon the escort's return, according to Cadwallader, Grant ordered the steamer to go to Chickasaw Bluffs; Cadwallader succeeded only in delaying the trip so that Grant arrived at dusk. Grant continued drinking aboard a sutler's boat (the sutler in question, Washington Graham, had known Grant in Galena). The general then mounted an aide's horse and dashed off into the woods. Cadwallader followed, caught up with the general, induced him to dismount, and then secured an ambulance for a return trip to headquarters, arriving at midnight.

Once again the stories of Dana and Cadwallader do not mesh:

aside from offering a completely different account of the activities of the cavalry escort, Dana says nothing about the matters described in such loving detail by Cadwallader. Other pieces of evidence contradict each other. James H. Wilson confided to his diary on 7 June, "Genl. G. intoxicated" (although he would have had to compose the entry on 8 June, for Grant did not arrive until midnight). Wilson did not witness the events Cadwallader described, but learned about them later; in fact, he told Hamlin Garland that he never actually saw Grant drink. Moreover, it is difficult to reconcile Cadwallader's story with a postscript Rawlins added to his letter of 6 June, stating that his "admonitions were heeded, and all went well." As he gave the letter to Grant on 6 June, it is difficult to believe that Rawlins could say this had he known of what Cadwallader claimed happened on 6 and 7 June—and Cadwallader made it clear that he had told Rawlins everything. Nevertheless, according to Benjamin Thomas, others also testified as to the essential accuracy of Cadwallader's story, although he failed to include this material in *Three Years With Grant*.[18]

What is one to make of all this? Despite superficial similarities, the Dana and Cadwallader accounts do not reinforce each other. Rather, they contradict each other in telling ways. To argue, as McFeely does, that "little about [Cadwallader's] story, including his claim to have been aboard, fails to make sense," is akin to making sure that the facts don't get in the way of a good story. In later years Cadwallader, Dana, and Wilson corresponded in a futile effort to reconcile these differences. Dana flatly denied that Cadwallader was present; Cadwallader then sought to salvage his story by asserting that Grant made two trips to Satartia, although it is clear that such was not the case. Other contradictions were equally obvious. Dana clearly recalled that Rawlins handed Grant his letter of 6 June before the general boarded the dispatch boat; Cadwallader later insisted that Rawlins composed the letter upon Grant's return.[19] Wilson endorsed Cadwallader's belief that there were two expeditions to Satartia as the best way to reconcile the conflicting reports, although his own typescript of his private journal during the Vicksburg campaign confirmed Dana's statement that Grant never made it to Satartia, and that he returned with the gunboats. Moreover, he concurred with Grenville Dodge's declaration "that on any important occasion, no matter when, as officer or civilian, Grant was absolutely abstemious."[20]

Moreover, Dana offered two accounts that contradicted each other. The version most often quoted by historians appeared in his 1898 *Recollections*, ghostwritten by Ida Tarbell: it mentioned nothing about drinking. In contrast, in 1887 Dana claimed that Grant was indeed "as stupidly drunk as the immortal nature of man would allow" on the steamer bound for Satartia. In this account, Grant pocketed Rawlins's letter, then took "an excursion up the Yazoo River"; he had chosen a "dull period in the campaign" to tie one on. The next day "he came out fresh as a rose" (recall the account in Dana's *Recollections*) "without any trace or indication of the spree he had passed through." Nothing was said about Grant's supposed continued drinking on 7 June or about a wild ride through the woods. According to Dana, when Grant drank, "he always chose a time when the gratification of his appetite for drink would not interfere with any important movement that had to be directed or attended to by him." However, as he well knew, Grant was on no pleasure excursion that day; indeed, he was involved in securing his rear lines. If we are to accept the 1887 version, then Grant got drunk on duty in such a way as to endanger not only his own life but also the security of the men under his command—and Dana, a representative from the War Department instructed to report such matters, betrayed his orders and covered it up.[21]

The documentary record flatly contradicts this image of a jaunt designed to break up boredom. Grant was not on some sort of lark during a lull in the action: he was on an important inspection trip to safeguard his position. Accompanying him was a man detailed to his headquarters in part to report back to Washington about his personal habits. To argue that Grant saw this trip as an opportunity to down a few drinks strains credulity. To accept Dana's story is to suggest either that Grant could not control his drinking (although the 1887 account makes it clear that the general timed his sprees) or that he did it almost as an act of defiance or contempt toward Dana, as if the campaign itself had proven his indispensability—for, after all, he had asked Dana to come along.

If one cannot thus accept the story Cadwallader tells, it does not follow that nothing happened on the trip to Satartia. Exactly what occurred remains a mystery. One reasonable supposition links Grant's illness with that tried and true remedy of a stiff drink. In a draft of his Rawlins biography, Wilson lent credence to this interpretation when he wrote that Grant "fell sick, and thinking a drink of spirits would do him good, took one with the usual unhappy result."[22] Perhaps this would explain both the stories of intoxication with Dana's decision not to report the incident to Washington, for what he had witnessed was not a binge but an accident. In contrast, Cadwallader's account strikes one as a tall tale told to impress others, a story hard to reconcile with the available evidence.

It is unfortunate that Cadwallader's story of the so-called Yazoo bender has come to dominate impressions of *Three Years with Grant*, for the book proves valuable in other ways. It confirms several other accounts of Grant's actions during the war, and in areas adds valuable information about Grant's generalship. For example, Cadwallader contradicts accounts that at the battle of Chattanooga Grant merely intended the Army of the Cumberland to take the rifle pits at the base of Missionary Ridge, for while Grant's initial orders were limited to that immediate objective, Grant's intention was to reform the assault columns and then send them onward and upward; the men simply anticipated his desires. He offers an illuminating examination of how war correspondents operated and how generals treated the press. Finally, he presents an intimate portrait of Grant and the men around him. Nevertheless, as Cadwallader himself acknowledged, it was not enough. He never got inside Grant. "Notwithstanding my long and intimate acquaintance with him I was obliged to acknowledge to myself that I did not quite know, nor wholly understood his character," he admitted. "There was always something in him withheld or kept back."[23]

NOTES

1. Michael Fellman, *Citizen Sherman* (New York, 1995), 126; Theodore Lyman, *With Grant and Meade from The Wilderness to Appomattox* (Lincoln, 1994 [1922; originally *Meade's Headquarters, 1863–1865*]), 359; William T. Sherman to Ellen Ewing Sherman, 6 June 1862, Sherman Family Papers, University of Notre Dame.

2. T. Harry Williams, *McClellan, Sherman, and Grant* (New Brunswick, 1962), 101.

3. Ulysses S. Grant to Julia Dent Grant, 25 April and 11 May 1862, *The Papers of Ulysses S. Grant*, ed. John Y. Simon, et al. (20 vols. to date: Carbondale, 1967–), 5:72, 116 [hereafter PUSG]; Grant to Elihu B. Washburne, 14 May 1862, ibid., 5:119; William T. Sherman to Ellen Ewing Sherman, 6 June 1862, Sherman Family Papers, University of Notre Dame.

4. Brooks D. Simpson, *Let Us Have Peace: Ulysses S. Grant and the Politics of War and Reconstruction, 1861–1868* (Chapel Hill, 1991), 37.

5. Frederick T. Dent, Ely S. Parker, and George K. Leet to James G. Bennett, 22 September 1864; Adam Badeau to Bennett, 23 September 1864; and Orville E. Babcock to Bennett, 24 September 1864, Cadwallader Papers, Library of Congress; Grant to Cadwallader, 23 September 1864, ibid.; John Y. Simon and David L. Wilson, eds., "Samuel L. Beckwith: 'Grant's Shadow,' " in Wilson and Simon, eds., *Ulysses S. Grant: Essays and Documents* (Carbondale, 1981), 123–24.

6. Simon and Wilson, "Beckwith," 123.

7. James H. Wilson to Sylvanus Cadwallader, 13 February 1887, Cadwallader Papers, Library of Congress.

8. James H. Wilson to Sylvanus Cadwallader, 22 February 1887, Cadwallader Papers, Library of Congress.

9. Frederick D. Grant to Sylvanus Cadwallader, 19 March 1896, and Horace Porter to C. A. Woodruff, 17 December 1890, Cadwallader Papers, Library of Congress; Cadwallader to James H. Wilson, 21 June 1897, Wilson Papers, Library of Congress.

10. *St. Louis Globe Democrat*, 11 February 1887, clipping in Cadwallader Papers, Library of Congress. Had this been true, then it follows that a good number of stories about Grant's drinking could not be true, for they involved the connivance of members of his staff or other people around headquarters. Even Horace Porter testified that after a hard day in the field Grant joined his staff "in taking a whisky toddy in the evening." Horace Porter, *Campaigning with Grant* (1897), 215.

11. Franc B. Wilkie, *Pen and Powder* (Boston, 1888), 205–9.

12. Paul M. Angle, introduction to Charles A. Dana, *Recollections of the Civil War* (New York, 1963 [1898]), 9; *Letters from Lloyd Lewis*, ed. Robert Maynard Hutchins (Boston, 1950), 15–16; Shelby Foote, *The Civil War: A Narrative* (3 vols.: New York, 1958–74), 2:416–21; William S. McFeely, *Grant: A Biography* (New York, 1981), 132–34. Richard Wheeler incorporated it in *The Siege of Vicksburg* (New York, 1978), 203–5; so did Samuel Carter III in *The Final Fortress: The Campaign for Vicksburg, 1862–1863* (New York, 1980), 245–46, and Jerry Korn, *War on the Missis-*

sippi: Grant's Vicksburg Campaign (Alexandria, 1985), 143–46, where it is embellished with a photograph of Grant's liquor cabinet. Comparing the descriptions of the jaunt in these several accounts provides an interesting study in textual analysis, not least because of the variations between the accounts and their efforts to overcome (or overlook) contradictions in the source material. Readers should use Dan Bauer's "The Big Bender" (*Civil War Times Illustrated* 27 (December 1988), 34–43, with great care, as it consists in good part of close paraphrases of other scholars' work.

13. Ulysses S. Grant III, "Civil War: Fact and Fiction," *Civil War History* 2 (June 1956), 29–40; Kenneth P. Williams, *Lincoln Finds a General* (5 vols.: New York, 1949–1959), 4:439–51; Bruce Catton, *Grant Moves South* (Boston, 1960), 464. Catton's role in the controversy is especially interesting. He had agreed to finish Lloyd Lewis's multivolume Grant biography after Lewis's death; Lewis, who had come across Cadwallader's manuscript, had accepted the story at face value. He had sanctioned the publication of the excerpt of *Three Years with Grant* in *American Heritage*; only later did he come to deny its veracity.

14. Grant to Stephen A. Hurlbut, 31 May 1863, *PUSG*; 8:297–98; Grant to David D. Porter, 2 June 1863, ibid., 8:299; Grant to Joseph A. Mower, 2 June 1863, ibid., 8:301; William T. Sherman to Grant, 2 June 1863, ibid., 8:300;

15. John A. Rawlins to Grant, 6 June 1863, *PUSG* 8:322–23. The heading of the letter indicates that it was written at 1:00 AM. Thomas erroneously notes that the letter was written on 8 June (page 110, note 3).

16. Charles A. Dana, *Recollections of the Civil War* (New York, 1963 [1898]), 90–91. Thomas's note on page 105 inaccurately renders Dana's account, claiming that Dana reported that the vessel reached Satartia.

17. Dana was quite explicit in denying that Grant switched vessels: "We came back with the same steamboat that we started with, arrived at Haines' Bluff in the night, and the General went back to his headquarters in the forenoon." This statement also casts doubt on Cadwallader's description of events on 7 June. Dana to James H. Wilson, 18 January 1890, Cadwallader Papers, Library of Congress.

18 *PUSG*, 8:323–25, contains a selection of pertinent material; Wilson is quoted in Hamlin Garland's research notes, Garland Papers, University of Southern California. Thomas's claim appeared in an exchange with Kenneth P. Williams in *American Heritage* 7 (August 1956), 106–11.

19. Cadwallader to Wilson, 31 August 1904, Wilson Papers, Library of Congress.

20. McFeely, *Grant*, 133; Vicksburg Journal Typescript (6 June 1863)

47, Wilson Papers, Library of Congress; Grenville Dodge to James H. Wilson, 4 November 1904, and Wilson to Dodge, 8 November 1904, and 17 February 1905, Wilson Papers, Library of Congress.

    21. *New York Sun*, 28 January 1887.

    22. Draft of Rawlins biography, 118, Wilson Papers, Library of Congress.

    23. Cadwallader to Wilson, 18 February 1887, Wilson Papers, Library of Congress.

ERRATA AND ANNOTATION TO BENJAMIN THOMAS'S NOTES

page 41	Cadwallader is referring to an incident at Collierville, Tennessee, where a Confederate force assailed Sherman and a small escort on 11 October 1863.
page 105	In 1890 Dana denied that Cadwallader was present on the Satartia excursion. Dana to James H. Wilson, 18 January 1890, Cadwallader Papers, Library of Congress.
page 110	In fact, Rawlins's letter to Grant was dated 6 June 1863—the day Grant *left* for Satartia. Thus Thomas is incorrect in assuming that Rawlins composed the letter upon Grant's return; moreover, the letter does not mention the trip to Satartia, which it doubtless would have if Cadwallader's story is true. Thomas insisted that the letter was misdated in a letter to *American Heritage* published in August 1956.
page 117	Grant visited Banks at New Orleans during the first week of September 1863; he fell from his horse 4 September.
pages 195–96	In fact, Wing's report covered only the action of 5 May.
page 255	Thomas's annotation is erroneous. Badeau did not revise the latter part of Grant's *Memoirs*; by that time Grant had severed relations with him. Grant composed the majority of the second half of that book (as an editor's note makes clear) after he fell seriously ill in April 1885; on 5 May he informed Badeau that their agreement was terminated. Badeau's suit for compensation was for the original amount agreed upon; he did not claim that he wrote the *Memoirs*, although his claims of assistance far exceeded his actual contribution.

Badeau first mentioned Rawlins's last-minute effort to head off Sherman's march in the third volume of *The Military History of Ulysses S. Grant* (page 157), and offers an explanation of the correspondence between Grant, Sherman, and the authorities at Washington that is consistent with the documentary record. Grant told Mark Twain of Rawlins's opposition during a visit at the end of April 1885. See *Mark Twain's Autobiography*, ed. Albert Bigelow Paine (2 vols.: New York, 1924), 2:145.

page 263   Sholes was most likely captured on 25 August 1864, when the 36th Wisconsin of the Army of the Potomac's Second Corps was heavily engaged at Reams's Station.

page 285   By early 1865 Ferrero was no longer with the Ninth Corps, but instead was with the Army of the James.

page 329   Grant and Lee did not sit at the same table. The table where Lee sat is in the Chicago Historical Society; the table Grant used is at the Smithsonian Institution.

Editor's Introduction

THE train slowed to a jerking stop beside the grimy depot at Jackson, Tennessee, and among the passengers who tumbled from the wooden cars into the dust and din and bustle of the Union Army base was a slim, nervous civilian in an odd fur cap, with a seamed and swarthy countenance and darting, restless eyes. His credentials bore the name Sylvanus Cadwallader, and identified him further as a war correspondent for the *Chicago Times*. Additionally, however, he had a secret mission.

Thirty-six years old when he arrived at the little town where General Grant had established his headquarters, Cadwallader had been born and educated in Ohio. Married to Mary I. Paul, a native of Vermont, and father of one child, a daughter, he had moved in his early thirties to Kenosha, Wisconsin, to edit a small newspaper. Then he and his brother-in-law, Edward A. Paul, bought the *Milwaukee Daily News*. Until the death of Stephen A. Douglas in 1861, Cadwallader had been a Douglas Democrat.[1]

Cadwallader was serving as city editor of the *Daily News*

---

[1] Census Returns, 1860. National Archives; George L. Dodge to B. F. Butler, August 30, 1865, Benjamin F. Butler Papers, Library of Congress.

when he received an urgent message from the owners of the *Chicago Times*. Their star reporter, Warren P. Isham, who had been assigned to cover Grant's movements, had overstepped his privileges and been shipped off to a military prison. Desperate for news from the Western army, the owners of the *Times* implored Cadwallader to undertake the formidable assignment of obtaining a personal interview with Grant and persuading him to order Isham's release.

Many persons regarded the *Times* as a malignant Copperhead sheet, and Cadwallader himself commented that it "delighted in seeing how near it could approach the line of disloyalty without incurring the penalty." He accepted the mission, however, and performed it without undue difficulty; but meanwhile he had manifested such singular talents as an on-the-spot reporter that he continued to serve in that capacity until the end of the war.

On arriving at Jackson, Cadwallader appraised the war correspondents assembled there as an ignominious lot. Some of them were not above "writing up" an officer in return for favors or money. Others eavesdropped around headquarters to obtain confidential information. Some vented personal spite against officers in the guise of news. Finding their conceit and arrogance insufferable, Cadwallader determined to keep aloof from them and to conduct himself with such dignity and circumspection as to gain the confidence of the military men whom he met in the course of his duties. As time passed, the scoundrels and incompetents among his colleagues were weeded out, and by the end of the war Cadwallader and others like him had elevated the war correspondent to an honored rank in journalism. In so doing, they gave the American press new power and prestige.

More than that, in keeping the American people informed of

what went on at the front, they effected a revolution in American journalism. For by the war's end the newspaper was no longer chiefly an organ of editorial opinion. News had become all-important. And the press, assuming the obligation of keeping the electorate informed, had become an indispensable adjunct of the democratic process.

As morale-builders, the war correspondents played a part in winning the war. "No people," Louis M. Starr has pointed out, "were ever more tightly bound by a sense of shared experience than the millions who read the dispatches. The underlying sense of solidarity prevailed over divisive factors, periods of black despair, peace sentiment, Copperheadism, because the day's news, however unsatisfactory, always whetted hope for the morrow." [2]

Franc B. Wilkie, a leading correspondent for the *New York Times*, granted that Cadwallader became the most capable of all the correspondents. Untiring in the pursuit of news, "he was not diverted in his search by fatigue, danger, or any other obstacle." [3] But diligence, courage, and resourcefulness were not enough to account for Cadwallader's unparalleled success in obtaining information, and for his ability to communicate it to his paper when other correspondents found their efforts unavailing. It became evident that Cadwallader enjoyed a favored status at army headquarters; according to rumor, he had gained it by helping a high-ranking officer out of a bad scrape. After the war, Wilkie wrote a book in which he referred to this incident and added: "I will not give the name of the high officer, but will only say that he was one in whom General Grant had a wonderful personal interest." [4] Now, from Cadwal-

---

[2] Louis M. Starr: *Bohemian Brigade* (New York, 1954), pp. 349–51.
[3] Franc B. Wilkie: *Pen and Powder* (Boston, 1888), p. 203.
[4] Ibid., p. 205.

lader's reminiscences, we learn the full details of the escapade and discover that the "high officer" was General Grant himself. And we also learn the measure of Grant's gratitude and how much it meant to Cadwallader.

A pass from Grant enabled the reporter to go anywhere he chose. Quartermasters were ordered to furnish him with transportation. He could draw subsistence from the commissaries. He was allowed to send off dispatches in Grant's official mail pouch. His tent was always pitched near Grant's; he messed with the members of Grant's staff; he was allowed to use staff horses. But Cadwallader won and kept his advantageous position by respecting confidences; his reminiscences contain information that he withheld from his dispatches.

Cadwallader remained with Grant all through the Union operations in southern Tennessee and northern Mississippi. Once he was captured in attempting to take news reports to Memphis for transmittal to the North, but talked his way out of the difficulty. He witnessed Grant's advance on Vicksburg and the investment of that citadel, though he was absent when it surrendered. Cadwallader states complacently but truthfully that during these operations the *Time's* coverage of news from Grant's army was "early, complete, and greatly superior to that of any competitor."

During the siege of Vicksburg, James Gordon Bennett, the enterprising editor of the *New York Herald,* learning of Cadwallader's superior talent or superior facilities for getting news, persuaded the reporter, for a consideration, to furnish him with information, not for publication, but for Bennett's eye alone. By this time Cadwallader had become convinced that Grant had no equal as a general, and his letters to Bennett were no doubt instrumental in obtaining for Grant the unwavering support of the *Herald* which never ceased until Grant became President.[5]

Cadwallader followed Grant to Chattanooga and covered the Chattanooga campaign for the *Times* while continuing to send confidential reports to Bennett. But field service sapped his strength, and when Grant went east to take command of all the Union armies in March 1864, Cadwallader resolved to return to Milwaukee, where his brother-in-law needed his help in editing the *Daily News*. Cadwallader severed his connection with the *Times,* but when Bennett learned of his intentions he took immediate action to keep him in the field. Frederic Hudson, manager of the *Herald,* summoned Cadwallader from Milwaukee to an imperative conference in New York. When the Army of the Potomac crossed the Rapidan River and began its advance on Richmond, Cadwallader was back at Grant's headquarters as special correspondent for the *Herald.*

Trying to make his way to Washington with full reports of the Battle of the Wilderness, and with a complete list of casualties, Cadwallader was captured for the second time. The Confederates took him for a general officer and refused to let him go, but he finally escaped by bribing a guard. His performance earned him a promotion: he was made the *Herald's* correspondent-in-chief, in which capacity he directed a staff of a dozen or more reporters. Bennett was determined to surpass all rivals both in news-coverage and in prestige, and Cadwallader was instructed to equip himself with the best horse he could buy, to procure a professional cook from Willard's Hotel, and to keep open house for distinguished visitors at the *Herald's*

---

[5] Unfortunately the James Gordon Bennett Papers in the Library of Congress contain only two relatively unimportant letters from Cadwallader.

field headquarters. He had a large tent for a reception room and another for a dining-room, with an old plantation darky in a white jacket to welcome visitors. Cadwallader felt certain that the *Herald's* ample outlay was more than repaid in good-will.

No paper excelled the *Herald* in its coverage of the Army of the Potomac as Cadwallader directed the far-flung operations of his corps of correspondents and saw to it that their dispatches went forward promptly to New York. When the military censors banned the use of the telegraph for press reports, Cadwallader organized a relay system of private messengers. Shuttling back and forth between City Point and New York City by boat and rail, they got the news to the *Herald's* office in something less than thirty-six hours. Each messenger was provided with a pass signed by Grant; Secretary of War Stanton had ordered that no other passes should be honored.

Again Cadwallader's intimacy with Grant and his staff became the subject of comment. Colonel Theodore Lyman wrote that "at Grant's headquarters, there is a fellow named Cadwallader . . . and you see the Lieutenant General's staff officers calling, 'Oh, Cad; come here a minute!' " [6]

Living close to Grant from October 1862 until the end came at Appomattox, Cadwallader was one of the few men—certainly the only civilian—who had a clear view of how the Civil War was fought at the command level. He observed many Union officers at close range: Sherman, Sheridan, Logan, Wallace, Thomas, Butler, Rawlins, Warren, Meade, and others. He appraises their military talents candidly; he describes their traits and habits.

Above all, Cadwallader gives us a superb picture of Grant;

---

[6] George Agassiz, ed., *Meade's Headquarters, 1863–1865: Letters of Colonel Theodore Lyman* (Boston, 1922), p. 359.

or, more accurately, a mosaic: little bits, pieces, and tidbits thrown in here and there, often when he is writing about something else. These pieces combine neatly to form a graphic pattern, and he binds them all together at the end with an edifying summary of Grant's character. Cadwallader probably settles once and for all the question of Grant and liquor. He treats the matter frankly, but with fairness and objectivity. And no one was better qualified to tell about it.

Cadwallader depicts Grant in the heat of battle, and Grant relaxing with his friends. Describing Grant's relations with his generals, he reveals him as a surprisingly good diplomat in army politics. We learn that Grant thought more highly of Sheridan than of Sherman, and we learn the reasons why. Accompanying Grant as he pursues Lee after the evacuation of Richmond, Cadwallader brings us the excitement of the last days of the war and finally allows us to sit in on the surrender at Appomattox.

Through Cadwallader's eyes we see Lincoln stopped by a sentry when he comes ambling into camp alone one day by a back way. Cadwallader describes Lincoln swapping yarns with officers, and takes us with him to the cabin of the *River Queen* when he goes there to acquaint Lincoln with the latest news from the front. He also describes Mrs. Lincoln at City Point, sorely trying her husband's patience. And throughout the narrative we watch Cadwallader and his fellow newsmen making journalistic history as they unfold the daily panorama of the war for persons throughout the Union.

Cadwallader, a man almost forgotten, emerges as a memorable character. Stolid, overweening, with the perseverance of a bulldog and the combativeness of a terrier, he never hesitates to tangle with an officer, no matter what his rank. A superb reporter and a born journalist, he must also have been a rankling thorn of a puzzling new type in the side of the military. If he did not "scoop" his rivals as often as he takes credit for, he did it frequently. And, more often than not, he did it, not by reason of his favored position, but through sheer determination and ingenuity. His methods of achieving news beats are shrewd and sometimes humorous.

After the war Cadwallader became head of the *Herald*'s Washington news bureau and lived with General Rawlins, Grant's chief-of-staff, in Georgetown until he brought his wife from Milwaukee to join him. In 1866 the Cadwalladers had a son, whom they named Rawlins. In 1868 the family returned to Milwaukee, where a third child, a daughter, was born.[7] From 1874 to 1878 Cadwallader was an assistant secretary of state in Madison, where he had charge of the working force dealing with insurance, the land office, and the auditor's accounts. Some time in the eighties he moved to Springfield, Missouri. Occasionally he wrote articles on various phases of the war for newspapers.[8] Various writers on the Civil War consulted him, and he claimed that he supplied most of the anecdotes about Grant in Albert D. Richardson's *A Personal History of U. S. Grant*.[9]

Cadwallader lived in San Diego, California, for several years, then moved to Fall River Mills, Shasta County, in the northern part of that state. In that remote little settlement, hundreds of miles from a library, where it would seem that he made his living as a sheep-raiser, he wrote his reminiscences, aided only by such books as he possessed, a file of the *New York Herald*, and letters he had written to his wife during the war. But

---

[7] Census Returns, 1870, copies in the Wisconsin Historical Society.

[8] See, for example, the *St. Louis Globe-Democrat*, Feb. 10, 1887; the *Milwaukee Sunday Telegram*, Sept. 2, 1888.

[9] Hartford, Conn., and Newark, N.J., 1868.

he had a retentive memory and made few major errors, though he slipped occasionally in spelling names. He finished the manuscript in 1896, when he was seventy years old. General James H. Wilson read it, made a few minor suggestions, and vouched for its accuracy. But it was never published. A number of years ago it was acquired by the Illinois State Historical Library. Not more than a half-dozen living persons have read it.

Notwithstanding the color and originality of Cadwallader's narrative, a great deal of editing has been necessary to make it suitable for publication. The part dealing with Cadwallader's newspaper activities after the Civil War is episodic and disjointed. To have included it would have destroyed the unity of the book, so it has been left out altogether. Cadwallader sometimes wandered off into the trite and trivial. He retold happenings that he had not seen but only read about. He interjected accounts of this or that person's post-war career. He repeated occasional passages, sometimes word for word. Thus, even that portion of the manuscript here printed has been severely pruned, deletions being indicated by the usual ellipses. All told, well over a third of the original manuscript has been excluded in order to make this book primarily an eyewitness account.

The wording of Cadwallader's text has been scrupulously respected, but deletions have made it necessary to change his chapter divisions. I have also split up Cadwallader's paragraphs, some of which ran on interminably. Names of persons have been left as he wrote them, with additions and corrections indicated by brackets when first mentioned; thereafter, however, the addition or correction has been made by me, whenever necessary, without the use of brackets. In three or four other instances I have helped him with his spelling, and I have frequently used commas in place of the semicolons for which he displayed an inordinate fondness. Where it seemed necessary to make editorial insertions to keep the story moving smoothly or to make it understandable, italic type has been used. Cadwallader titled his manuscript *Four Years with Grant*. I have subtracted one year for the sake of accuracy. Specialists desiring meticulous information of one sort or another may wish to consult the original manuscript; but if my editorial labors have not been misdirected, the text as here presented should be more enjoyable and more enlightening than the original to readers generally.

I am deeply grateful to Alfred W. Stern and Clarence P. McClelland, trustees of the Illinois State Historical Library, for permission to publish the manuscript. E. B. Long, editor of the *Personal Memoirs of U. S. Grant* (Cleveland and New York, 1952), has drawn on his vast knowledge of the Civil War to make many valuable editorial suggestions; and I also wish to express my thanks for aid of one sort or another to Harry E. Pratt, Illinois State Historian; Margaret Flint, reference librarian of the Illinois State Historical Library; Clifford L. Lord and Margaret Gleason, of the Wisconsin Historical Society; Margaret Scriven, of the Chicago Historical Society; Ruth A. Presleigh, county clerk of Shasta County, California, and her deputy, Ruth Sweigert; Earl S. Miers, Robert V. Bruce, Louis Starr, Edmund Crozier, Ralph G. Newman, and Neva B. Deffenbaugh. The editorial suggestions of Joseph M. Fox, of Alfred A. Knopf, Inc., have been of great assistance. My daughter, Martha Thomas, made her first venture into historical research by drawing rough sketches from which some of the maps were prepared. And ever ready with encouragement has been my wife.

BENJAMIN P. THOMAS

Springfield, Illinois

MAPS

THREE YEARS WITH
GRANT

CHAPTER

One

DURING the forepart of 1862 I was city editor of the *Milwaukee Daily News*, badly broken down in health, and seeking some less exhausting occupation. The following Special Order from Gen. Grant commanding the Department of the Tennessee, to Gen. Sherman, commanding the District of Memphis, afforded me the first opportunity for doing so:

Major General W. T. Sherman, commanding United States forces, Memphis, Tennessee.

August 8th 1862.

General:—Herewith I send you an article credited to the Memphis correspondent of the Chicago Times, *which is both false in fact and mischievous in character. You will have the author arrested and sent to the Alton Penitentiary, under proper escort, for confinement until the close of the war, unless sooner discharged by competent authority.*

I am very respectfully
 Your Obedient Servant.
  U. S. Grant,
   Major General, &C.

The correspondent alluded to was Mr. [Warren P.] Isham, a brother to the wife of Wilbur F. Storey, the great editor of the Chicago *Times*. He had been a writer for the *Times*, and upon the breaking out of hostilities was sent to the field as a war correspondent. The *Times* had an immense circulation in the armies of the south-west and was very sensational in character. It delighted in seeing how near it could approach the line of actual disloyalty without incurring the penalty. Mr. Isham was considered one of the most brilliant correspondents in that department, but was never sufficiently careful and guarded in his statements. He had been cautioned by General Grant once or twice before this against giving such free range to his imagination. This last offense was that of sending off for publication a "cock and bull" story about a fleet of rebel iron-clads at Pensacola, which he claimed to have received by "grape-vine" telegraph through the Southern Confederacy.

Neither Grant nor Sherman were given to subterfuges, and the text of the order bears evidence that neither of them, at that date, were positive that Isham was the author of the article complained of. But it was a dragnet that soon had him in its meshes.

The order could not have been placed in the hands of a more willing officer in the department. Gen. Sherman had been treated harshly and unfairly by the "jingo" press of the whole north, for a year previous. Because he had predicted a long and bloody war, and declared that hundreds of thousands of troops would be required to end it, he was ridiculed in northern newspapers, and finally pronounced "crazy." This exasperated him greatly, and embittered him against war correspondents till the rebellion was ended. The arrest and punishment of Isham was to him a labor of love. . . .

About the middle of October 1862 I received at my home in Milwaukee, the following telegram:

"Can you go to the army of the Tennessee for us?" signed Storey & Worden.[1]

I replied: "Yes."

The second dispatch of same date inquired: "When?"

To which I answered: "Immediately."

"Come to Chicago by the first train," was the final dispatch for that day.

On arriving at the *Times* office I was put in possession of the facts concerning Isham's arrest and imprisonment, and informed that the object of my trip would be to secure his release, if possible. I had never seen either Storey or Worden till then; knew nothing of Mr. Isham but what I learned from them in this conversation; had no acquaintance either with Gen. Grant or any member of his staff; and at first objected to the undertaking. The interview ended, however, in my starting at once for Jackson, Tennessee, where Gen. Grant's headquarters then were, as a duly accredited correspondent of the *Times*, to avoid betraying the chief object I had in view.

Before leaving Chicago Messrs. Storey & Worden supplied me with scores of letters from influential men of the state of all shades of political opinion, asking for Isham's release from prison. Armed with these and a letter of credit from the firm, I boarded a morning train for Cairo. The cars were crowded with officers returning to the army from furloughs and hospitals, every one of whom professed more or less acquaintance with Grant, Sherman, [William S.] Rosecrans, [John A.] McClernand, [Lewis] Lew Wallace, and the long list of western generals coming into prominence. They also professed to know the minute details of every skirmish, battle or campaign which

---

[1] Storey and Ananias Worden were co-owners of the *Times*.

had occurred in Tennessee. They could tell just how, when and why each successive step had been taken—its origin, consummation or abandonment.

I was naturally interested, and a good listener. It happened frequently that some staid old farmer who had one or more sons at the front, but knew nothing himself about marches and battles, was considerably mystified by what seemed to him such contradictory accounts of the same affair, but the voluble, rollicking narrative of the last speaker generally dimmed the recollection of its predecessors. As all united in affirming what everyone wished to hear—that the valor of our troops had never been equalled on earth—every listener was charitably inclined to make allowance for discrepancies. "He might have slipped a leetle in his recollection, you see. But, twas a mighty entertainin story, now wasnt it?"

The scribe kept his countenance serene, passed from group to group, expressly disclaimed knowing anything about the matters under discussion, and seemed to give such credence to the statements of others, that he was soon voted a good fellow. He was also given an immense amount of valuable, inside, information—"all in confidence you know"—about men and measures, by officers and privates. These confidential communications revealed the following facts: "Grant was used up at Belmont—he was drunk all day—his troops were driven from the field—[Maj. Gen. Benjamin M.] Prentiss of Illinois had been sacrificed at Shiloh—McClernand was the coming man, perhaps—Lew Wallace had few equals, perhaps no superiors—Rosecrans was the most brilliant officer in the west—Sherman was crazy—but Grant; well, he just now commanded a department; he never did amount to anything, and never would; he had been kicked out of the United States Army once, and would be again; he was nothing but a drunken, wooden-headed tanner, that would not trouble the country very long, &c, &c."

It was manifest that most of the talkers were from the Army of the Cumberland, under Rosecrans. Others were from Crawfordsville, Indiana, where Lew Wallace raised the 11th regiment of Indiana Volunteer Infantry.

A curious phase of those times was that in public opinion wisdom was vouchsafed to soldiers in exact proportion to the number of wounds each received in battle. Zack Chandler's [2] theory that bloodletting must precede a satisfactory settlement of the war was being verified. A knowledge of grand strategy and statesmanship, of tactics and political economy, of squad drill and foreign diplomacy, was superabundant in every convalescent hospital. There could be no wisdom found to plan or execute equal to that of the "stretcher and ambulance." The dullest private whose scalp had been furrowed by a minnie ball had a prescriptive right to be heard in preference to the hosts of unwounded. To him who had been twice or thrice wounded, however slightly, was conceded a superiority over his comrades that can be but faintly understood at the present day. These Sir Oracles were often bigoted, despotic, and ignorant, but the nation loved to bow down to them, and make parade of such subserviency. Veterans were not common then, but a sorrowful abundance soon followed.

But night came on. Officers and privates mainly reclined on blankets and knapsacks and wandered away in broken dreams. When within a few miles of Cairo, a couple of officers at the forward end of the car I was in got into a violent wrangle about the respective merits of Grant and Rosecrans, which gradually attracted everybody's attention. I was at the

---

[2] Zachariah Chandler, United States Senator and Republican boss of Michigan.

back end of the car and noticed that a small, dark complexioned, quiet, unobtrusive man sitting opposite to me was an eager listener to the dispute in front. He kept edging forward, a seat at a time, as he had opportunity, and was soon near the noisy champions of the armies of the Tennessee and Cumberland. The Rosecrans man repeated all the stereotyped accusations against Grant so much in vogue at the time, and asserted many of them to be true from his own knowledge; told how shamefully Grant had behaved at Shiloh; [3] and finally silenced, if he did not convince, his opponent.

At this juncture my little, bilious fellow-passenger arose, stepped in front of the man who professed to have such damaging knowledge of Gen. Grant, and quietly asked the gentleman his name. The latter replied pompously that he was Capt. Blank of an Ohio regiment, giving its number.

"You seem to know all about the battle of Shiloh," continued the little bilious questioner.

"I have a right to know," replied the Captain, bracing up, "I went through it from beginning to end."

The two men stood confronting each other in silence, the Captain considerably nettled by the manner of the questioner; the latter stony and cadaverous in expression, but emitting a torrent of scorn, wrath and hate from his glittering eyes. The little game-cock commenced deliberately again:

"I am always willing to overlook and forgive misstatements about men and events—"

"But I am not mistaken about what happened, and what came under my own observation," hotly replied the Captain.

"—but," continued the little one, "when a man pretending to

---

[3] Grant allegedly was negligent in ignoring the order of Gen. Henry W. Halleck to entrench when in the presence of the enemy and in allowing himself to be surprised.

be a gentleman, and an officer, makes slanderous charges against a friend of mine; claims to have witnessed what I know never occurred; and to have heard orders which I know were never given, I intend to clinch his lies on the spot. You are a liar I know. You are a coward, I believe. I'll bet ten to one you were not in the battle of Shiloh."

The Captain sprang to his feet and began to bluster and threaten to fight. Some of his comrades urged him to defend his honor by throwing his assailant head foremost through the car window. Every one in the car crowded forward. Till then but two men had avowed themselves for Gen. Grant. But the audacity of the smaller man, and his determined defense of an absent friend against all odds, struck a responsive chord in most of those present. A general roar of shouts, yells and guffaws burst from all.

The Captain saw the tide was against him and wisely adopted the role of discretion at fearful expense to his valor. He demanded the small man's name, blustered and swore fearfully, but committed no breach of the peace.

"My name is of no consequence," the small man replied to all questioners. "If I must get into a public row, I prefer to do so unknown."

The fitful glare of the single lamp in the car revealed a small gold cord down the outside seam of his trousers, and beyond this there was nothing in his dress or appearance to denote rank or service. Just then the train ran into Cairo, and in the confusion of a night change from car to steamboat, I lost sight of both men. Two days after this the small man was introduced to me as Lieut. Theodore S. Bowers, Judge Advocate on the staff of Gen. Grant. . . .[4]

---

[4] Bowers, at this time thirty years old, was an aide to Grant. Always passionately devoted to him, he became one of that small intimate group

On arriving at Jackson, Tenn., I consumed twenty-four hours in deciding upon some systematic line of procedure to obtain Mr. Isham's release. I was supplied with more letters and petitions uniting in the request, than such a person as Gen. Grant could ever be induced to examine. I soon decided to not unmask this budget of correspondence at present, and to make any future use of it depend upon conditions and circumstances which should arise later on.

I was first of all (to outward appearance at least) a correspondent of the Chicago *Times*. To maintain this character I must visit Gen. Grant's Headquarters and obtain permission to remain within the military lines of his Department, with authority to pass from place to place as an army correspondent. So assuming a confidence very much beyond what I really felt, I presented myself to Major [John Aaron] Rawlins [Grant's adjutant general] and handed him my letter of credence from Storey and Worden. He was ceremoniously polite—altogether too polite and formal I felt, to promise well for the chief mission on which I had been sent. After a few commonplace remarks concerning newspapers and war-correspondents in gen-

---

of officers which Grant kept with him throughout the war, and rose to the rank of lieutenant-colonel. He was killed by falling under the wheels of a train when returning from a visit to West Point with Grant in 1866. Cadwallader stated: "Incidents and anecdotes revealing Col. Bowers' character crowd on my mind by dozens, one of which I cannot forbear mentioning. . . . While sitting idly at headquarters one evening after the Surrender of Vicksburg discussing the probable time of the paymaster's next visit, Bowers drew from his pocket a five cent piece fractional currency and declared that was all that kept him out of bankruptcy. After a general laughter at his exhibit, Gen. Grant tossed him a silver twenty-five cent piece, saying: 'Here's a stake, Jo.' Beyond a joke nothing was thought of it at the time. But Bowers had Grant's words engraved on the coin and carried it as a pocket piece as long as he lived. He would sometimes exhibit it modestly to intimate friends in his sentimental moods; view and handle it carefully and tenderly; and treasured it as the apple of his eye."

eral, Major Rawlins relieved himself from the burden of my further entertainment, by politely and formally introducing me to such members of the staff as were present.

At that time nearly all army correspondents were in bad odor at all army headquarters, and were always secretly held to be a species of nuisance that needed abating. In many cases official hostility was openly expressed, and hindrances put in their way as to collecting and transmitting army news. This unfriendliness was especially prevalent among "West Pointers" and U.S.A. officers. The war was half over before Gen. Sherman could forbear being rude, if not positively insulting, to every correspondent with whom he was thrown in contact, unless the individual came into his presence bearing the unqualified indorsement of some of the general's influential friends, and studiously kept the nature of his avocation in the background.

Candor compels the admission that as a class, the first instalment of correspondents sent to the armies deserved no high rank in public or official estimation. Some unduly magnified their importance as the representatives of leading metropolitan daily newspapers. Some were so lacking in conventional politeness as to make themselves positively disagreeable wherever they went. Others were base enough to make merchandise of personal mentions in their correspondence. Others almost unblushingly took the contract of "writing up" some Colonel to a Brigadier Generalship, for a specified consideration in dollars. And still others were sufficiently ignoble to fasten themselves upon some Colonel or Brigadier, and pay their bills, whiskey bills and horse hire, by fulsome and undeserved praise of their patrons and protectors in every communication sent back for publication.

There was also still another class, more despisable if possible than those already mentioned, who would purloin papers and orders, hang around officers' tents secretly at night hoping to overhear conversation that could be used by their papers. . . . A small proportion only of the whole number possessed the rudimentary qualifications of common honesty, tact, and the ability to discriminate between legitimate and illegitimate news from the seat of war. In the end, "the survival of the fittest" corrected all this. At the close of the war, good standing at Army headquarters equalled a patent of nobility.

In view of this status of army correspondents, I resolved upon an entirely new line of procedure. This was first to sustain my own self respect and secondly, to so govern my intercourse with military men in the Dept. as to deserve theirs. I decided to procure my own outfit, to ride my own horses and pay my own expenses liberally rather than parsimoniously. That if the exigencies of the service required me to enter a military "mess," to pay my full *pro-rata* share of all its expenses and to accept no hospitalities on any other conditions. I also decided to make all calls at Regimental, Brigade, Division, Corps & Army headquarters rather formal than otherwise at the outset; to make them brief, and never to allow them to interrupt official business.

My calls at Army h.d.q. were therefore regular and very short ones. I simply inquired if there was any news suitable for publication that they were at liberty to give me; asked for copies of special or general orders; and bowed myself out at once. I never allowed myself to hang around as if to gather news by eavesdropping on official conversations, and never presumed to take a seat without urgent invitation. It was not long before I began to observe the effect of this conduct in more cordial receptions and more extended conversations.

In the meantime I had made the acquaintance of Col. Thomas Lyle Dickey, then chief of cavalry in that Dept., from Ottawa, Ill. I was surprised to find him a son of the Rev. Wm. Dickey of Bloomington, Ohio; a nephew of Rev. James [Henry] Dickey [5] for many years pastor of the Presbyterian church at South Salem, Ross Co., Ohio; and nephew also to Mr. James Dean of the same place with whose family I was intimately acquainted while at the Academy there. He was surprised and pleased to make the personal acquaintance of one so often mentioned in correspondence between himself and his relations. We had many mutual acquaintances and friends which led to intimacy and friendship between ourselves.

This seemed to open a way for my approaching General Grant upon the real object of my mission to his headquarters. So inviting Col. Dickey to dine with me I made him my confidant; exhibited my petitions, letters, &c.; and said to him frankly that were I in Gen. Grant's place I would never read such a mass of matter. The facts were simply these: Isham had been imprisoned for misbehavior; the *Times* did not question the propriety of his imprisonment, and admitted Gen. Grant's right to decide what was fit matter for newspaper publication concerning military affairs within his Department. Mr. Isham's friends asked for his release solely on the grounds that he had been sufficiently punished. His family needed his earnings for its support and were then dependent on others for their daily subsistence. If, as the *Times* believed, Gen. Grant's only desire was to stop literary buccaneering in his army by making an ex-

---

[5] Dickey's first name was Theophilus, not Thomas. He was a lawyer and Democratic politician, and the son, not the nephew, of James Henry Dickey.

ample of some representative man, it had certainly been accomplished by Mr. Isham's incarceration which must convince all concerned that such conduct as his would not be tolerated.

Col. Dickey agreed with all of this and was pleased to learn that the *Times* took a reasonable view of the matter. It was arranged between us that I was to keep all these letters and petitions in my own custody until he had an opportunity of presenting the case to the general. This occurred the next day when on a ride to Gen. [John A.] Logan's headquarters, Dickey introduced the subject to Grant. The latter inquired how long Isham had been in the Alton Military Prison and on learning that it was two or three months, admitted it to be a severe discipline for the offense. A staff officer was sent northward the next day charged with the duty of releasing Isham from custody.

The boundaries of the District of West Tennessee left in Grant's command by the departure of Halleck for Washington City, July 17th, 1862,[6] was only defined by the Mississippi river on the west, the Ohio and Tennessee rivers on the north and east, and reached indefinitely South and Southeast. By an order of the War Department, October 28, 1862,[7] Grant was formally placed in command of what was thenceforth called the Department of the Tennessee. The troops under his command after the second battle of Corinth, fought September 4th, 1862,[8] were substantially the three corps commanded respectively by Gens. Charles S. Hamilton, William T. Sherman and James B. McPherson, with department headquarters at Jackson, Tenn. . . .

---

[6] Henry Wager Halleck had been appointed military adviser to President Lincoln and general-in-chief on July 11, 1862.

[7] The appointment was made on October 25.

[8] The Second Battle of Corinth occurred on October 3 and 4, 1862.

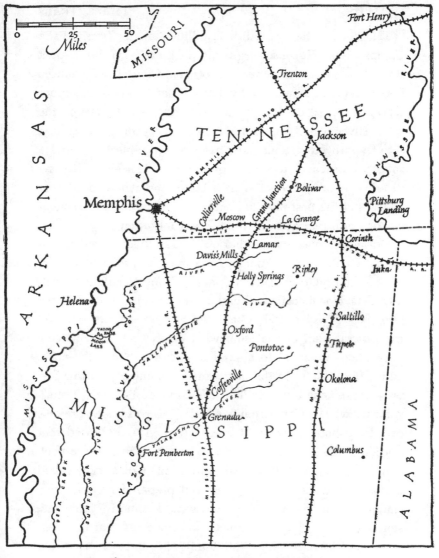

GRANT'S OPERATIONS IN SOUTHERN TENNESSEE
AND NORTHERN MISSISSIPPI

Taking advantage of a lull in military affairs I visited the
Camps of all Wisconsin regiments in these corps, and spent
several days at the headquarters of Gen. Charles S. Hamilton.
He always entertained royally, but on that occasion the dinner
service equalled the bill of fare. He had elegant ware on the
table, silver plated knives and forks, some good glass ware, a
set of approved champagne glasses, white table linen, and a
smart "contraband" to wait upon the mess. It seemed like civilization to be seated at such a table, and when the dinner
ended and the post-prandial chat was stimulated by excellent
cigars, mud, rain and "hardtack" was forgotten. . . .

During the pleasant weather of Sept. and Oct. all the troops
in that Dept. were recuperated in camp, furnished with commissary and quartermaster supplies, paid up to date, all available detachments called in, and a general consolidation of the
army accomplished. Gen. Grant had in the meantime outlined
the general plan of that somewhat celebrated "Tallahatchie
Expedition" intended to approach Vicksburg from the north
and east by land. As the last formal preliminary to this forward movement Gen. McPherson's corps at Bolivar, [Tenn.],
was reviewed by Gen. Grant and staff. This was the first review
of a large body of troops I ever witnessed and showed that
portion of the army to be in superb condition in every respect.

A day or two after this, (Nov. 3rd, 1862) Col. Dickey called
me aside and inquired if I was well prepared for an active
campaign. He pointed to a car, with locomotive attached,
standing on a switch, and quietly informed me that the General would leave for the front 35 miles beyond Bolivar within
an hour, and said that if I would board the car, asking no
questions, none would be asked me. The guards evidently had
their instructions for they allowed me to pass. On the train
Dickey advised me to stop at Bolivar, procure a mount and

outfit, and be ready for an early start in the morning; and said that Grant and staff would return from the extreme front to Bolivar before midnight. I acted upon the advice, ordered a very early breakfast at the hotel, naming the hour, and went to bed.

Upon going into the dining room for my breakfast next morning, (Nov 4th) as ordered, I was surprised to find Grant & staff already at theirs. The only vacant seat was at the side of the Gen. who seeing my hesitancy and confusion kindly bade me be seated with the remark that "no apologies were needed," and the conversation went on without interruption. Col. Wm. S. Hillyer of the staff, and afterward provost marshal of the Dept. of the Tennessee, was telling a string of practical jokes which had recently been played upon the 124th Ills. Regt. that had arrived a few days before.

It seems the 124th came down to Bolivar in all the pride and circumstance of war. They were newly enlisted men, had never seen a day's service, could not be formed in a straight line in an hour, but had new tents, new arms, a full band, trunks full of clothing, and most of the comforts of home life. The old "vets" in camp pounced upon the new comers at once, and victimized them unmercifully every day. When a detachment of the 124th was sent out for forage they naturally brought in chickens, turkeys, ducks, geese, pigs, sheep, butter, eggs, vegetables and such other delicacies as they could find. The "vets" surrounded them on their return, tried them before a pretended court-martial, confiscated most of the choice edibles, fined them for a breach of military discipline, and as Hillyer told the story, actually collected these fines! Finally a night or two before this the "vets" made an organized and well planned raid upon the sleeping members of the new regiment, stole the tents from over the heads of nearly half of

them, and actually got away with them without waking a man
or an officer. Hillyer was a brilliant conversationalist, a capital
story teller, and had us all in uproarious laughter till breakfast ended. . . .

Our horses were at the hotel door before breakfast was finished, and the general, staff and escort were soon in the saddle
following the army. The ride was a leisurely one most of the
day. Gen. Grant usually rode alone at the head of the cavalcade, but occasionally an officer would dash up to his side and
ride with him for a mile or two. The staff rode in couples
without much regard to rank. During the forenoon I was in
some way thrown by the general's side for a half hour, and had
my first conversation with him on military affairs. This was
necessarily brief, and only amounted to the information that
our destination was La Grange as a base for the present. We
talked longer of Illinois horses, hogs, cattle, and farming than
of the business actually in hand. It was Grant's habit, as I afterward learned, to divert conversation into side channels when
desiring relief from official business, or not wishing to impart
information.

He rode that day his somewhat celebrated clay-bank stallion
"Jack," which he purchased at Galena with borrowed money
when he was in desperate straits to raise enough to equip himself as Colonel of the 21st Illinois Volunteer Infantry. While
riding by his side I saw the first of the only two manifestations
of temper he ever exhibited in my presence. An orderly came
dashing up with a dispatch and carelessly rode on to Jack's
heels. Grant turned in his saddle and rebuked him sharply,
saying there were few things he disliked more than to have a
careless rider run onto his horse's heels. The other occasion
was during the second day of fighting at the Wilderness when
Aides and Staff Officers came thronging to headquarters bring-

ing the news that Gen. Lee was turning his right flank under
Gen. [John] Sedgwick, and rapidly getting into our rear. These
repeated messages of what seemed to the Union officers the
beginning of disaster and defeat provoked him to say in sharp
terms, that "While Gen. Lee was getting into our rear we certainly ought to be able to get in the rear of Gen. Lee." In other
words he was willing then and there to change fronts with the
Confederates and stake the fortunes of the contest on one decisive battle.

We followed the cavalry into La Grange in the evening of
that day and established headquarters in a comfortable dwelling house near the center of the village. . . . We remained at
La Grange several weeks owing to delays in receiving expected reinforcements, and repairing railroads.

Our knowledge of the country between La Grange and
Holly Springs was quite limited; and the strength of the enemy which held and over-ran the intervening territory, was
also an unknown quantity. Ample preparations for all emer-
gencies must be made. Gen. Sherman was sent to Memphis to
command that district and repair the Memphis & Charleston
R.R. as far east as La Grange. He was also to reorganize all
newly recruited regiments, and all convalescents fit for duty,
and have a column of troops ready to cooperate with the main
army when it should start southward from La Grange.

During the march from Bolivar to La Grange, stragglers
from McPherson's corps were often scattered over the country
for miles on each side of the line of march, and were frequently lawless and destructive. In addition to plundering
houses of food, clothing, silverware and jewelry, they in several instances applied the torch to everything combustible on
large plantations, and left smouldering ruins behind them. On
one occasion Gen. Grant dispatched an officer to the scene of

these outrages to find and arrest the guilty parties if possible, but his mission proved unsuccessful.

Gen. Hamilton's command behaved even worse than Mc-Pherson's. Its line of march from Corinth to Grand Junction was marked nearly every mile of the way by burnt buildings and fences, and was literally shown by clouds of smoke in daylight and pillars of fire by night. It had an immense concourse of camp followers who stole horses, mules and vehicles along the route for their own transportation, and robbed houses of everything they fancied. Many infantry regiments had scores of animals loaded with mess stores usually carried in haversacks, and with the arms and accoutrements of the men in the ranks. In one of my first letters from La Grange to the *Times,* I stated the facts fully, and commented on them freely.

After the letter was dispatched I began to reflect seriously upon the consequences to myself. Gen. Grant might be as greatly displeased with me as he had been with my predecessor, Mr. Isham. Subordinate officers were reasonably sure to be offended by my statements, brand them as "another batch of copperhead lies," in that "copperhead newspaper, the Chicago *Times.*" A dozen lively quarrels with regimental commanders seemed inevitable, and I wished the letter unwritten, or that I had at least modified some of its strongest invectives.

I waited for the return of my communication in print with some anxiety, and seized the first paper containing it to see how it actually appeared in the after light of cooler reflection. To my consternation it was even more hot and vindictive than I remembered to have written. Yet there it was as it came from cold type, and no escape from my responsibility was possible.

I had only a week before obtained permission from Major Rawlins to have my mail matter sent to me at headquarters in his care. My letter in the *Times* made me hesitate twenty-four hours before calling on him for my mail, but I ventured into the Adjutant's office after dark one evening, hoping to escape particular observation. As I passed the open door to Gen. Grant's room on my way out, he beckoned to me to come in, and began turning over a mass of newspapers on his table till he found the *Times*. Pointing to my letter in it he said he supposed I wrote it. I said that I did. He then went on to say that the troops had behaved shamefully on the march, in violation of general orders, (copies of which he handed me), but that he was powerless to do more at the time to prevent it, that such unsoldierly conduct could not be stopped without the hearty cooperation of regimental officers—that he could not stop the march of his army to establish courts of inquiry and courts-martial—that if he caught a soldier engaged in such acts of vandalism, he should feel very much inclined to have him shot on short notice—he said my strictures were just, and fully deserved—and that if I never wrote more untruthfully than this, he and I would never have any difficulty concerning my correspondence.

He also stated that he was engrossed with his own affairs and responsibilities and should not attempt any censorship over letters and dispatches from his department in advance of their publication. The newspapers and their employees must determine what to publish, and what to withhold, and that he should make correspondents personally accountable by sending them out of the lines if they sent off improper dispatches concerning real or fictitious affairs. He furthermore volunteered this important information: That all correspondents from his department would be accorded full liberty at all times to state as fully as they pleased, all the facts and details of any army operations already completed; but they could not be safely allowed to publish any predictions as to what would, or would not, be done in the future.

As may be imagined, my satisfaction was extreme. Singularly no one seemed offended by my letter, and no one ever expressed to me the slightest dissatisfaction with it.

I was not long in learning that Grant and Rawlins abominated cotton buyers as a class. In private conversations to the end of the war he always spoke of them as a gang of thieves. Meantime I inadvertently got into a difficulty with a cotton buyer and upon his complaint had been arrested by the Provost-Marshal, Col. John E. Smith, of the 45th Ill. Regt. The man finally exonerated me, withdrew his complaint, and signed a complete retraction, which was witnessed by Col. [George Clarke] Rogers, 15th Ill., and J. B. McCullagh, then correspondent of the Cincinnati *Commercial,* and afterwards the famous editor of the St. Louis *Globe-Democrat.* Having secured this document I went to the fellow's room, gave him a specified time to get out of the department, notifying him plainly that we could not both live within the lines of that army. For this threat, and for having been caught in the act of giving him a good pommeling in his own room, I was again arrested on his charge of disorderly conduct. Although an entire stranger to Col. Smith he allowed me to go free upon my promising to appear for trial when wanted. I doubtless had Col. Smith's full sympathy, for he reported the whole affair the same day to his old Galena friend, Major Rawlins.

That evening upon stepping into the Adjutant's office Rawlins called me to his desk and said he had heard of a slight misunderstanding between myself and a cotton thief named Fairchild, and inquired if I had gotten out of it satisfactorily. For answer I handed him the cowardly retraction. Without saying a word he stepped into Gen. Grant's room and showed it to him. He soon returned beaming with satisfaction and pronounced the affair the best thing which had happened in a month, and said he was sorry I had not broken every bone in the rascal's body.

Gen. Grant always thwarted the operations of all cotton-buyers who came within his lines as far as he possibly could without interfering with other departments of the government, and some were sent out of the department on short notice; but Mr. Chase, Secretary of the Treasury, inaugurated a system of trade permits to special government agents for the purchase of cotton which were so exercised as to cover much rascality which military commanders could not prevent. These agents were not long in learning that Grant and Rawlins were their implacable enemies, and that no persuasions, appliances nor artifices could deceive or mollify them for an instant. . . .[9]

---

[9] There is no doubt that favoritism and corruption were encouraged by the system of trade permits, administered by the Treasury Department, whereby cotton, which was sorely needed in the North, might be purchased within the enemy's lines. Cotton-buyers were detested by the military men, not only because of the sharp practices they employed, but also because they supposedly aided the enemy and were enriching themselves from the war. The system was a frequent cause of controversy in Lincoln's Cabinet. See *The Diary of Gideon Welles,* John T. Morse, Jr., ed. (Boston, 1911, 3 vols.), II, 138–40, 159–63.

C H A P T E R

Two

ABOUT the middle of November a reconnaissance in force was made as far southward as Lamar by a portion of Gen. Mc-Pherson's corps, which developed the Confederate position on the Coldwater, four miles north of Holly Springs, in strongly intrenched earthworks to contest the crossing of that river. McPherson accompanied the troops and commanded in person. . . .

A few days after this our cavalry found the Confederate line so weak that it dashed into Holly Springs and captured a few officers and men. Among the prisoners taken were Capt. Clark,[1] of Gen. [Earl] Van Dorn's staff, and Capt. [L. B.] Harris, on the staff of Gen. [Mansfield] Lovell. For reasons which I never knew they were paroled immediately by Gen. Grant and returned under a flag of truce, borne by Lieut. [Edward T.] Sherlock of the headquarters escort. I accompanied them, and on the way to Holly Springs, rode most of the time by the side of Capt. Clark. I was greatly surprised to learn that he was a graduate of Amherst College; was at one time a mem-

---

[1] Captain Henry Clark of Gen. Sterling Price's staff. Price and Van Dorn were co-operating in opposing Grant's advance.

ber of Governor [Erastus] Fairbanks' family in Vermont; that he had gone south a few years before to practice law; had formed a partnership with Roger Barton of Holly Springs; subsequently married Mr. Barton's daughter; and as usual in such cases, became a rabid secessionist. He responded to the first call for Confederate troops in Mississippi; became a Captain in 1st Miss. Infantry, and marched to Pensacola upon the outbreak of the rebellion.

When we arrived at Holly Springs late in the afternoon Capt. Clark insisted on my being his guest till morning, and Capt. Harris took Lieut. Sherlock with him for supper. The privates were quartered in a hotel. The return of the prisoners was a great surprise to their families and friends, and an informal and congratulatory reception was given them that evening at Capt. Clark's.

The ladies greatly outnumbered the gentlomen, as was to be expected. Time passed very pleasantly—in conversation, with an occasional witty allusion to the war, but all were politely and studiously inoffensive. During the evening I was conversing awhile with a Miss Mortimer, and found her to be an intellectual, scholarly and charming woman. Our chat finally took a more direct turn upon war topics than either of us perhaps intended, and she expressed her ultra proslavery sentiments without much reserve. I finally ventured the remark that I was surprised to hear a northern woman entertaining such opinions. "I am no northern woman," she retorted sharply.

Just at this moment there was a lull in the buzz of conversation around the room, and my remark, and her reply, were heard by all. I noticed that a general relaxation of countenance spread over the faces of nearly all in the room, expressing restrained risibility. I concluded my random shot had struck near the mark, and begging her pardon for the personal allusion, said that I knew her to be a northern woman by birth and education, if no more. Her friends began to laugh and shout that she was fairly trapped. She was very anxious to know what foundation I could possibly have for such an opinion. I could only reply that there was generally something indescribable, but real, in the language of three-fourths of the people of the United States that marked the section from which they came, as in which they were educated. That some faint idioms, and a Boston precision of speech, made me think her from New England. It turned out that she was born in Montpelier, Vt. and educated in that state. She had come south as a teacher and was at that time the head of the Female Seminary in Holly Springs.

In the morning by Capt. Clark's invitation Lieut. Sherlock and myself accepted his escort through the city that we might see that its reputation for beauty was actually deserved and we then started on our return. On arrival at the Confederate outposts, near the Coldwater, we were informed that we could not proceed homeward and that we were charged with violating the privileges of a flag of truce by riding through the streets and presumably spying out the defenses of the place. Our statements of facts were of no avail. We reiterated over and over again that we had only ridden through a few of the streets on the special invitation of Capt. Clark as an act of politeness to his guests; that we knew nothing, (nor did we care) about the defenses of the place; and demanded that the rights and privileges of the flag be instantly recognized. To this demand very little was answered, but we were told very decidedly that we would have to remain. No threats or expostulations availed; a turbulent crowd of hundreds collected around us; and our situation was soon one of peril.

At this juncture Capt. Clark appeared. Having learned of

the intention to detain us at the lines he had mounted and ridden hastily to our relief. He came through the crowd furiously, pushing aside officers and men, until he was at our side —began on the officer in command by saying that our detention was a damnable outrage—that we had ridden abroad only at his request—that we had suggested to him before starting its possible impropriety—that our behavior had been that of officers and gentlemen while on the way from La Grange, and afterward while the guests of himself and Capt. Harris—and that if we were not allowed to depart instantly he would go back to La Grange himself if he had to go on foot, and voluntarily surrender himself a hostage for us. We were very ungraciously allowed to depart without further molestation.

Shortly after this, the combined movement of the three corps was ordered. Hamilton and McPherson marched southward, practically following the line of the Mobile & Ohio R'y., Sherman started from Memphis a day or two in advance and by parallel roads to the westward, and by the last of the month was at College Hill, ten miles from Oxford forming the right of the line. McPherson and Hamilton had in the meantime marched through Holly Springs to the Tallahatchie where a feeble effort at resistance was made. Our occupation of Oxford took place without any fighting worth mentioning and headquarters were established there early in December.

Our advanced cavalry upon entering the latter place and getting hold of some liquor, behaved scandalously and robbed the people right and left of everything they fancied. It was nothing uncommon for them to hold up a darky and take his watch, paying in green express labels stolen from the depot. The University of Mississippi was located here and the place was a sort of literary center for the state. The Hon. Jacob Thompson, Secretary of the Interior under Mr. Buchanan,

lived here. He left his home and property on our approach
and the place was looted by negroes and white men until
everything was destroyed. . . .

As we were entering Holly Springs I suggested to Gen.
Grant that it would afford me an excellent opportunity to re-
pay Capt. Clark for his kindness. He assented emphatically and
quickly, and told me to make arrangements for the protection
of his family and property. I galloped to his residence where I
found Mrs. Clark and two or three friends at the front gate in
a terrible state of excitement and fear. Her servants were on
the sidewalk, and neighbors and negroes in a crowd were soon
assembled to know what my visit portended. Mrs. Clark was
almost hysterical and seemed to think the town would be destroyed and the inhabitants subjected to all the barbarities of
medieval warfare.

I had some difficulty in convincing her that the personal
safety of herself and family was quite as well insured by the
presence of the Federal troops as they ever had been by those
of the Confederacy. Our occupation would work some incon-
veniences and hardship as a matter of course, and this could
not be helped; but beyond these, there was no cause for uneasiness. I promised to extend all necessary protection to her
from the troopers who had already run down half the pigs and
chickens, and entered all the meat houses of the town.

As we stood talking at the gate two or three cavalrymen
came tearing round the corner of the house after a chicken.
"See there, see there," she exclaimed. "That's the way they
have been doing all day." I suggested that the loss of a few
chickens cut little figure in the war, and advised her to make
up her mind to lose them all, and everything else good to eat,
that was not securely guarded.

I recommended her to have her servants carry into the

house, upstairs, everything from the out houses; and to set apart for a storehouse one upper room, put in it immediately all household valuables of every kind, including their best clothing; to lock the door and carry the key herself and never trust it to any one else until better times returned. She was inclined to resent this imputation of her servants' honesty; but I told her it had been our uniform experience that the negroes stole first, and then deserted from their old masters, and she ought not to consider hers an exception.

Obtaining the number of her servants, I proceeded to the provost marshal, Col. John E. Smith, my former acquaintance at La Grange, and had the names of Mrs. Clark, her family of four children, and eight servants, entered upon the rolls for protection. I also made arrangements at once with our commissary to supply them with one full ration each, daily, during our stay. Taking a private, detailed for guard duty, I went back to the house, informed Mrs. Clark of what had been done, and told her in the presence of the detail, what his duties were. He could not keep away all intruders, but no one should enter her house without her consent, and the guard would enforce this order carefully.

I then went into the front room and said to her privately that this was a lonesome and disagreeable job for the sentry— it was already raining—and advised her to invite him into the front room, where he could watch the front gate through the window. She at first declared she would never do this, but without noticing the rudeness of the remark, I went on to say that at any time when she had an extra meal prepared, she ought to invite him to share it with the family. This brought out the reply that she "never would invite a Union soldier to eat at her table as long as she lived"; but added that "she knew she ought to, but it seemed a great humiliation."

I told her it was not; that many privates were men of intelligence and education; and very few would ever presume upon it to intrude on her. I further said to her that if he were treated kindly he could be of untold advantage to her. He would draw and carry home her daily rations and save her the annoyance of standing in a line of black and white mendicants for hours, provided he thought he would receive some kindnesses in return. Besides this, the average soldier would, if he was of Sherman's corps, manage to "pick up" about as much more. I gave her an idea of the character of rations that it would be to her interest to draw, assuring her that no one person could eat it all daily, and the accumulation ought to be of such things as the South could not furnish, and as were not perishable.

Headquarters were at Oxford for several weeks afterwards. The Infantry and pioneer corps were pushed forward repairing the railroad and all bridges as far south as Yock-na-pa-ta-fa.[2] The cavalry drove Pemberton's forces to Coffeyville some miles south of this on the R'y. I was ahead of the staff with the infantry and took that opportunity of again visiting all Wisconsin Regiments there.

I was especially impelled to this by letters from home concerning the unsatisfactory condition which had existed for months in the 17th (Irish) Wisconsin Infantry. This was mainly raised in Milwaukee and officered by Col. [John L.] Doran, Lieut. Col. [John J.] Jefferson and Maj. Adam [G.]

---

[2] Cadwallader seems to be confused here; at least he has confused the editor. I have failed to locate any town named Yock-na-pa-ta-fa. Plate CLIV in the atlas accompanying *The War of the Rebellion . . . Official Records of the Union and Confederate Armies* shows a river in this vicinity named the Yohnapatapha. Union commanders referred to it as "the Yockna" or Yockna Creek, and in one case the Yocknapatalpha, so it may have had variant spellings. Today it is called the Yocona. The novelist William Faulkner calls this region the Yocknapatawpha country.

Molloy [Malloy]. Col. Doran's convivial habits unfitted him for usefulness and finally made him so obnoxious that the regiment was on the point of mutiny. Some time before this, charges had been preferred against him for drunkenness; he in turn preferred charges against his accusers; and a court martial was ordered by Gen. John McArthur. . . .

While these were pending I visited their camp and on my return Rawlins questioned me closely as to its condition, the feelings of the men toward their officers and asked me pointedly what I thought would end these constant quarrels. I told him frankly that Doran should be removed and Maj. Malloy, who had been in the regular army, made its colonel; that if the Regiment was assured that such a change would be made, the delay of a court martial could be avoided and good feeling restored. There was another feature that added gravity to the situation—their chaplain, Father Mignault, was a disturbing element. He probably left the regiment at Vicksburg as I do not remember him after that date.

My advice was acted upon; Malloy became colonel and commanded [the regiment] to the end of the war [and] rose to the rank of Brigadier. . . .

[*By mid-December, Sherman, acting under Grant's orders, was preparing to embark for the vicinity of Vicksburg with some 30,000 troops, and as part of the general plan to reduce that stronghold, Grant sent Colonel Dickey, with seven or eight hundred picked cavalry, to cut the Mobile and Ohio Railroad. Cadwallader accompanied this cavalry expedition.*]

The first day's march was leisurely made and we went into camp early to prepare for sharp work the next day. Soon after midnight the men were quietly aroused, mounted and formed in silence, and led by guides to the vicinity of Pontotoc. A half hour halt was made there to feed horses, when the command pushed rapidly ahead a few miles east to where the roads separated which led to Tupelo and to Okolona, both stations on the Mobile & Ohio R'y. and about twenty miles apart. Here the force was divided and an attempt made to surprise both places. The right-hand road to Okolona was taken by a column under command of Major Datus E. Coon[s]. . . .

The boys led by Major Coons dashed into Okolona, made a few prisoners, captured some stores, seized the telegraph office before an alarm could be given and then quietly posted themselves to await the arrival of a passenger train about due. But the engineer probably received some signal of danger for he suddenly came to a stop, and instantly reversed his engine.

As soon as this was discovered the dismounted cavalry made a break for the train already in motion to the rear. There ensued an exciting and laughable scene. Some soldiers were clambering up the sides of the tender and engine; others were trying to catch it before it got under full headway; and still others firing at the engineer and fireman in a reckless way which only endangered their comrades. No one had taken the precaution to have the track blockaded, or torn up in the rear, as might have been done by a small detail.

Meanwhile the passengers rallied to the aid of the trainmen, and the few cavalry men who actually boarded the cars were knocked off, and the whole train escaped. Maj. Coons spent the next twenty-four hours in destroying the public stores, and the railroad each way as far as possible. He rejoined the main command near Pontotoc on its way back to Oxford. . . .

Col. Dickey and myself accompanied the other column under Col. [Edward] Hatch and reached Tupelo about 10 P.M. The place was taken without resistance, but nothing of value was captured. The main part of the command was marched back several miles that night (I never knew why) and was in the saddle twenty-five consecutive hours excepting the thirty minutes spent in feeding at Pontotoc. The next two days were spent in destroying the railroad. This was quite effectually done by tearing up the track, burning bridges and heating and bending the rails from Saltillo, north of Tupelo, to Okolona on its south.

Upon the return march we went into camp the first night on the plantation of Mrs. Sample, an old lady who had lived there about a quarter of a century. She had colored men for overseers; had a day school to which all colored children were sent and taught to read; and had then over one hundred slaves on the place. They were well fed and clothed, had religious instruction every Sunday, and were happy and contented in their lot. No one of them left her to follow us the next morning. Forage, meat, flour and all supplies were abundant. Mrs. Sample's first and only request was that nothing should be wasted or destroyed, as the very lives of her colored people depended upon her stores. She refused compensation for what we used. Col. Dickey in compliance with her request took the keys to her supply houses, had the issues therefrom made under official supervision, had details cooking up food for the return, and watched her stores carefully.

In answer to our inquiries she said she had in times past, been arrested and fined for teaching her slaves to read, but of late years had not been interfered with. She thought her neighbors' hearts had been touched by her patient determination to teach her black people to read their Bibles; and their judgments also convinced them that an intelligent "chattel" was more valuable than an ignorant one. Her two colored foremen, educated by herself, were her active men of business who raised and sold her crops and bought supplies. As we were leaving next morning she mentioned that her worst anxiety was how to obtain salt for putting up meat, as it was not to be had at any price in the Confederacy. She accepted Col. Dickey's offer to send a team to Oxford for salt, and a six-mule team was loaded and sent to her a few days after our arrival there. We sent the outfit through our lines in safety. This was the only instance of a patriarchal or beneficent condition of slavery that I ever saw in the Confederacy.

On the 18th within eight or ten miles of Pontotoc, we began to meet darkies of all ages and sexes running away from the town. They brought the news that a large cavalry force under Gen. Earl Van Dorn had been going northwest through Pontotoc all day. Some placed the number at 15,000, but it was generally thought to be from six to eight thousand. Occasionally a white man was met, who corroborated the darkies.

Proceeding with great caution by a road diverging to the right, the head of our column reached the heights, three miles northeast of Pontotoc about 2:00 P.M. Here we remained all the afternoon. We could plainly see Van Dorn's men marching along the road, crossing our line of retreat. A little before sundown our own troops headed into town. On reaching the village, flankers were thrown out and Dickey's whole force, well closed up, passed across Van Dorn's rear on a trot, in plain view of his rear guard, who merely turned in their saddles and watched us without halting for an instant.

Guides were seized, all extra wagons and baggage burned, and a forced march made towards Oxford until three o'clock next morning. Then a halt was made until daylight. All bridges were torn up in our rear and every precaution taken to retard pursuit. Dickey seemed to think that Van Dorn would certainly pursue him, and that if he could manage to escape with his force well in hand, it would cover him with glory and

the affair take rank with Zenophens [Xenophon's] retreat of
the 10,000.

A little reflection should have led to a different conclusion.
Every man, woman and child in Pontotoc saw us pass eastward
three days before. Van Dorn doubtless had full information as
to our number, purpose, and accomplishment. He was after
larger game. Time was an important element and he did not
so much as halt his column when Dickey appeared in his rear.

The federal officer should have fought against all odds. He
should have attacked, retarded, delayed and harassed Van
Dorn's advance at the cost of his whole command, if necessary,
till Gen. Grant at Oxford could have been notified of the facts.
This error of his judgment cost the government millions of dollars and practically retired Col. Dickey to private life.

Leaving the troops to move on under Col. Hatch, Dickey,
myself and four orderlies pressed ahead to Oxford and reached
there about four o'clock in the afternoon of December 19th.
Dickey began his report to Gen. Grant, narrating the events
day by day, to which the general listened without much apparent interest until he reached his account of Van Dorn's
movement northward. Grant was instantly on the alert—inquired particularly as to its appearance—estimated strength—
the day and hour of its passage—the particular road it moved
on, etc., etc.

Without waiting for Col. Dickey to finish, but without any
intention, probably, of rudeness, he walked out of the house
into the road and started unattended to the telegraph office at
the depot, a quarter of a mile away. Sitting down there he
wrote and sent off dispatch after dispatch northward, notifying
post commandants of Van Dorn's approach and his undoubted
intention of cutting our line of communication somewhere between Oxford and Jackson. All small detachments were to be

called in, and extra precautions taken to prevent surprise. This was before dark and ten or twelve hours before Van Dorn's entrance into Holly Springs.

Col. [R. C.] Murphy of the Eighth Wisconsin who was in command at the latter place, at first denied receiving this dispatch in time; but his denial was subsequently shown to be untrue. The facts seem to have been that he and Major [John J.] Mudd, who commanded the cavalry there, were out at some entertainment until towards midnight—that this entertainment, like Tam O'Shanter's, made them a trifle over bold. They easily persuaded themselves that there was no immediate danger. Mudd declared that all the roads had been patrolled leading in that direction, for miles that day, and that neither Van Dorn nor any other enemy was near.

In 1882 I spent a night with one of Van Dorn's officers in south west Missouri. He said they reached our outposts on two roads about midnight—that they halted, rested, ate lunch, and waited for the fixed hour to commence the attack. He says Van Dorn's entire command lay on these roads several hours, all within three to five miles of the public square of Holly Springs, and that there were no pickets out that deserved the name. Every one was captured, no alarm was given, and Van Dorn rode undiscovered into Holly Springs. I believe he told the truth.

Col. Murphy was openly disgraced and Dickey sent north on detached service until the close of the war. Socially these two officers were much alike. Both were elegant conventional gentlemen, fond of song and story; but neither of them evinced much soldierly aptitude and both failed on the crucial test.

This was Col. Murphy's second failure. He narrowly escaped a court martial for his conduct in hastily evacuating

Iuka and leaving a large amount of government stores to fall into the hands of Gen. [Sterling] Price which he had been left to destroy. He had previously been driven out of Tuscumbia by Price and had been left at Iuka to bring away or destroy the stores there if he was unable to hold the place. He had abundant warning of Price's approach, but abandoned Iuka and all its stores before Price appeared.

In contrast to this conduct was that of Col. [William H.] Morgan of the Twenty-Fifth Indiana, commanding at Davis' Mills, a few miles north of Holly Springs on the railway. Van Dorn appeared there on the morning of the 21st and demanded its surrender. Col. Morgan promptly refused and prepared for a vigorous defense. He trained an old six pound smooth bore (the only piece of artillery he had) on the only approach from the south, a corduroy road through a swamp for a half mile, and stationed a line of sharpshooters in range also. Van Dorn underrated the resistance he would encounter and ordered a cavalry charge. By a detour around the swamp he could have had smooth ground for an attack.

As the head of his column filed onto the road such a storm of grape and ball was turned on it that it came near filling the swamp on both sides of the road with dead men and horses. The column was thrown into confusion and the sharpshooters picked off the officers unmercifully for awhile. The time gained by Col. Morgan enabled him to erect some barricades of brush and wagons formidable to cavalry, and by the time Van Dorn was ready to attack on some other line, the post was too strong for any sudden assault. Van Dorn was on a raid to cut Grant's communications, and had no time to spend in sieges. Those posts that could not be taken by surprise, by a dash of cavalry, were passed by.

Van Dorn's column passed on rapidly to a point on the

Memphis & Charleston R'y. a few miles west of La Grange and by a detour to the right struck the Jackson and Miss. R'y. again a few miles above Grand Junction, toward Jackson [Tennessee]. By this time our cavalry were close on his heels and the infantry were making forced marches to intercept him on his probable line of retreat. The wily general had accomplished his purpose, which was to show Gen. Grant the impossibility of maintaining such a long line of communication. He hastily turned southward before he could be caught. We followed him as far as Ripley and abandoned the hopeless chase.

On receipt of the news of the capture of Holly Springs on the morning of the 20th, Gen. Grant loaded a train with infantry under Col. Cal. C. Marsh, of the 20th Ill. with orders to run the train as near to Holly Springs as possible, debark the troops, and retake the place. The forces under Col. Marsh was deemed sufficient to do this with certainty, but other troops were sent to the same point to support the movement.

Col. Marsh was by nature a brave and impetuous man; had distinguished himself as a colonel on several occasions, stood well up on the list for promotion for Brigadier General, and had for a long time been soliciting an opportunity to win his star. When the occasion presented itself, his judgment, or his courage, failed him. He halted the train seven miles south of the town without an enemy in sight, or an obstruction in his road; formed his troops in regular battle array and marched cautiously to Holly Springs. His movements were so deliberate that it was night before he arrived and he found all the stores destroyed and the last of Van Dorn's cavalry leisurely riding out of town. He lost the military opportunity of his life, and never regained his former standing in the service.

This raid of Van Dorn's seems to have been part of a general plan; for at the same time Gen. [Nathan Bedford] Forrest, who commanded the Confederate cavalry in the district of Memphis, attacked and captured post after post on the R'y. from Jackson to Columbus. His strategy was the same as Van Dorn's. He would surprise, or capture, a place, take a few prisoners, destroy all stores, and as much of the R'y. as possible and ride rapidly to the next place. Like Van Dorn, he lost no time by investing a place.

Gen. Nathan B. Forrest was one of the ablest cavalry officers developed on either side, especially for partisan warfare. Bold and reckless, almost to a fault, he often accomplished by sheer audacity and celerity of movement, what could never have been done in any other way. His thorough topographical knowledge of the country enabled him to take advantage of every road and bridle path, of every stream, timber land and plain, and thus avail himself of the most desirable places for offensive and defensive fighting. He had the sympathy and confidence of the inhabitants of that section of country, thus gaining information of the strength or weakness of all Union forces in his proximity. He was quick to take advantage of our errors, and the exact moment in which to strike.

He was the only Confederate Cavalryman of whom Gen. Grant stood in much dread in the Dep't. of the Tennessee. When raids were made or threatened, Grant's first inquiry was "who commanded" it. If Rodney [Philip Dale Roddey] or [Joseph] Wheeler, he would make some light remark, showing he did not think it very formidable; but if Forrest was in command he at once became apprehensive because the latter was amenable to no known rules of procedure, was a law to himself for all military acts, and was constantly doing the unexpected, at all times and places. . . .

So much destruction was made by Van Dorn and Forrest on these raids that Gen. Grant seems to have for the first time realized the impossibility of leaving his base of supplies so far in the rear, in so hostile a country. On the 23rd of Dec. headquarters were moved back to Holly Springs and the troops were gradually drawn back to the Tallahatchie river.

The news of the capture of Holly Springs caused great rejoicing at Oxford. The citizens thought Grant's army would be starved into surrendering. This feeling of joy turned into one of consternation when his troops began to supply themselves from the surrounding country, thus making the Confederacy feed his army. Trains of wagons, heavily guarded, were sent out by scores, for twenty-five miles on both sides of the road from Yocknapatafa to Holly Springs, and stripped the country of all food for men and animals. Mills were erected, grain ground, fat stock driven in and slaughtered by thousands, and abundant supplies obtained. To people's inquiries as to what the inhabitants should live upon, Gen. Grant advised them to move further south. His army would not be allowed to starve while there was anything to live upon within reach.

Finding that all telegraphic and railway communications with the north were so badly damaged that ten days or two weeks would be consumed in repairs I left headquarters December 24th for Memphis with public and private dispatches to be transmitted from there.

I stayed that night with Capt. Philip Trounstine who commanded a Company of Ohio cavalry, in pursuit of Van Dorn. Capt. Trounstine was the son of Martin Trounstine of the heavy and well known clothing firm of A. & J. Trounstine & Co. doing business for many years on Pearl & 3rd streets, Cincinnati. So far as I know he was the only cavalry officer in the service that was of Hebraic extraction. He enlisted early and served creditably to the end.

On the morning of the 25th I left him, taking the dirt road along the R'y. to Memphis.

A few miles west of La Grange (at Moscow) I was startled by a shot from the timber to the left and the "zip" of a minie ball. As no one appeared in sight I thought it might possibly come as a random shot from some hunter. I was soon undeceived. The first was followed by others in rapid succession and I ran a gauntlet of musketry fire for a half mile without seeing anything but the smoke of some guns.

About noon, within a few miles of Collierville, the scene of one of Gen. Sherman's after exploits and narrow escape from captivity,[3] I stopped at a cross road to rest, and to feed the horses, myself and negro servant "Jerry." No men were about the house but the woman was very unwilling to have me stay, or furnish me food or forage. I offered to pay her handsomely. There was abundance of corn and sheaf oats in sight, but she positively refused to furnish me anything.

Disregarding her wishes, we took the bridles off and fed our horses. I then offered to pay her for any cold provisions she had. This was also refused. I was unable to account for her disinclination to accommodate us, and for her nervous and agitated condition. Seeing that we were determined to remain, she finally told me plainly to mount and ride for my life—that a troop of Confederate cavalry had just crossed the road, and were then feeding and watering their horses within a half mile of us, just out of sight in the timber. We thought her advice good, and it took just ten seconds to be in the saddle.

---

[3] Cadwallader evidently refers to Sherman's near capture by Confederate cavalry when he was sleeping in a log house near Decatur, Mississippi, on February 12, 1864. But that incident took place many miles from Collierville. See Memoirs of General William T. Sherman (New York, 1875), I, 391.

We had not ridden two hundred yards until we heard a bugle sounding the "assembly" in the timber, but we rode away without discovery. About two miles west of Collierville, at the end of a lane where the road turned obliquely to the right into some thick woods, we found ourselves face to face with a detachment of Confederate cavalry coming toward us. There was no time for a horse race, or escape. A command to "halt" accompanied by the click of carbines was promptly obeyed. This was a part of a Tennessee regiment under Capt. Scales, which Van Dorn had thrown out to the west to patrol the main roads leading to Memphis and pick up such stragglers as might have run away from Holly Springs. I was placed in charge of an orderly Sergeant, who was directed to shoot me if I attempted to escape, and marched back towards Collierville through which we had just passed.

As a cold drizzling rain had set in, Capt. Scales took advantage of the first cotton gin he came to near the road, and ordered me brought into his presence. He questioned me very closely, said he should have to strip and search me thoroughly, for he believed I was bearing dispatches from Grant to Memphis. To all of my denials he turned a deaf ear and continued to ply me with a torrent of questions concerning the position and strength of Grant's forces, the pursuit made of Van Dorn, and other things affecting his safety. I finally convinced him that my own protection demanded my silence. After a conference with his lieutenants he said he was in no condition to take prisoners and must either hang me or turn me loose. As I had seemed to tell a straight story he had decided to give me another lease of life.

I thanked him for this and then began to question him concerning the condition and resources of the Confederacy. Taking from my pocket a handful of cigars I offered him one with the remark "that they were probably no luxury to one in the Confederate Service, where tobacco was so common"; but was surprised by his saying that it was the first cigar he had smoked for more than two months. The cigar-makers, he said, were in the army; cigars were held at fabulous prices; while raw tobacco was plentiful. My supply was soon distributed, and a pleasant half-hour conversation took place. Jerry then came up with my horses and I directed him to bring me a canteen that was slung to his saddle under his poncho, out of sight. I opened it, took a drink myself, as I assured the Captain laughingly, to prove it was not rank poison; handed it to him with the request that it be passed around. This he said was the first whiskey he had tasted for over three months. I mounted and started off, followed by Jerry, when the Captain called to me to halt, saying he could not allow the darky to go. I told him Jerry had been my servant for some time, and I could not afford to part with him; that he certainly ought to go if I did; when with a wave of the hand he replied "go ahead, one darky more or less don't count in the Confederacy."

Owing to the almost impassable conditions of the roads I made slow progress; stayed all night at Germantown a few miles east of Memphis and rode in early the next forenoon. A large amount of telegraphic matter was sent off during the day, and taking the four o'clock P.M. boat for Cairo, I was soon on my way to Chicago.

C H A P T E R

Three

I HAD a pleasant week at my home in Milwaukee and returned to Memphis, January 10th, 1863. I then learned that
Gen. Grant had abandoned all territory south of the Memphis
& Charleston Railroad, and that most of his troops were on
the march to Memphis. The general and staff were hourly
expected, but did not arrive until nearly daylight Saturday
morning. Headquarters remained in Memphis until the last
week in January. . . .

[*During Cadwallader's absence Sherman had been roughly
handled in his effort to take Vicksburg, and his failure, along
with the constant Confederate harassment of the Union supply lines, had induced Grant to draw back. While Cadwallader waited at Memphis, he was on the alert for news from
Sherman.*]

There was an episode connected with Sherman's expedition
which so far as I know has never appeared in any account of
that campaign. In an order issued Dec. 18th, Sherman had forbidden all citizens, traders and women to accompany the
army; and if any citizen should be detected disregarding or
violating the order, he was to be seized and put into the

ranks, or set to work as a deck hand on some of the transports.
In defiance of that order Thomas W. Knox, correspondent
of the N.Y. *Herald*, smuggled himself on board one of the
transports, accompanied, I think, by Richard Colburn of the
N.Y. *World*, Junius Henri Browne, of the Cincinnati *Gazette*,
A. M. [Albert H.] Bodman, of the Chicago *Tribune* and Albert D. Richardson of the N.Y. *Tribune*. These correspondents
witnessed Gen. Sherman's attack and repulse at Chickasaw
Bayou. Gen. Sherman got wind of their presence and ordered
their immediate arrest.

The correspondents must have had some "friend at court"
who gave them instant information of the order. They managed to reach [Admiral David D.] Porter's flagship and were
allowed to stay on one of his vessels, and were thus beyond
the jurisdiction of Gen. Sherman. They very naturally re-
venged themselves by writing their various accounts for publication to Sherman's disadvantage; revived the old story of his
being crazy; and could without much apparent malice put him
in a very unenviable light. So far as public sentiment in the
north was concerned his failure was an overwhelming con-
demnation on its face.

This affair had a sequel. When Gen. Grant arrived in front
of Vicksburg, in command, Knox returned as a correspondent
and upon charges preferred by Gen. Sherman, was arrested
and courtmartialed. I have always suspected that the court
was selected with a view to Knox's final acquittal and a sort
of left-handed vindication of Gen. Sherman. Such was at least
the result. The feeling was almost universal that Sherman's
conduct in attempting to court martial Knox was unworthy of
his position.

Knox's punishment consisted in his being sent out of the
Dep't. He went directly to New York and Washington, and re-

turned in a few weeks with the President's permission to remain in the field. He was naturally triumphant for a few days;
but Gen. Grant soon informed him in a private conversation
that his return was very ill-advised. That while he admitted
the authority of the President to issue such permits in all general conditions, yet there might occur special occasions when
the commanders themselves would be better judges of the
necessity, or propriety of what should, or should not be allowed within their own lines, than the President possibly could
be at such a remote distance. That in his opinion this was a
case in point, and that he could not afford to antagonize so
valuable an officer as Gen. S. for so trifling a reason. He assured him that future trouble was certain to ensue if he remained within Sherman's reach, and gave him to understand
that he need not appeal to headquarters for protection. Knox
took the hint—and the first steamer up the river. . . .

[*About this time, Grant, resolving to assume personal charge
of the operations against Vicksburg, sent Captain F. E. Prime
and Lieutenant James H. Wilson, engineers on his staff, to
Young's Point, on the west bank of the Mississippi, to make an
inspection of the Williams Canal, begun in 1862 by Gen.
Thomas Williams, C.S.A., but never completed, as a possible
means of putting his army south of the city without running
past its batteries.*]

I accompanied these two officers on the little steamer Cata-
houla and arrived there Jan. 28 (I think) and proceeded in
their company to the upper end of the canal and followed it
clear through to its mouth, a few miles below the fortifications
on the opposite shore. The river at that time was moderately
full, barely high enough to fill the shallow ditch, but not high
enough to decide positively upon the practicability of its use.
It was standing full of still water, without any current what-

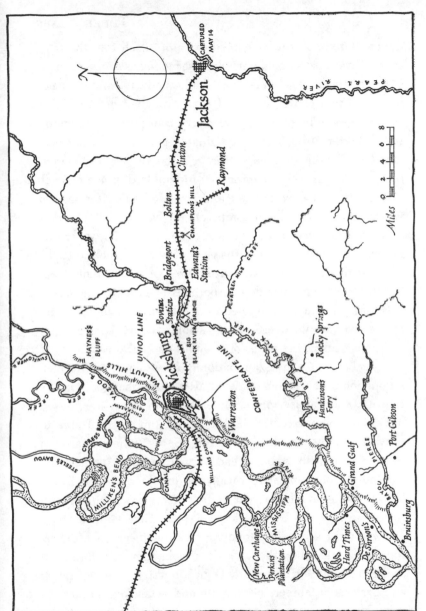

GRANT'S OPERATIONS AROUND VICKSBURG

ever and quite as much inclined to empty itself into the river above Vicksburg as below it. My first feeling was one of great disappointment. The canal was shallow and narrow, and not one-tenth part of the work had been expended on it which I foresaw would be necessary for heavy transports, to say nothing of Porter's ironclads. The valuable part of the work consisted in clearing its course through the timber and underbrush. This was well done for a considerable distance on each side of the actual excavation and rendered the after task of widening it, if need be, a comparatively easy one.

Its radical defect was that it left the river at its upper end nearly at a right angle with the current which ran close to the shore at that place, and very little force of the current swept into the canal. Another defect, perhaps even more important, was that unless it was doubled in depth, any subsequent raise of the river would overflow the whole country before water sufficient to float the transports would enter the canal.

I was back from my examination in a few hours and formed an opinion of it which was never afterwards changed. On the return of the engineer officers later in the evening, I expressed my opinion very freely to both of them, but was not able to draw from either much confirmation. Capt. Prime was a quiet reticent man with whom I had very little acquaintance and was never communicative to anyone except officially. Lieut. Wilson had graduated a year or two before from the Military Academy, and had been ordered west to Gen. Grant's Dept. He was for a short time topographical engineer on McPherson's staff, and when the Vicksburg campaign took form and shape, was transferred to Grant's headquarters. He was quick and nervous in temperament, plain and outspoken on all subjects, but would not say much to me on this matter until he had made his report to Gen. Grant. I was given to understand that he fully agreed with my estimate of the ditch. . . .

Gen. Grant states in his Memoirs that he arrived at Young's Point January 29, 1863. He came a few days before we expected him on the steamer Magnolia, which was retained as his headquarter boat until we left Milliken's Bend toward the latter part of April. . . .

Gen. Grant's inspection of the canal on the day of his arrival must have satisfied him that its plan was defective, for orders were immediately given to the troops arriving daily to commence some important alterations of it. One of these was to commence from a half mile to a mile above its head, and take it into the river at an acute angle with the current, and also to widen and deepen it throughout. This work was pressed forward with all the force that could work at it, until the rise of the river, which came soon after, did actually overflow about all of Young's Point and rendered its further prosecution impossible. It had been so nearly completed that one or two light draft vessels had traversed nearly its entire length. Our delay in completing the work had been so great that the Confederates had planted batteries on the opposite shore exactly opposite its mouth by which an enfilading fire could destroy vessels in the lower two-thirds of its length. As a matter of historical interest it may be stated that very little water ever ran through it, and the theory that a small stream once diverted into it would soon widen and deepen it, until it became the main channel of the river, was completely exploded.

The overflow of the Mississippi that winter and spring was extraordinary in volume and extent. The troops in front of Vicksburg were soon driven from their camps to the levee which became the only ground above water for many miles.

The army was compelled to retire to Milliken's Bend, twelve miles up stream. Military operations were necessarily suspended except in attempts to secure new lines of approach to Vicksburg through the numerous bayous and waterways which this phenomenal overflow seemed to make practicable.

It does not appear from any of Gen. Grant's orders, communications to Washington, or from his private or public utterances then or afterward that he ever placed much reliance upon any of these inland transportation schemes; but he foresaw that the stage of high water would last for months, and that the army would be in better condition by reason of such temporary work and occupation than by laying idle in camp. The public sentiment at the north gave outbursts of impatience at the delay; and intrigues were at work to remove Grant, and place McClernand, or someone else in his place. It was apparent that continued activity was the only condition on which he could hold his position. . . .

The Yazoo Pass expedition, the most celebrated perhaps of all, was undertaken about March 1st [1] by which it was intended to transport a heavy body of troops from its upper end, eight miles below Helena, Ark., eastward into Moon Lake, which emptied into Coldwater river, and this into the upper Yazoo. The shallowness of the water prevented the passage of fully half the transports and ironclads, and occasioned delays that enabled the Confederates to erect an exceedingly strong fortification, known as Ft. Pemberton, at the junction of the Tallahatchie and Yalobusha rivers. This fort was entirely surrounded by water for several miles when our transports arrived in its vicinity. There was absolutely no road by which infantry could reach it. It was too strong to be reduced by the

---

[1] Work on this waterway was started several weeks before March 1, and the attempt to pass troops through it began on February 24.

force which could be brought to bear upon it; and the ironclads could not get close enough to do the work. Part of the
troops commenced the return trip to the Mississippi on March
21st arriving at Milliken's Bend on the 23rd.

The next attempt of importance, if not in the order of date,
was known as that of Steele's Bayou. This bayou debouched
from the west, or right, bank of the Yazoo about halfway from
its mouth to Haynes's Bluff; and extended northward about
seventy-five miles. It was very tortuous, filled with logs of
decaying trees, overhung with cypress and tangled growths,
and found to be exceedingly difficult to navigate. Gen. Sherman was in command; and two gunboats from Porter's fleet
led the procession up the Bayou. Knowing the difficulties to
be encountered the troops were loaded upon light-draft transports. The old and less valuable ones had been selected. There
was no lack of water on this route, but the vessels were torn
to pieces and the deck houses stripped off by overhanging
branches. In many instances great notches from one to two
feet deep had to be cut into cypress trees on each side of boats
to allow the guard rails to slide through. Not a plantation or
clearing broke its dreary solitude for forty miles. Birds, fish,
snakes, turtles and alligators were the only living things we
saw while traversing its dark and gloomy labyrinths.

On emerging into the Deer Creek plantations, we found the
Bayou so narrow and shallow that persons could jump from
the boats to dry land on either side. As usual we were surrounded by darkies, young and old, who rejoiced in our coming, gave much valuable information, recognized us as true
friends, and on the return accompanied us in large numbers
to Young's Point and Milliken's Bend.

As usual also the Confederates began to appear in the distance and to show a determination to stop our advance, if

possible. Porter's "ironclads" finally were several miles ahead of the infantry transports. Soon firing was heard in the extreme advance, and it became apparent that the enemy were trying to impede and harass the gunboats. No fears were entertained for their safety however until an appeal for aid came from Porter to Sherman.

The infantry made a forced march to their relief and found them in what seemed to the "dough-boys" a ridiculous predicament. The Confederates had dumped one or two kilns of brick into the channel in front of the boats so it was impossible for them to proceed; and had then gone deliberately to work felling trees in the creek in the rear. Sharpshooters were in tree tops commanding the ironclads and every one who appeared on deck was a target for prize shooting. The Admiral and his boats were at their mercy and would have been starved into a surrender beyond all question without outside aid!

Gen. Sherman raised the siege, helped to remove obstructions in the rear, and enabled the fleet to back out. A reconnaisance showed that Deer Creek and the Sunflower would not permit the passage of vessels, and the expedition was considered a failure, and the return commenced.

Being then a war correspondent on the *Times* my ambition was to secure a newspaper "beat." I selected three of the ablest darkies I could find, took possession of the best skiff on the Bayou, put on board extra oars, a supply of hard tack and bacon, and started back in advance of the troops. We rowed all night and arrived next forenoon at a point opposite Eagle Bend on the Mississippi where the bayou was only a mile from the river, just in time to catch the mail boat for Memphis and Cairo, putting the Chicago *Times* three days ahead of all competitors.

A few parting compliments to Admiral Porter seem in order. At the risk of being thought dogmatic, and of standing alone in this opinion, I pronounce him by all odds the greatest humbug of the war. He absolutely never accomplished anything if unaided. He bombarded Vicksburg for months; threw hundreds of tons of metal into the city; never hit but one house and never killed a man. The Confederates laughed at him. He attacked its batteries, and those of Haynes's Bluff, and was driven from both. Gen. Grant in his Memoirs, page 463, Vol. I, mentions Porter's passage of Vicksburg with several vessels, in a way to convey the impression that these were the first to accomplish that feat. My recollection is vivid that Grant had previously prepared several old hulks of steamboats; called for volunteer crews; and actually ran five or six safely past, losing only one. Also, that Porter subsequently followed with his fleet from very shame. The same thing occurred substantially afterwards at Grand Gulf; Porter fought the Confederate batteries one whole afternoon and hauled off whipped. Grant was compelled to run transports past these batteries and ferry the river at Bruinsburg a few miles below. . . .

Add to this that Porter was vain, arrogant and egotistical to an extent that can neither be described nor exaggerated and you have his calibre completely. He possessed many polite accomplishments; but very few qualities of a great naval commander.

It is one of the anomalies of human existence that the most enduring personal attachments are often formed between persons of the widest dissimilar characters. The warm personal friendship which existed between Grant and Porter was a case of this kind, and lasted unbroken throughout their lives. Porter's enemies accused him of selfish dissimulation, but Grant's professions of esteem were always sincere. Of all the great

men mentioned in history, not excepting King James the 2nd
of England, Gen. Grant was the most easily imposed upon by
those he believed to be his friends, and many sorrowful instances of this could be adduced till the end of his life.

I omitted to mention in the order of their occurrence a number of incidents which deserve statement. When Gen. Grant
decided to retain the Steamboat Magnolia as his headquarter
boat he was compelled to issue an order forbidding civilians
occupying staterooms, seats at the dining table, or in being in
any manner quartered upon, or fed from the vessels. Guards
were stationed at the gangplanks day and night to exclude
every one not connected with headquarters. Gen. Rawlins informed me privately that I was an exception to that order, and
that I was given the privilege of selecting any stateroom not
occupied by the staff, and making any arrangement that
pleased me best for meals on board, or on shore. I remained
there until the boat was discharged from the service at Milliken's Bend.

For a few weeks after we arrived at Young's Point a large
proportion of the dead were buried in a strip of bottom land
laying between the river bank and the levee. As the water rose
to the level of the river bank, in some places, this bottom was
converted into a mud hole and quagmire, until teams that
were still contriving to drag through to the transports for supplies would often strike the end of the box or coffin and heave
it clear out of the ground. Generally these were buried a
second time, a little deeper. For another period thereafter, the
dead were buried in the side of the levee (there being no other
dry ground for miles), until the levee was literally honey-
combed by such excavations.

On one occasion the father of a dead soldier came from
the north with a metallic casket, disinterred the remains of his

son who had died of smallpox from the bank, and left the empty box on the side of the levee. That night one of the negro, roustabouts on the Magnolia brought this discarded smallpox coffin to the lower deck of the vessel and used it to sleep in for fully a week before he was detected. Singularly the contagion did not spread, but fumigations were in order for a while.

Immediately after the departure of Thomas W. Knox from the Department, as previously mentioned, Mr. Finley Anderson presented himself at headquarters as Knox's successor. He remained but a short time, visited Capt. [Charles Rivers] Ellet's fleet which lay on the river a few miles below Vicksburg and decided to accompany him on his expedition up Red River. Anderson seemed completely infatuated by the promise of excitement and adventure, and no persuasions could induce him to forego this trip. Leaving his personal effects in my care to be shipped to his mother in New York City, if any accident befell him, and in company with Mr. A. H. Bodman, correspondent of the Chicago *Tribune*, he started.

The fate of the campaign is historical. Ellet's fleet was practically destroyed. Bodman escaped capture by floating away from a sinking vessel on a cotton bale; but Anderson preferred the chances of captivity to those of drowning. He remained on the vessel until taken off by the Confederates and was confined a year in a southern Texas prison. Bodman escaped and brought back the first detailed account of the disaster.

Mr. Anderson returned to New York early in 1864 and found that his widowed mother had been the especial charge of the New York *Herald* during his absence, and that his personal account in that office was credited with full pay for the whole time of his imprisonment, and a blank space left for estimated expenditures. He was soon sent as a correspondent to Culpeper Court House. He was wounded in the Wilderness at the side of Gen. [Winfield Scott] Hancock; and afterwards was induced by that officer to relinquish his position on the *Herald* and accept that of Assistant Adjutant General on his staff. He held this place under Hancock to the end of the war and the muster out of the veteran reserve corps which Hancock had been authorized to recruit during his convalescence from wounds received at Gettysburg. Anderson seemed to be absolutely fearless in danger, and this was the quality that first attracted Hancock's notice.

About the middle of February (I think the 12th) I visited Lake Providence and learned on the morning after my arrival there that Gen. Hulburt [Stephen A. Hurlbut], at Memphis, Col. [Jeremiah C.] Sullivan, at Jackson, and Col. [James M.] True, at Trenton, had at about the same time, but without intentional concert of action, susceptible of proof, suppressed the circulation of the Chicago *Times* within their jurisdictions. In one or two instances their orders had been enforced to the extent of seizing and destroying the papers found in the hands of newsboys and dragging the innocent vendors to the Provost Marshal for punishment, before they knew of the orders.

On the Mississippi river Gen. Hurlbut's order was carried to the length of threatening severe fine and punishment to anyone found with a copy in his possession. A system of terrorism was attempted, which if carried out, would have prevented the circulation of that paper in the Department. The reasons for such action were personal and political so far as these officers were concerned, but originated largely in the envious suggestions of the publishers and correspondents of rival papers. The *Times* had acquired a wonderful circulation throughout the U.S.—the largest by far, to that date, ever secured by any newspaper outside of the Atlantic cities. Its news from the western armies was early, complete, and greatly superior to that of any competitor.

Gen. Grant had run up to Lake Providence during the night on the headquarter boat and arrived about daylight. I had a conference with Rawlins, concerning the suppression of the *Times* by these commanders. I took the ground that their procedure was unwise and unjust; that any paper which the Sec'ty. of War permitted to be published should also be permitted to circulate in all the armies of the U.S.; and that it was certainly true that if the *Times* or any other newspaper, was to be prohibited in the Dep't. of the Tennessee, it should be done by the Dep't. commander alone; that it would not do to vest such discretionary power in the hands of district commanders, because one paper might be suppressed at one place, another at another place, and so on indefinitely according to the caprice or prejudice of every officer commanding a post.

Rawlins assented to this unqualifiedly, but did not know how the Gen. might view the matter. I spoke to Gen. Grant concerning it as soon as he emerged from his stateroom, and presented the case in the same way to him. He said without a moment's hesitation that my positions were well taken, and that while he disliked the general tenor of the *Times* as much as any officer in his Dep't. he nevertheless admitted the right of anyone to pay for it and read it. A special order was sent to those officers countermanding their action. . . .

I returned from a hurried trip to Memphis, and arrived at Milliken's Bend, Saturday, April 18th. I was met at the gangplank by A. D. Richardson, Junius Henri Browne and Richard Colburn, my fellow correspondents, who informed me headquarters were several days ahead, and nearly all the troops withdrawn from Milliken's Bend.[2] These gentlemen had secured a government tug, had it thoroughly protected, as they supposed, by cotton bales, and had all arrangements made to run by the Vicksburg batteries that night. They were in high glee over their success in securing this method of transportation and urgently solicited me to join them. I took an hour to consider the matter and decided to take my chance through the mud. As my horse and equipments had gone on with headquarters the best I could do was to secure a government mule, a thrown away cavalry saddle and bridle, and one or two extra blankets. Thus mounted I took to the road, over which the army had preceded me.

I soon overtook Hon. Sherard Clemens, member of Congress from Wheeling, Va., in the last old Congress. He was the man who fought a duel with O. Jennings Wise two years before this, and was crippled for life by a pistol shot in his thigh. He married a Mrs. Grove, not far from Richmond, Louisiana, who owned a six thousand acre plantation well stocked with field hands. Our army marched through this plantation and destroyed an immense amount of property. Clemens was a strong Union man and was down there to look after his interests.[3]

As we were riding across his place, we found a couple of straggling soldiers asleep on one of his sofas, worth at least one hundred dollars, in an old shed nearly in the center of a cotton field. Clemens' father-in-law was a great rebel, who abandoned a plantation equally valuable, a few miles above, and upon the approach of the Union army drove the negroes

---

[2] Union headquarters had been moved from Milliken's Bend to Perkins's plantation, on the west bank of the river, a few miles above Grand Gulf.

[3] According to the *Biographical Directory of the American Congress*, Sherrard Clemens, a Buchanan Democrat, served for a time in the Confederate Army.

of both places to the western part of the state. Clemens and myself slept that night in the same room he was married in three years before. The house was stripped of its furniture; the magnificent grounds torn to pieces; one of the pianos stood in the yard with the strings torn out and the sounding board showing that it had been used as a feed trough for army mules.

I lay awake half the night listening for the batteries of Vicksburg to open on my friends, the correspondents, but for some reason the attempted passage was delayed until the next night. The tug was sunk and sixteen of the thirty-five persons on board were captured while floating to shore on cotton bales. Among the captured of course were the three correspondents. We received the first news of their misfortune from some rebel papers brought within our lines a few days afterwards. The next day I arrived at headquarters, then at Perkins' plantation, and remained there until the army moved below to cross at Bruinsburg. . . .

Up to this time nearly every projected movement on Vicksburg had proven a decided failure. The army was becoming discouraged; and during its stay in the swamps and bayous of Young's Point and Milliken's Bend had lost heavily from the unsanitary condition of its camps. Public feeling in the North had also become excited and troublesome. The cry of "On to Vicksburg" was as common as "On to Richmond." Gen. Grant's enemies were industrious and persistent in their efforts to have him removed from command. Many leading newspapers were openly demanding it. Public opinion had set so strongly in this direction because of the great length of time spent at Young's Point and Milliken's Bend, fruitlessly as it seemed to the nation at large, that his staunchest friends found it difficult to defend him.

The government was finally almost compelled to take some

action in the premises. Adjutant General Lorenzo Thomas was thereupon sent from Washington City to the theater of Grant's operations on a double mission. One of these was to examine the condition of the "contraband" camps on the Mississippi river, and if possible organize negro regiments there. The other, and most important, duty assigned him was to investigate affairs about Vicksburg with a view to Grant's removal. It was asserted in some quarters that he came clothed with authority to do this, if in his opinion it seemed advisable.

Contrary to public expectation Gen. Thomas became so interested in negro regiments that he seemed unlikely to reach Grant's headquarters before midsummer. He stopped at nearly every landing on the river and spent what seemed to be an unnecessary time at each, until he was suspected of purposely evading the disagreeable subject. However this may have been, the impatience at the capital became so great that Hon. Charles A. Dana, First Assistant Secretary of War, soon followed Gen. Thomas with full power to carry out the instructions previously given to the former so far as Gen. Grant was concerned.[4]

There was another potent but unexpressed reason for sending Gen. Thomas on this mission. He was the ranking Adjutant General in the United States Army, and never worked harmoniously with Secretary Stanton of the War department. His obstinacy and intractability were a constant source of irritation to the latter, who could brook no opposition to his own will. Mr. Stanton managed to have Thomas sent away from Washington, so that Gen. E. D. Townsend could assume the func-

---

[4] Dana had not yet been appointed First Assistant Secretary of War, and it is unlikely that either he or Thomas had authority to remove Grant from command, though Dana may have been instructed orally to observe Grant's habits.

tions of Adjutant General, as the next in rank. The latter was obsequious and time-serving—knew which side of his bread was buttered—and became a plastic instrument for executing Stanton's high-handed and tyrannical administration. . . .

Mr. Dana reached headquarters a day or two after the army had started from Milliken's Bend, and perhaps mindful of Mr. Lincoln's motto: "Never swap horses while crossing a river," he wisely delayed action for awhile.

Gen. Grant had been apprized by friends of Mr. Dana's visit and its probable object. A conference of Staff officers was held, the situation was explained by Rawlins, and a line of procedure agreed upon. The paramount object was to keep Mr. Dana quiet until Grant could work out his campaign. Several of the staff could scarcely be restrained from open manifestations of their hostility, but wiser counsel prevailed. Col. [William S.] Duff, chief of artillery, pronounced him a government spy, and was more inclined to throw him in the river, than to treat him with common civility. But Rawlins took a sensible practical view of the situation, and said: "I am surprised, Col. Duff, at your discourteous and unmilitary remarks. Mr. Dana is the First Assistant Secretary of War, and an official representative of the government. He should not be left in a moment's doubt as to the cordiality of his reception. He is entitled to as much official recognition as Mr. Stanton, or any other high public functionary. I shall expect you to see that a tent is always pitched alongside Gen. Grant's, for Mr. Dana's use as long as he remains at headquarters—that sentries are placed in front of it—that orderlies are detailed for his service—and a place at mess-table specially reserved for him."

A suitable horse and equipments were provided for Mr. Dana's use and the entire staff, including Col. Duff, were properly deferential. Dana was not long in becoming an enthusiastic admirer of Gen. Grant's military ability, and remained his staunch friend till the war ended. Thus again was imminent danger averted by the wisdom and tact of Rawlins, and Grant spared to become the greatest military chieftain his generation produced.

Mr. Dana was shrewd enough to see that much which had been urged against Gen. Grant was untrue, or unjust, and undoubtedly thought it would be unwise to remove him from command on the eve of important movements, or in the middle of a campaign. This authority could be exercised later on should failure seem to justify it. Should the campaign prove successful, his delay would be completely vindicated. He therefore sacrificed personal comfort, adapted himself to the situation, shared the fatigues and deprivations of the march, and remained at headquarters till Vicksburg surrendered. . . .

CHAPTER

Four

[*With Grant's army posted on the west bank of the Missis-*
sippi below Vicksburg, Porter brought his ironclads and trans-
ports down past the dangerous batteries by night, and on
April 30 ferried Grant's troops to the east bank. A sharp fight
took place at Port Gibson, but the Confederates fell back, and
Grant set up his headquarters at Grand Gulf. Then, cutting
loose from his base and subsisting on the country, Grant began
his advance on Vicksburg by way of Raymond.]

The stories and anecdotes circulated, then and since, relating
to Gen. Grant's being separated from his Headquarter train
for days at a time, depending on borrowed horses for passing
from one command to another, sleeping on the ground without
blankets or covering of any kind; and having no baggage but
a toothbrush, are so literally true that no exaggeration is possible. The headquarters train could not be brought to the front
for several days after the battle of Port Gibson, and his horses,
servants, mess-chest, and clothing, except what he had on,
were too far behind for any communication. He rode a naked
saddle tree for a week which had nothing but stirrups for
upholstery. . . .

From about May 3d till the afternoon of May 4th I remained behind in Grand Gulf to get off my dispatches for the North, quite an amount of matter having accumulated in my note-book for lack of any safe and speedy conveyance. Soon after daylight Monday morning I mounted a captured mule, with such equipment as could be hastily obtained, and took the road leading by way of Hankinson's Ferry to Vicksburg. The ride, notwithstanding the annoying peculiarities of an illy broken mule, was one of the most delightful of my life. It was a well traveled thoroughfare, along elevated ridges, through dense forests (sometimes for miles) of large magnolias, then in full bloom; or through thickets of black haw, and wild plums, along the creeks and small brooks which I frequently crossed, past acres and acres of mayflowers (mandrake) also in bloom, and by Virginia rail fence at every plantation presenting an impenetrable hedgerow of sassafras and wild grapevines.

The grass was growing luxuriantly, birds were singing joyously, and everything seemed to be putting on the beautiful garments of spring-time. The fragrance of bud, blossom and flower became absolutely oppressive, until the forenoon sun had partially dissipated it. Occasional stragglers and slightly wounded men pushing ahead in pairs and squads to rejoin their commands were the only human beings I encountered for several hours.

Toward noon when in the vicinity of Hankinson's Ferry I passed to the front of the advanced infantry then moving by that road, and passed into the highly cultivated and well improved farm lands stretching along Big Black. In a lane separating two farms I saw a group of children that had just been dismissed from school on account of the approach of our army. As soon as the children saw me they took to the fence corner thickets, like a covey of quail, and it required considerable persuasion on my part to induce them to come out of hiding and answer some friendly questions. They had been taught to believe that the "Yankee Army" was a horde of vandals.

On reaching the school house the teacher saluted me from the doorsteps and begged for the privilege of a few minutes conversation. She came from central New York, a year before war was declared between the North and South, and was never able thereafter to get through the lines on her way homeward. She said the people had been uniformly and uncommonly kind to her, had mitigated the hardship and distress of her isolation from friends and home, had paid her wages as fully as was possible under the circumstances, and had generously shared with her all obtainable supplies of dry goods, clothing, &c. But she was too intensely "Union" in sentiment to feel comfortable with such environments, and her daily prayer was for "Home, Home, sweet, sweet Home." The arrival of Gen. Grant's army gave her the first look into a northern face for two years, and intensified her determination to get away.

I tried to reconcile her to a few weeks delay by assuring her that Vicksburg would soon be in our hands and the Mississippi open from St. Anthony's Falls to the sea. She answered that this hope, so long deferred, had made her sick at heart, that the chances of war were too uncertain for her ease, that with Gen. Grant's permission she could go at once.

I escorted her to headquarters, presented her to the general and saw her depart in half an hour to make arrangements for starting northward next morning. Grant also tried to persuade her to remain where she was a short time longer; explained to her that the only transportation back to Milliken's Bend would be an army wagon or ambulance, that her route would be through and past an army of men; that she would not see a white woman's face on the entire trip; and the only protection and escort he could give her would be written orders to Army officers and Steamboat Captains to furnish her free transportation and subsistence as far as Cairo, Illinois, and such personal assistance as a courier and bearer of dispatches could give her between himself and Milliken's Bend. She accepted the conditions joyfully, and started the next day.

She subsequently wrote to me announcing her safe arrival home, with far less hindrance and annoyance than she was prepared to encounter; and expressed warm feelings of gratitude on her own part, and that of her relatives and friends, for my kindly interest in presenting her to Gen. Grant and doing all in my power to provide for her comfort and safety on the road.

During the delay at Hankinson's Ferry, Gov. Oglesby [1] of Ill. and Hon. Elihu B. Washburne, member of Congress from the Galena District of that state, arrived at headquarters on a very short visit. The governor brought with him a barrel of whiskey which was generously distributed by the drink (or canteenful in a few instances). On leaving, the governor turned over to Col. Duff and myself all that remained in the barrel with the jocular remark that we seemed to be the only persons who could be safely trusted with such a valuable commodity. We filled and secreted as many canteens and bottles as we could obtain, and had a small store in reserve when the barrel was finally emptied. This reserve lasted us, and a few of our friends, until the morning of the investment of Vicksburg, May 18th.

It will give some insight into the habits and character of

---

[1] Richard J. Oglesby was not elected Governor of Illinois until November 1864. The visitor was Governor Richard Yates, who reviewed Grant's Illinois troops and delivered a speech. See Charles A. Dana's letter to Stanton of April 27, 1863, Stanton Papers, Library of Congress.

Gen. John A. Logan, at that time, to state that he often rode from his headquarters to ours, at night, after his troops had gone into camp, a distance varying from five to ten miles, attended by a single staff officer or orderly, ostensibly on some business with Gen. Grant, but in reality to have a convivial hour with Col. Duff. He was, as yet, not up to the conventional requirements of a Brigadier General. A great change came over him in after life, when I think he renounced his earlier political habits of drinking and swearing. He was developed and broadened by the times, and grew up to requirements of the eminent military and civil positions he afterwards held.

But during this same campaign I saw him on one occasion (after he became a brigadier general), with nothing on him in the way of clothing but his hat, shirt and boots, sitting at a table on which stood a bottle of whiskey and a tin cup, and playing on the violin for a lot of darky roustabouts to dance. When the exercise began to flag, which it generally did at short intervals in the face of such temptations, potations were indulged in by player and dancers. Yet he was never accused of drunkenness—was not intoxicated from the beginning to the end of the war, so far as came to my knowledge.

On the night of May 13th [2] I was a guest at Gen. [John Milton] Thayer's headquarters a couple of miles south of Fourteen Mile creek, on which all three army corps rested at that date. . . . Gen. Thayer then commanded a brigade in Sherman's Corps, afterward became Major General, Governor of Nebraska, and United States Senator from that Commonwealth. As the head of Sherman's advance approached the heavy timber which skirted the creek it was harassed by a venomous fire from sharpshooters in the tree tops, and by an

---

[2] This must have been May 11, the night before the battle at Raymond on May 12.

occasional wild shot from a Confederate cannon somewhere beyond the timber. The column was halted; the road cleared for the passage of artillery, and the First Missouri Battery of Light Artillery ordered to the front to shell the woods and drive out or develop the enemy in front.

As this battery passed me, on the gallop to go into position, one of the drivers with whom I had a slight acquaintance, saluted with a hurrah and dashed ahead. I was holding my watch in my hand, noting the time. The timber was soon cleared of sharpshooters and the column again put in motion. On riding forward to where this battery had opened fire, I found a detachment just heaping up the dirt on the shallow grave of one of their comrades, and was startled to find it was that of my "driver acquaintance."

A piece of clapboard was placed at the head of his grave rudely inscribed with his name, rank, and the command to which he belonged; and as his battery marched off leaving him "alone in his glory," I looked again at my watch and found that only twenty-nine minutes had elapsed between the time of his passing me in robust health, and the march of his comrades away from his newly made grave. But nothing more could be done. The corps was in the face of impending battle. It could not be stayed an instant for the loss of one man—or hundreds of men—and he was fortunate to receive even this hasty burial by the hands of his friends.

Soon after this the roar of cannon a few miles to the right signaled the attack by Logan's division of McPherson's corps, upon the Confederate General [John] Gregg, who resisted his advance with great spirit and determination. Although having less than six thousand troops, and being greatly outnumbered by Union troops, Gregg fought with such obstinacy that the tide of battle was not hopelessly set against him for three hours. He was at last compelled to withdraw hastily from the field he had held so gallantly, with a loss of three hundred and five killed and four hundred and fifteen left as prisoners in our hands.[3] McPherson lost sixty-six killed; three hundred thirty-nine wounded; and thirty-seven missing. I entered Raymond with McPherson's advance and before night had dispatched north a very complete list, for the circumstances, of all casualties, with the names, rank and regiments of nearly all the killed and wounded belonging to the Union army.

That afternoon and night refugee "contrabands" came swarming into our lines by hundreds. They were of all ages, sexes and conditions, and came on foot, on horses and mules, and in all manner of vehicles, from the typical southern cart, to elegant state carriages and barouches. Straw collars and rope harness alternated with silver plate equipments, till the moving living panorama became ludicrous beyond description.

The runaway darkies who had made sudden and forcible requisition upon their old masters for these varied means of transportation, generally loaded their wagons and carriages with the finest furniture left in the mansions when their owners had abandoned them at our approach. Feather beds and tapestried upholstery seemed to possess a peculiar charm and value to the dusky runaways. A black boy named Jerry, probably fourteen years old, who came to headquarters at that time, was taken by Rawlins as a body servant, and attended him till the war ended. On settling in Washington City in 1865, Rawlins kept him in his family, gave him quite a fair education, and had no more sincere mourner at his funeral than this faithful black boy Jerry.

Another boy named Willis attached himself in the same ca-

[3] Gregg reported his losses as 73 killed, 229 wounded, and 205 missing. Francis Vinton Greene: *The Mississippi* (New York, 1884), p. 143.

pacity to Col. Duff and remained with him till his expiration
of service at City Point. He then became mine by adoption, as
he claimed; but he certainly adopted me instead of my adopt-
ing him; and would doubtless be with me today, had not
Count Saldatankoff of the Grand Duke Alexis' retinue during
his visit to the U.S. over a quarter of a century ago, taken an
especial fancy to him and prevailed on Willis to accompany
him to Russia.

Even then he made one irruption on me in Milwaukee
afterward. He became homesick—wanted to see his "ole
Mammy "—in Arkansas—came to New York as a full fledged
Marine on a Russian War vessel—was furloughed for three
months and supplied with clothing, and cash to visit his "ole
Mammy"—joined his vessel at the expiration of his furlough—
and is presumably a loyal subject of the Czar, as I write this
brief account of his career. He asserted stoutly that "de Count
Saldatankoff, was a mitey nice man—de nicest man he eber
seed," excepting myself—and expected to remain in his service
till death separated them. . . .

The night of May 12th was spent by me on an army cot in
Col. Duff's tent. About midnight, or soon thereafter, Gen.
Grant came into the tent alone, in the dark, and requested a
drink of whiskey. Col. Duff drew a canteen from under his pillow and handed it to him. The general poured a generous po-
tation into an army tin cup and swallowed it with great apparent satisfaction. He complained of extraordinary fatigue and
exhaustion as his excuse for needing the stimulant, and took
the second, if not the third drink, before retiring.

A light was struck upon his entrance, so that he knew of my
presence; but he made his request, and drank the whiskey in
an ordinary manner, as if it was a matter of fact procedure
which required no particular apology. His stay in the tent did

not exceed twenty or thirty minutes. He sat on the edge of Duff's cot, facing mine, and apparently addressed himself to me as much as to Duff.

This was the first time I ever saw Gen. Grant use any spirituous liquor, and I was a little surprised by his openness in asking for it, and drinking it, before me. My intercourse with him to that time had been casual or accidental rather than intimate and confidential as it afterwards became; yet there was nothing evinced in word or behavior, from which I could infer that he desired the slightest secrecy or concealment concerning the object of his midnight call. The occurrence was never mentioned by me, excepting perhaps to Rawlins, until after the close of the rebellion. I think Col. Duff did suggest to me after the general's exit from the tent, that in view of Grant's reputation for excessive drinking, and his peculiar surroundings at that time, the affairs of state as well as my personal interests, might be best promoted by discreet silence, inasmuch as the general did not know that anyone occupied the tent with him until concealment was out of the question.

But I put a different construction upon his indifference, which was fully borne out by after events. The general knew that Gov. Oglesby [4] had left nearly a half barrel of whiskey in the joint care of Col. Duff and myself on taking his departure from headquarters a few days before. I also subsequently learned that Duff had catered to Grant's inordinate desire for stimulants long before this, and continued to do so till his "muster-out" at City Point. Rawlins suspected him of doing so, but had no positive proof of the fact for more than a year after this. Duff did not rise from his cot during Grant's stay that night, but lay stretched out at full length, except when he half

---

[4] See above. p. 66, footnote 1.

rose on one elbow to join the General in his drinks, and to
volunteer "success to our campaign, and confusion to the
Whole Confederacy." But little was said by Grant in response
to these sentiments, beyond an expression of satisfaction at
what he had thus far accomplished, and a cheerful hope and
belief that Vicksburg would soon be ours.

From the date of Sherman's arrival at Hankinson's Ferry,
till we fought the battle of Raymond, foraging upon the enemy
was brought to the highest stage of efficiency. Army wagons
by scores and hundreds were sent out daily from ten to fifteen
miles, escorted by infantry details sufficient to protect them
from any sudden foray of Confederate Cavalry. They returned
at nightfall groaning under the weight of impressed supplies,
and increased by the addition to the train of every vehicle, no
matter what its description, that could bear the weight of a
sack of grain, pieces of salt meat, or pails full of butter, eggs,
honey or vegetables.

Fine carriages were often brought in loaded with corn fodder (blades stripped from the stalk in the fall, dried and bound
into sheaves), sheaf oats, or anything eatable by man or beast,
that was conveniently at hand. Horses, mules and cattle were
brought by droves of hundreds. I frequently saw horses, cattle
and mules, of all ages and condition; milch cows and calves;
sheep, goats and lambs; turkeys, geese, ducks and chickens,
driven together in one drove. Other details of men slaughtered
a sufficiency to supply the army each night. Corn and corn
meal was abundant. Salt, sugar, coffee, and sometimes a small
quantity of "hardtack," were the only issues then made from
our supply trains coming from Grand Gulf. The country was
much richer in food products than we had expected to find it.
If owners could establish their loyalty they were given regular
vouchers for everything taken—if not, not.

CHAPTER

Five

[*General Joseph E. Johnston, attempting to reinforce General Pemberton at Vicksburg, had recently reached Jackson, the capital of Mississippi, with some 12,000 troops, and was expecting more. Pemberton commanded more than 30,000. Grant, with about 40,000, some of whom had not yet crossed the river, sought to prevent a junction of the two Confederate forces and to defeat them in detail. On May 14 McPherson and Sherman struck heavily at Johnston, forcing him to abandon the city of Jackson. He retreated northward in an effort to make contact with Pemberton. Grant moved quickly to keep his army between the two Confederate forces. Cadwallader entered Jackson with the Union advance.*]

. . . As soon as the fire of the Confederate batteries was silenced, Fred. Grant (a stout goodnatured son of the General who accompanied the army all through the campaign) and myself, started for the Capitol at full speed to secure the large Confederate flag which waved from a staff on the roof. We supposed ourselves far in advance of anyone connected with the Union army. We dismounted hurriedly in front of the building, ran upstairs till we reached those leading from the garret to the roof, where we met a ragged, muddy, begrimed cavalryman descending with the coveted prize under his arm. To say that our disappointment was extreme but mildly expresses the state of our feelings. We were beaten and compelled to admit that to the victor belongs the spoils.

I pushed on to the Bowman House, then the principal hotel in the city, and found its office and corridors filled with Confederate officers and soldiers, some of whom were wounded and disabled men from convalescent hospitals; others who were doubtless bummers, skulkers and deserters who fell out of the Confederate ranks as Johnston's army retreated across the river; and a large concourse of townspeople and civilians who chanced to be there from other parts of the State. I ran the gauntlet of unfriendly observation; secured a room at once; and wrote dispatches for the Chicago *Times*, with scarcely a moment's relaxation, till Gen. Grant's courier was ready to take the road for Grand Gulf, with government dispatches, announcing his victories at the capital of Mississippi.

Grant and staff arrived at the Bowman House soon after I did, which diverted attention from me. He occupied the room that night which was said to be same one Gen. Johnston had slept in the night before. Many calls were made upon him by citizens asking for guards to protect their private property, some of which perhaps were granted, but by far the greater number were left to the tender mercies of Confederate friends.

Gen. Sherman was charged with the provost duty of the city and was directed to remain with his corps till all the public property used by the Confederacy had been destroyed and its usefulness as a great Confederate railroad center put past the possibility of being speedily re-established. Foundries, machine-shops, warehouses, factories, arsenals and public stores were fired as fast as flames could be kindled. Many citizens

fled at our approach, abandoning houses, stores, and all their
personal property, without so much as locking their doors.

The negroes, poor whites—and it must be admitted—some
stragglers and bummers from the ranks of the Union army—
carried off thousands of dollars worth of property from houses,
homes, shops and stores, until some excuse was given for the
charge of "northern vandalism," which was afterward made by
the South. The streets were filled with people, white and
black, who were carrying away all the stolen goods they could
stagger under, without the slightest attempt at concealment,
and without let or hindrance from citizens or soldiers. Of
course this was mainly stopped as soon as Sherman had fairly
and formally assumed control of affairs; but the era of stealing
and plundering lasted through the evening and night of the
14th, I believe. In addition to destruction of property by Gen.
Sherman's orders, the convicts of the penitentiary, who had
been released by their own authorities, set all the buildings
connected with that prison on fire, and their lurid flames added
to the holocaust elsewhere prevailing. . . .

A rather laughable affair took place at the Bowman House,
if correctly reported, when Gen. Grant before leaving, demanded the bill for headquarter entertainment. Sixty dollars
was the sum demanded by the proprietor for all their accommodations. Lieut. Colonel Wilson thereupon took out a $100
bill in Confederate paper and handed it to the landlord. The
latter seemed thunderstruck and said that he had expected to
be paid in U.S. coin, or greenbacks, or the charges would have
been much higher. "Very well," said the Colonel, "charge
what you please. We propose to pay you in Confederate
money." It was finally settled on the latter basis at 90 dollars.

Whether literally true or not in this particular instance, such
discriminations were constantly made in all intermediate terri-

tory. When outside of our own lines, I never paid less than
ten dollars in Confederate money for a single meal, although
that much was never demanded, and I was quite as willing to
give twice that for a satisfactory dinner. I had an abundance
of it that cost me nothing, and there was no other way in
which I could properly use it. On one occasion I gave an old
darky a One Hundred Dollar bill for a bridle rein. After I had
convinced him that it was indeed a note of that denomination
he threw up both hands joyfully and exclaimed: "'Fore God
dat will buy a mule." I advised him to so invest it, and rode on.

On the morning of May 15th I made an early start from
Jackson for the front and arrived at McPherson's headquarters
late in the afternoon. A disagreeable rain set in which lasted
all night. It added greatly to the fatigue and discomfort of
the marching troops, but did not materially delay them. All
were in position on the morning of the 16th, excepting McClernand. Some of his divisions were behind and otherwise out of
place, although he marched on a shorter line than McPherson
to the point of convergence. Thus he unwittingly added to the
long list of shortcomings another black mark in Gen. Grant's
book of remembrance.[1] I messed that night and next morning
at Gen. Logan's headquarters, slept under the friendly shelter
of one of his tents, and was up early anticipating coming
events. Grant and Staff spent the night at Clinton.

Logan's division of McPherson's Corps had the advance in
the morning and moved out of Camp early and briskly, expecting to encounter Pemberton in the forenoon and having
the honor of opening the battle which all agreed was now in-

---

[1] McClernand was ready at 9.30 a.m., but did not receive Grant's
reply as to when he should attack until 2 p.m. But his advance was slow.
Matthew Forney Steele: *American Campaigns* (Washington, 1943),
p. 411.

evitable. Logan and myself were near the head of his column, after an hour or two of marching, when we reached a road coming obliquely into ours from the one on which McClernand's advance was to be made, and [Alvin Peterson] Hovey's division of the latter's Corps was already half past.

Logan was compelled to halt till Hovey had passed this intersection, and then start on squarely in Hovey's rear. I rarely ever witnessed such an exhibition of rage, profanity and disappointment as Logan then gave. The air was just blue with oaths, till speech was exhausted. McPherson's arrival a few minutes after was the signal for another outburst. But there was no apparent remedy. Hovey had the road by right of prior occupation, but Logan's division was avenged before nightfall.

In the meantime McPherson learned of Pemberton's proximity, and sent word to Grant urging him to come to the front. By half past seven in the morning Grant and staff were on the road from Clinton, and arrived at Champion's plantation lying in front of the ridge or hill on which the battle was fought, just as Hovey opened fire on the enemy's left and commenced the day's engagement. . . .

The road on which Hovey and McPherson marched passed across the north end of Champion's plantation till it reached the western border of the lowland when it turned to the left, and ascended to the northern end of the timbered land which extended a mile or two southward, when it turned westward again on its way to Vicksburg. On the crest of this ridge facing eastward, Pemberton was found in line of battle awaiting McClernand's attack. Hovey's division followed the road up the sloping end of the ridge and fell upon Pemberton's left under Gen. [C. L.] Stevenson with such impetuosity that it was driven pell-mell in the utmost confusion and disorder before it could be reinforced from the rebel center and right. As it was rolled back it became stronger and stronger until it rallied, reformed, and was reinforced; when it in turn repulsed Hovey severely, following up its advantages to the extent of sending it flying back over the ground it had just so gallantly won.

Between the end of Hovey's splendid charge, and Stevenson's equally successful counter-charge, there ensued a lull in the firing, while each was preparing for a second contest. I was lying on the blue grass in Champion's front yard, with Grant and staff near by in the shade, when I asked Rawlins if I had not better ride up in the timber and "see what was going on." He thought it the proper thing to do if I felt so inclined, whereupon I mounted and started. I soon found a few dead, and many wounded.

Coming to an abandoned four-gun battery of six-pound Confederate cannon which Stevenson had been obliged to leave behind him, I stopped to examine them. Several of the horses lay dead in their harness, and dead men in blue and gray were also plentiful. The forest as far as I could see was torn and trampled. While there, trying to get some slightly wounded men to run the cannon back towards the rear, the fighting was fiercely renewed some distance ahead of me, and I was not long in discovering the tide of battle had turned in my direction. The rattling musketry fire came nearer and nearer; the noise and storm of battle grew louder and stronger every minute; and very soon some rebel guns commenced a furious cannonade on Hovey's broken, retreating ranks. The air was filled with the roar of battle; and with leaves and twigs from saplings and trees. Next, the road and woods was filled by the slightly wounded, and stragglers, who came singly and in squads, until it seemed as if the whole command was irretrievably routed.

I was not long in deciding that my point of observation

ought to be further to the rear, but I was determined to not add to the panic by any exhibition of haste! But as I now write after the lapse of forty years since the date of that battle, several of which often placed me in positions of greater danger, I never felt more like hurrying in my life. My pride in making a show of courage, which I was far from feeling; and in setting a good example to others; enabled me to ride at a moderate pace till I had passed to the front of Hovey's disorganized men.

At the foot of the hill in the open ground I met Gen. Grant and told him precisely what I had just witnessed—that Hovey's division was destroyed for the time being—and would soon come over the brow of the hill, with very little show of military formation. Turning to McPherson, who just then rode up, Grant said: "Cadwallader reports that Hovey is being driven back." McPherson replied that he also had just been informed of it. Grant spoke up with great quickness: "Then I would move Quimby [2] into line here," and pointing with his finger said: "I would place a battery here; and another there."

These dispositions were made just as Hovey's stampeding men poured over the crest. Hovey's troops were passed through the ranks of Quinby's brigade, reformed in its rear, and returned valiantly to the encounter which continued for at least two hours. As the rebels emerged from the timber in pursuit of Hovey the two batteries so opportunely posted, opened fire and staggered them back. Quinby started up the slope bearing to the right, and Hovey soon advanced along the line of his previous march and flight. Logan passed the north end of the ridge and turned southward. [Marcellus M.] Crocker's division came into line between Hovey's right and Logan's left, when the real battle began. . . .

---

[2] Isaac Ferdinand Quinby commanded the 7th division.

Impressions of great events recorded at the time are often of more value than after reflections and philosophising. For this reason I append a few extracts from a letter written by me that evening to my wife in Milwaukee, Wisconsin:

> *Champion's Hill,*
> *18 miles east of Vicksburg,*
> *May 16th 1863.*

. . . We have had another terrible battle. Though not so stupendous as some, not so many troops being engaged, it has been as hotly contested as any could be. The rattle of musketry was incessant for hours. Cannons thundered till the heavens seemed bursting. Dead men, and wounded, lay strewed everywhere. I have been riding day and night throughout this campaign. The army is absolutely nomadic. We march and fight alternately. I find it impossible to get a list of the killed, for "dead men tell no tales," and in these cases no one tells for them. Missing, means dead in this army. My heart sickens at the suspense many families must suffer. I saw Col. Gab [Gabriel] Bouck and Lieut. Col. Beale [Samuel W. Beall] of the 18th Wisconsin, after today's fighting. No officer in that regiment is killed or wounded. Col. [Charles R.] Gill's regiment (the 29th Wis.) was in the battle. Don't know how it fared. Publish these items of information in the Milwaukee Daily News, *on account of the families interested. I promised to write for them, but this publication will be better. Gen. Grant has defeated Pemberton today quite badly. Vicksburg must fall now. I think a week may find us in possession—it may take longer, but the end will be the same. . . .*

When the battle of Champion's Hill was over, I sat down to write my account of it for publication. Joseph B. McCullagh, then correspondent of the Cincinnati *Commercial* and after editor of the St. Louis (Mo.) *Globe-Democrat,* consulted me as to the best name to give it in our dispatches. We expected to transmit the first newspaper accounts from the field, and concluded that it would be permanently fixed in the public mind by any suitable name which we should use in concert. We agreed at once upon the name and dated our letters from "Champion's Hill."

Two days after the battle was fought the name by which it should be known in history was under discussion at headquarters. Gen. Grant said that in pursuance of the common usage of military commanders in fixing locations of battles by imperishable names of streams, mountains and well known places, he had given it the name of "Baker's Creek" in his official dispatches to the War office. I told him he was too late—that it was already named—that I had christened it "Champion's Hill" in my correspondence—that the newspaper dispatches giving it that name would reach every hamlet in the United States—that this would be its popular designation for one generation at least—and that millions of people would read of it by that name in my dispatches, while his official report naming it Baker's Creek, was growing mouldy in the pigeon-holes of the War Department. He laughingly replied that my prediction might prove true, but that he thought he ought to have the one small privilege of naming it.

By rapid work, good management, and the judicious expenditure in fees to couriers and others my dispatches were speedily transmitted and were published three days in advance of all others. They were copied by New York city papers in the absence of any from their own correspondents, and were read from the clerk's desk in the House of Representatives at Washington, D.C. I received many complimentary letters from the north concerning them; and the Albany (N.Y.) *Argus*

stated editorially that all eastern newspapers had been obliged
to depend on the Chicago *Times* for nearly two weeks, for the
latest news from Grant's Army.

Had Mr. McCullagh's dispatches to the Cincinnati *Commercial* been published before mine, he might justly have
claimed that he naméd the battle; but as I, on that occasion,
made what is termed a "newspaper beat," this honor belongs
to me. Gen. Grant calls it "the battle of Champion's Hill" on
page 518, Volume I of his Memoirs, and very few people know
it today by any other designation. I have been sorry ever since
that I did not consult the general as to its name, before sending off my dispatches.

Gen. Grant's headquarters on the night of the 16th were a
few miles west of the battleground. The only shelter I could
obtain was the porch of a log cabin which was full of wounded
Confederate soldiers. I was soon sound asleep in spite of all
surroundings but was waked up near midnight by some one
attempting to crawl over me. It proved to be a delirious soldier, struggling about in the dark and groaning in agony. I
changed my berth to the protection of an oak tree for the balance of the night, and had no further disturbance. . . .

The early morning of the 17th found me at Big Black where
the Union advance was busily engaged all day in collecting
material for building bridges across the river to replace those
destroyed by Pemberton. This was done by tearing down the
dwelling houses, barns, stables and cotton gins nearest at hand,
and flooring the cotton bale and timber floats which were
bound together and anchored in the river.

The Confederate forces were all withdrawn to the west, or
right, bank of the river, excepting Gen. Mart [Martin E.]
Green's Missouri brigade, which had been left on our side pro-

tected in front and on both flanks by what he considered an impassable bayou. Pemberton's artillery was posted to cover Green's brigade and to contest our passage of the river. On his arrival Grant rode to the river bank above the head of the bayou and opposite Pemberton's left. As he, and a few of the staff who accompanied him, emerged from the brush into plain view from the other bank, a murderous fire was opened on them by Confederate sharpshooters. They took to cover instantly, and providentially no one was hurt.

As our troops came up they were put into position for forcing a passage of the river as soon as darkness would conceal the movement if the bridges were finished. The fighting on the 17th at Big Black was confined to the batteries, till nearly noon when Col. Mike [Michael K.] Lawler, commanding the brigade on our right, with its right flank resting on the river, made one of his characteristic dashes across a small cotton field, plunged into the bayou in line of battle where the mud ranged in depth from the men's knees to their armpits, scrambled through and out of it, stormed the rebel riflepits and swarmed over their cotton-bale breastworks with irresistible impetuosity. Lawler's men suffered severely from the musketry fire on their advance, and from the rebel batteries on the opposite shore of the river covering the position, but nothing could check them for an instant. It was at the same time the most perilous and ludicrous charge that I witnessed during the war.

General Lawler was a large and excessively fat man—a fine type of the generous, rollicking, fighting Irishman. His cherished maxim was the Tipperary one: "If you see a head, hit it." He saw Green's brigade in a false and vulnerable position, and could not forbear impulsive action. He was precisely the kind

of officer to make an assault, and ask permission to do so afterwards. I cannot say positively that he acted in this case without orders, but I always supposed that he did. . . .

During the night of the 17th Pemberton retreated on Vicksburg and the Federal troops crossed at all points unobstructed,
very early on the morning of the 18th. Gen. Grant says the
crossing was at eight o'clock, by three bridges. I know that I
crossed on one of them before sunrise, and that infantry was
ahead of me. He also fixes the time of Lawler's charge of the
day before at about nine o'clock. I express the conviction with
considerable diffidence in the face of such authority, that it
was nearer twelve than nine o'clock.

With the maneuvers and marches between Jackson and the
Big Black, which resulted in separating and keeping apart
Gens. Johnston and Pemberton and driving the latter behind
his intrenchments at Vicksburg, may be said to have ended the
tactical features of the campaign. They were splendid beyond
description—almost beyond conception—are scarcely equaled
in history—and may be profitably studied for all time. They are
certain to be handed down to posterity as military classics,
for the imitation of future generations.

CHAPTER

Six

EARLY on the morning of May 18th 1863 the whole Union force was in line of march from Big Black to Vicksburg. . . . I rode some distance ahead of our advance at one time, and came in sight of some Confederate soldiers who had stacked arms and were lying in the grass in the shade. My first thought was that it would be dangerous to ride up to them, and that it might also be impossible to get safely away. But a moment's reflection dissipated my fears. They were far behind Pemberton's rear guard, and probably preferred being taken prisoners, to remaining longer in the rebel army.

As I rode up to them slowly they rose to a sitting posture and smiled good-naturedly. "What are you doing here boys," was my first salutation. "Well sir, we've been waiting for you to come along" was the reply from an Irishman who was the spokesman of the squad. "You want to be taken prisoners I suppose." "Well, that's about it sir," was the response. So ordering them to "fall in," I actually marched them back on the road till I found an officer to whom I could turn them over. It was a broad travesty on war; but a manifestation of what we afterward learned to be a wide-spread feeling in Pemberton's army.

At another place on the grassy lawn of a deserted plantation house near the road, the house servants and field hands were assembled to witness the approach of "Massa Linkum's sojers." Their delight was shown in every conceivable way. One old gray headed toothless darky attracted particular attention by his ludicrous speech and contortion of body. He would sit on the grass with his hands locked in front of his knees, immovable as a statue for a few minutes. Then he would tumble back on the grass swinging his arms, and kicking his feet in the air, and screaming at the top of his voice: "Glory, hallelujah, glory, hallelujah. Dis is de year of jubilee, sure nuff. Bless God, bless God. I never spected to see dis day." Then he would come to a sitting position for a few minutes, and roll on the grass screaming again.

As we approached a tumble-down sort of log cabin near the road a poor sickly looking woman stood at the gate waving a little Union flag. Without halting Gen. Grant directed a staff officer to inquire who lived there. He soon reported that it was the family of a river pilot whose former home had been in Illinois. He had been pressed into the Confederate service as a pilot until his health gave way, and then lay in the cabin a very sick man. The general directed the staff-surgeon [Henry S.] Hewitt to return and give what medical advice and assistance seemed necessary. After riding on a few minutes in silence he directed another officer to return and place a guard to protect the premises; and still another to see that the family was supplied with needful commissary stores. The sick man received daily medical attention till he was able to bear the trip north, when Grant furnished the family free transportation and subsistence as far as Cairo. . . .[1]

---

[1] Cadwallader related the above incidents to Albert D. Richardson for use in his *A Personal History of Ulysses S. Grant* (Hartford, Conn., and Newark, N.J., 1868).

The night of the 18th was spent by Grant and staff at an unpretentious farm house two or three miles back of our lines, which was abandoned by the owner at the approach of the Union army. A few negroes remained on the premises, and did all in their power to accommodate their distinguished guests. But there was not a pound of provisions of any kind to eat. The headquarter train did not arrive till nearly morning. About one o'clock at night some of the colored people caught, dressed and stewed a solitary turkey somehow left behind. This was divided fairly among the hungry, and to most of them was the only mouthful of food eaten from daylight on the 18th till about the same time on the 19th. But no complaints were heard. Mind for the time triumphed over matter. The successes of the day were so gratifying that men dropped down and slept happily till morning.

The 19th was spent mainly in skirmishing along the front to develop the enemy's position and force, and to push our lines as far ahead as possible. In the afternoon an assault was made with some hope of carrying the rebel works in a few places, but nothing favorable resulted, excepting to enable us to get better positions further in the advance. The 20th, and forenoon of the 21st were spent in desultory firing and skirmishing without accomplishing much. Here for the second time I record my impressions of the campaign as written at that time to my wife in Milwaukee, Wis.:

In front of Vicksburg,
May 21st 1863.

. . . *Nothing like this campaign has occurred during this war. It stamps Gen. Grant as a man of uncommon military ability—proves him the foremost one in the west; if not in the nation. The plan, although suggested by Rawlins and Wilson was his own. For almost the first time for a year, he was not interfered with from Washington, and the result has been five hard fought battles in two weeks; a march of two hundred miles; the capture of over six thousand prisoners; the taking of sixty pieces of field artillery and nine heavy siege guns; besides destroying small arms, ammunition, and Confederate state property beyond computation; and finally the close investment of Vicksburg from every quarter, and forcing the evacuation of Haynes's Bluff on the Yazoo that has heretofore given us so much trouble. I think it brilliant. All his plans have worked to a charm. The enemy have been deceived as to his strength and intended movements at all points. Supplies have been brought forward at tremendous effort. The men have been on half rations part of the time, but foraged on the country for the balance, and have not really suffered for food. The constant marching and fighting has been wearing on them, and many have fallen out of the ranks exhausted. Our loss in killed and wounded since crossing the Mississippi, is probably between six and eight thousand. . . . Officers high in command, including some of the General's staff, believe firmly that we shall be in Vicksburg within a week at farthest. Their means of judging are superior to mine of course, and cause me to doubt my own judgment—which is that the place will hold out for at least another month.*

My estimate of Federal losses were at that time too large. I have no official reports before me as I write, But Gen. Grant in his Memoirs, gives his losses in all these engagements, in killed, wounded and missing, as only four thousand three hundred and seventy-nine (4,379).[2] He places the number of

---

[2] The figure Grant gave was 4,386. The official figure through May 21 is 5,279.

prisoners captured at over six thousand, but says that as many more had been killed and wounded. He also states that his forces captured twenty-seven heavy cannon (instead of nine as stated in my private correspondence), and sixty-one pieces of field artillery, instead of sixty as made in my estimate. My information may have been given me at the date of my letter, by Grant, or Rawlins, but its substantial accuracy has been a source of satisfaction to me ever since.

On the afternoon of the 22d, as I then recorded it (although Gen. Grant says it was at ten o'clock in the forenoon), the general assault was made which became historical. The rank and file of the whole Union army seemed to think that owing to continuous defeats, and the demoralization which resulted as a consequence, the entire line of Confederate fortifications could be carried, by making an attack upon all quarters at once. Corps, division and brigade commanders were in consultation with Grant upon its advisability and the prospect of success; and so far as I then knew, or could afterward learn, all advised the attack. That it proved a disastrous failure is known to all readers.

Anticipating the assault I rode to a point between McClernand's and McPherson's Corps that promised reasonable protection, but was soon compelled to take refuge in a canyon, or gully, near by. From this I had a fair view of the fort or point upon which McClernand directed his principal movement, but could not see much of the field across which his advance was made.

The cannonading from both sides was terrific. The air was filled with solid shot, percussion shells, and about every kind of missile ever thrown from heavy guns. At this time we were using many Hotchkiss shells having wooden bases fastened to metal points with wire and strips of tin. These were so imperfectly manufactured that the wooden base was blown off a large proportion of them before they reached the enemy. When fired over the heads of our advancing columns, it was a common remark that they killed more of our own men by flying to pieces prematurely, than the killed and wounded of the enemy combined. However this may have been, they came swishing, buzzing and clattering around me in considerable numbers, but none of them touched me or my horse.

As McClernand's advance neared the rebel works, it came into plain view from my place of shelter. It had been so mercilessly torn to pieces by Confederate shot and shell that it had lost nearly all resemblance to a line of battle, or the formation of a storming column. Officers and men were rushing ahead pell-mell without much attention to alignment. The small number in sight could no longer be mown down by artillery, as the guns of the forts could not be depressed sufficiently.

When they crossed the deep ditch in front of the earthworks and began to ascend the glacis, they were out of musketry range for the same reason, excepting from one or two salients within reach. A straggling line, continually growing thinner and weaker, finally reached the summit, when all who were not instantly shot down were literally pulled over the rebel breastworks as prisoners. One stand of our colors was planted half way up the embankment and remained there till a daring Confederate ventured over, and carried it back inside. Many stragglers took refuge in the ditch outside the earthworks and remained there till they could crawl away covered by darkness. I cannot pretend to say how much time was consumed in what I have been describing. But it seemed to me hours before firing subsided enough to warrant my crossing the field and returning to headquarters.

I then learned that McClernand signalled Gen. Grant that

he had carried the rebel works on his front—asked for reinforcements to hold them—and also requested the attack to be
vigorously pressed at all points, to prevent concentration on
him. Grant was somewhat incredulous, and had the dispatch
repeated, fearing some mistake in its transmission. He then
ordered Quinby's brigade lying near McClernand's right to be
moved to his support at once. This was done quickly as possible.

But instead of using Quinby as a support to his own troops,
McClernand ordered them to the front in the forlorn hope of
retrieving the fortunes of the day, and attempted to make a
second assault, with some of his own demoralized troops on
Quinby's flank. One of his Colonels flatly refused to obey this
order and declared that he would take the consequences of
his disobedience rather than lead his men to certain death. Col.
Jo Mower, in command of the brigade sent from Quinby,
looked the ground over with the eye of an able commander,
and exclaimed: "Great God, no man can return from this
charge alive." He accordingly took off his watch and handed it
and what money he had to a personal friend who remained
behind, requesting him to forward all to his wife. He led his
men gallantly into action and fell dead at the first line.[3] The
whole affair was miserable and inexcusable to a point past
endurance.

Gen. Grant says in his Memoirs that he occupied a position
from which he believed he could see as well as McClernand
what actually took place, but that he did not see the success
reported to him by signal. He nevertheless sent him reinforce-

---

[3] Cadwallader is in error here. Brigadier General Joseph A. Mower
later served under General Banks in Louisiana, and under Sherman in
Georgia and the Carolinas. At his death, on January 6, 1870, he was a
major general, commanding the Department of Louisiana.

ment. It is morally certain that he saw but little of the assault and its consequences. Had he been near enough to obtain a clear view of it, his guilt would have exceeded McClernand's, and instead of reinforcing him he should have peremptorily withdrawn him from the field.

I remember distinctly that I gave to Grant and Rawlins the first complete account of its failure—stated that I was within plain view of the rebel earthworks—that McClernand never gained a footing inside of them—and that the small number of his men who actually reached the crest, or scrambled over it, were there yet as prisoners. I was questioned closely concerning it; and shall never forget the fearful burst of indignation from Rawlins, and the grim glowering look of disappointment and disgust which settled down on Grant's usually placid countenance, when he was convinced of McClernand's duplicity, and realized its cost in dead and wounded.

McClernand had commenced his attack. He expected to succeed. But that he ever carried any part of the fortifications on his front, as he signaled Grant he had already done, was absolutely false. This was a fair sample of Gen. McClernand's victories. Added to a rather long list of vexatious shortcomings which had been constantly accumulating against him for months, and his uncontrollable itching for newspaper notoriety which led him to scribble long fulminations from his headquarters which he called congratulatory orders, or addresses to his corps (in violation of the rules of the War Department and of Gen. Grant's orders), determined the latter to remove him from command. This was done, and the thirteenth army corps was thereafter under Maj. Gen. Edward Otto [Otho] Cresap Ord till the latter was taken east.

Gen. John A. McClernand belonged to that class of officers who were taken from civil life at the beginning of the war and made full Major Generals without any previous military training or experience, because of their supposed political influence in their respective states. Nathaniel P. Banks, Benjamin F. Butler and too many others, were of the number. Every such major general proved a signal failure. I cannot remember a single instance where any Major General of volunteers rose to that rank, and held it by merit, who did not at least commence as low in rank as a Colonel, and gained promotion, and military knowledge and usefulness, by first serving with his men. The list of such as these is long and brilliant. But they first served an apprenticeship to war.

Since I am recording incidents connected with this celebrated campaign against Vicksburg, rather than attempting a complete history of it, I shall dismiss this day's bloody work by saying that the corps of McPherson and Sherman made gallant and heroic attacks at all points on their fronts, with no better success than McClernand. They were everywhere repulsed, but were not guilty of sacrificing the lives of their men needlessly. From that time forward, regular military approaches were made, and siege operations proper began.

The rebel fortifications were not constructed in continuously straight or curved lines, as civilians sometimes suppose, but were exceedingly irregular, owing to the rough face of the country they traversed. It was rolling or hilly everywhere and badly cut up by ravines and gulches. The line of fortifications would be pushed out on all bold prominences and retired around the heads of ravines instead of crossing them.

One of these projecting salients named Fort Hill was on the main Vicksburg and Jackson dirt road; [4] and was made as near impregnable as such a place could well be. It was directly in

---

[4] Fort Hill was a half mile or more north of the Jackson road.

front of Logan's division of the 17th Corps, and had been as nearly approached as was possible on covered ground. During the darkness of night a detail of men advanced into the open field fully half way to Fort Hill, and threw up earthworks before daylight revealed the movement to the enemy. Shot and shell of nearly every calibre and character were rained upon it all day long from Fort Hill; but it could not be hammered down, and the Confederates dared not risk a sortie to capture it.

The chief difficulty now lay in reinforcing it, getting supplies of rations and ammunition into it, and especially in moving heavy siege guns to it. But all this was finally accomplished in a few days and nights through ditches and covered ways; its parapets strengthened and raised by using gunny sacks filled with sand; until the time had come for mounting the heavy ordnance at the embrasures prepared for the pieces. This proved the most deadly work of all. It was within less than half musket range from the rebel lines where a strong force of sharpshooters were stationed day and night to pick off every federal soldier who exposed enough of his body to afford a target. An old hat held up on a stick or ramrod would be riddled with minnie balls instantly. Many of our men had been killed, and it became nearly certain death to half the detail who were set at work about the embrasures. In spite of all that could be done by Gen. Logan and his Chief of Artillery, Major Stohlbrand [Charles S. Stolbrand], the men dodged, and shirked, and became badly demoralized.

Here was the first and only instance in which I ever saw Gen. Grant guilty of what the soldiers called: "foolhardy bravery." He had gone into the cramped exposed redoubt to see how the work was progressing and noticing the reluctance with which the men could be brought to the open embrasure, deliberately clambered on top of the embankment in plain view of the sharpshooters, and directed the men in moving and placing the guns. The bullets zipped through the air by dozens, but strangely none of them touched his person or his clothing. He paid no attention to appeals or expostulations, acting as though they were not heard; and smoked quietly and serenely all the time, except when he removed his cigar to speak to the men at work. His example shamed the men into making a show of courage; but several were wounded before he left the place. He was probably not exposed to fire many minutes, but the time seemed long to those who were present. It was a wholly indefensible procedure.

During the progress of the siege the Union batteries probably fired twice as many shot and shell as the Confederates. The latter may have been short of ammunition towards the close, but they also depended upon the character of their works. These were ably planned and constructed. If at the end of continuous, heavy and concentrated fire from our guns, the face, or the crest, of an earthwork should be torn to pieces, all damages would be repaired at night, and the morning sun would show a dazzling array of white cotton gunny sacks filled with dirt and sand in the breaches made the day before. These white sacks afforded excellent targets for artillery practice, and bets were daily made as to the number of shots some particular gunner would require to dislodge one. The second or third shot would generally hit the mark. . . .

CHAPTER

Seven

THE INVESTMENT of Vicksburg and opening of water communications northward was the signal for a large influx of civilians. Sanitary and Christian Commission agents arrived with immense quantities of provisions, clothing and hospital supplies from all the northern cities and states having troops in that department. There was some waste and misuse connected with these distributions undoubtedly, but the benefits so far outweighed all these, that the good was wholly incalculable.

It was a case also in which givers were as much blessed as recipients. The fires of patriotism were rekindled at home and in the field. The soldier was made to feel that he was not forgotten when governors of States vied with the humblest citizens in their commonwealths in expressions of gratitude and contributions to the welfare and comfort of the men at the front. All wars are great levelers of social distinctions, and these latter agencies were potent factors in the work.

With them came also something unheard of before. The Lombard Brothers of Chicago (Julius and Frank) had acquired more than merely local fame in concert singing; and were employed and sent to the army in front of Vicksburg to visit all headquarters and hospitals (and all regiments so far as practicable), to give free concerts to enliven the monotony of camp life, and to cheer and inspire the troops by their excellent singing. The lines and Camps were made vocal at night for several weeks, and the uproarious encoring and applauding which was always given them, proved how heartily and deeply the soldiers appreciated the entertainment. "Old Shady," "Dixie," "The Battle Cry of Freedom," "Old John Brown," "The Star Spangled Banner," "Columbia," "Home Sweet Home," "the Mocking Bird," and dozens of other patriotic and sentimental songs were excellently—exquisitely—rendered, interspersed with comic songs, such as the "Irishman's Shanty," & "Widow Machree," which had the run of popular favor in those days. Occasionally operatic selections and solos were artistically rendered. But the ballads and home songs of the nation were the standing favorites, and thousands on thousands were alternately convulsed with weeping and laughter. These songs were better than rations or medicine to many a poor homesick private, and brought healthy sentiments and inspirations in place of morbid unhealthy ones.

At this time also came a considerable addition to the number of duly accredited war correspondents among whom were Frank [Franc] B. Wilkie (then of the New York *Times*, but for nearly a quarter of a century afterward on the Chicago *Times*), and De Bienville [De Bow] Randolph Keim, of the New York *Herald*. Mr. Keim remained with McPherson's corps after the surrender of Vicksburg, until halfway from Chattanooga to Atlanta in 1864, when Gen. Sherman ordered his arrest for publishing a minute account of the Confederate Signal Code just then discovered by Federal Commanders. The personal friendship of McPherson and staff for Keim, caused him to receive warning in time to evade the execution of Sherman's order, but he was as effectually banished from Sherman's army, as Knox had been in 1863. It was a very ill advised publication, and proved Keim's deficiency in judgment. Sherman could not be greatly blamed for expelling him from the army.

The newly arrived correspondents remained on transports and steamboats at Chickasaw Bayou, where they could board and lodge comfortably; visited the lines of the army occasionally; and wrote glowing accounts of the progress of the siege on marble-top tables in the ladies' cabin of some palatial Mississippi River steamboat. Among them was J. B. McCullagh, then on the Cincinnati *Commercial*. After the war he was Washington City correspondent for the same paper—subsequently succeeded Charles A. Dana as managing editor of the Chicago *Republican* till the great fire in 1873 [1871]—then became an editorial writer on the St. Louis (Mo.) *Globe-Democrat*, under William McKee (its chief owner) until the death of the latter—and from that time till his death was the editorial manager of that great daily. As an army correspondent he was not noticeably superior to his associates, but I have always considered him the ablest Washington Correspondent of my acquaintance, with the single exception perhaps of Gen. H. V. Boynton, the present Nestor of that ilk. Mr. McCullagh was born of Irish Protestant parents; was brought to the United States in infancy; was instinctively American from feeling and principle; and became at maturity, one of the ablest journalistic managers in the country.

To the list should also be added Mr. [William] Webb, on the St. Louis *Democrat* before its consolidation with the *Globe*. . . . Richard [T.] Colburn, of the New York *World* (captured with A. D. Richardson and Junius Henri Browne while attempting to run the blockade in front of Vicksburg) returned soon. He was a stub-and-twist Irishman, claiming to be English, with sufficient assurance to brow-beat the Confederate authorities into releasing him on account of being a British subject.

The corps of correspondents so far as I have mentioned them, was possessed of remarkable newspaper ability as a whole, but showed the widest divergent individuality. Wilkie was phlegmatic, cynical, severe in invective, well informed on political economy, and indolent by nature unless stirred into action. He served Mr. Storey, editor of the Chicago *Times,* in a confidential relation, and was one of the strongest, sturdiest political writers on that paper. Mr. Keim was polite, vivacious and accomplished in manners, and literary in all his tastes. He was never quite up to Mr. Bennett's estimate of a first class war correspondent because he could never obtain his own consent to send off a dispatch until he had subjected it to the severest literary and scholarly scrutiny; whereas James Gordon Bennett, Sen. exalted late news far above fine writing. . . .

I boarded and lodged for awhile with Capt. E. D. Osband, Co. A, 4th Illinois Cavalry. This company was detached from the regiment and assigned to headquarters for escort, orderly and fatigue duty when Grant became Department Commander, and remained with him until he was ordered to the Military Division of the Mississippi in October 1863. Osband was the proprietor of a cigar and tobacco stand under the Tremont House, Chicago, raised a company of Cavalry and became its captain soon after the commencement of hostilities, was breveted Brigadier towards the close of the rebellion, and leased a cotton plantation on the Upper Yazoo on the return of peace, and shared the common fate of all northern adventurers at that time. He incurred the hostility of all his southern neighbor planters, was ruined in business, and barely escaped alive.

Grant's headquarters were at a point directly in rear of where the corps of Sherman and McPherson came together, and about five miles from the center of the City. The situation was well chosen on a pleasant elevation, in the edge of a strip of timber which afforded protection from the glaring, burning mid-day sun, made drainage and sanitary conditions easily secured, and was also near to a brook of running water kept from pollution. The escort company was immediately adjoining, and the whole headquarter encampment was constantly well policed. In the light of after experience it seemed altogether too near the Confederate fortifications for safety. But I do not remember that a single hostile shot or shell invaded its precincts. There were no "Whitworth" guns in Vicksburg to carry destructive bolts from four to six miles (as frequently occurred at Petersburg), nor were any very long range guns brought to bear upon us.

Having comparative freedom allowed me, I selected Capt. Osband's quarters as my abiding place for the facilities it afforded me for instant communication with the general and staff at any hour of the day or night; for the certainty of having my horse well-cared for, and near at hand; but above and beyond these, that I could keep constantly within sight of all Gen. Grant's personal movements; his receipt of news from all parts of the line; and the arrival and departure of couriers and bearers of dispatches.

If I was a trifle too late in depositing my correspondence in the general's mail pouch, or if a courier was hurriedly and unexpectedly started with dispatches up the river (or elsewhere), my arrangements were such that when he was mounted and had received his final instructions, he came past my tent and took everything I had in readiness. This enabled me to keep from one to two days ahead of my less fortunate competitors. Even when the headquarter "pouch" went north by the same boat which carried the army mail, it often arrived alone at Cairo. It was always "preferred" matter, whereas the great mass of mail sacks, had often to lay over a day or two at Memphis.

The main road from general headquarters to those of Gen. Logan crossed a ravine (on a high bridge) which led up to a salient in the rebel works. This ravine was an open one, and the enemy stationed a corps of sharpshooters in this salient whose especial duty it was to observe and fire upon all persons and teams attempting to cross it. They killed so many men and horses that it was soon abandoned by teams and trains, but single horsemen would often ride quietly to the edge of the timber cover, and then putting spurs to their animals dash across the open ravine and bridge, at full speed, and be out of range of minnie balls before they came whizzing and zipping from the fort.

Late one afternoon I decided to return by the bridge rather than take the circuitous obstructed road around it. I was accompanied by an orderly and explained the danger to him, directing him to ride up close to me and keep in that position when we charged across the bridge. But his horse was not equal to the emergency—could not be quickly brought to the necessary burst of speed. He fell considerably behind me, and when I halted in the timber on the other side he came riding up slowly, considerably bent forward, and said he had been hit somewhere by a ball.

An examination showed that a bullet had gone through his clothing, passed beneath the skin in the pelvic region and entirely out through his clothing on the opposite side. He was somewhat faint at first from the shock, but insisted on remaining in the saddle and riding on to headquarters. I rode by his side to support him if necessary, but none was needed. The staff surgeon examined him at once, and pronounced it a fatal injury. The neck of the bladder was cut or ruptured so that urine oozed out through the wound. He died before morning. This unfortunate and fatal occurrence put an end to running this gauntlet of Confederate fire. It may be that the advanced surgery of today would save many lives when similarly wounded; but at that time if the bladder, or an intestine, was cut, the man was given up to die, as absolutely incurable, and nothing beyond an alleviation of suffering was ever attempted. . . .

We were constantly receiving news that Gen. Johnston was advancing to raise the siege. Gen. Frank P. Blair . . . made a reconnaissance in force for fifty miles without encountering any Confederate troops. Reinforcements began to arrive from the north. On the third of June Gen. [Nathan] Kimball's brigade from Hurlbut's Command at Memphis arrived and pushed out ten or twelve miles northeast of Haynes's bluff; some cavalry was posted near him also; and these troops were charged with the duty of patroling the country within their reach; to forage upon the country to the fullest extent; bringing in all food, grain and live-stock found, if possible, and to destroy the balance; and to tear up bridges and obstruct roads should an enemy appear. Some light-draught transports, two or three dispatch boats, and an occasional gun boat from Admiral Porter's were running irregularly between Chickasaw Bayou and Satartia, about one hundred miles up the Yazoo by water.

During the first week in June (I think it was, although I cannot fix the precise date because all my correspondence was destroyed in the great Chicago fire) I ran up to Satartia, to satisfy myself concerning affairs in that quarter, in the steamboat Diligence, Capt. Harry McDougall of Louisville, Kentucky, commander. Everything was quiet. So far as I could learn no one was expecting Gen. Johnston's arrival, and no Confederate troops were in the vicinity.

On the return trip next day we met another steamboat, having on board Gen. Grant, and a small cavalry escort, under Capt. Osband, on their way to Satartia also. Grant was acquainted with Capt. McDougall (having used the Diligence on other occasions) and concluded to transfer to it, and order it back to Satartia again. As the vessels approached each other we were signalled to stop, the other boat ran alongside of the Diligence, and Grant with those accompanying him, came aboard the latter vessel. She was turned about and started up stream at once.

I was not long in perceiving that Grant had been drinking heavily, and that he was still keeping it up. He made several trips to the bar room of the boat in a short time, and became stupid in speech and staggering in gait. This was the first time he had shown symptoms of intoxication in my presence, and I was greatly alarmed by his condition, which was fast becoming worse.

Lieut. H. N. Towner, of Chicago, acting A.D.C., was the only staff representative aboard. I tried to have Towner get Grant into his stateroom on some pretense, and not allow him to come out till sober. But he was timid, and afraid the General would resent it, and punish him in some way, for his interference. I then went to Capt. McDougall to have him refuse the general any more whiskey, in person, or on his order. This the Captain said he could not do—that Gen. Grant was department commander with full power to do what he pleased with the boat, and all it contained.

Finding persuasions unavailing, I commenced on McDougall with imprecations and threats. I assured him that on my representations he would, and should, be sent out of the department in irons if I lived to get back to headquarters. He knew something of the vindictive feelings Rawlins had for those who supplied Grant with liquor, and finally closed the bar room, and conveniently lost the key in a safe place, till we left the boat.

I then took the General in hand myself, enticed him into his stateroom, locked myself in the room with him (having the key in my pocket), and commenced throwing bottles of whiskey which stood on the table, through the windows, over the guards, into the river. Grant soon ordered me out of the room, but I refused to go. On finding himself locked in he became quite angry and ordered me peremptorily to open the door and get out instantly. This order I firmly, but good-naturedly declined to obey. I said to him that I was the best friend he had in the Army of the Tennessee; that I was doing for him what I hoped some one would do for me, should I ever be in his condition; that he was not capable in this case of judging for himself; and that he must, for the present, act upon my better judgment, and be governed by my advice. As it was a very hot day and the State-room almost suffocating, I insisted on his taking off his coat, vest and boots, and lying down in one of the berths. After much resistance I succeeded, and soon fanned him to sleep.

Before he had recovered from his stupor we reached Satartia, when another source of trouble arose. He was determined to dress and go ashore; and ordered Capt. Osband to debark the escort men and horses. Poor Osband was now in a dilemma. To obey orders and land just at night in such a miserable little hamlet, filled with desperadoes and rebel sympathisers, with

but a handful of troopers to protect the general, seemed sui-
cidal. To disobey would lead to—he knew not what. I came to
his help by promising to take upon myself the responsibility of
shooting or hamstringing every horse on the vessel. We soon
agreed that under no conditions whatever would we go ashore
ourselves, or permit the General to do so.

I returned hurriedly to Grant and in the end persuaded him
to abandon all thought of going ashore that night.[1] His first
intention was to mount and return overland to his headquarters in front of Vicksburg, through a section of country as
hostile as any in the Confederacy, and without any knowledge
whatever of the roads traversing it. I have never doubted but
he would have ridden off into the enemy's lines that night if
he had been allowed to do so. During the night the boat
started down stream on the return trip—tied up once for a
short time till the moon rose, and was at Haynes's Bluff in the
morning.

Grant was duly sober by this time [2] I think and sent a part
of the escort out to Gen. Kimball's camp (or it may have been
Gen. Cadwallader C. Washburne's [Washburn's] camp) to
obtain news from [there]. The Diligence tied up at the landing
to await their return. I supposed all necessity for extra vigilance on my part had passed, and was almost "thunderstruck"
at finding an hour afterward that Grant had procured another

---

[1] Charles A. Dana, who also accompanied Grant on this trip, reported
it tactfully in his *Recollections*. According to him, "Grant was ill and
went to bed soon after we started." Dana says that when the boat
reached Satartia, he knocked on Grant's door to report that the place was
infested with guerrillas and to ask if they should turn back. Grant was
"too sick to decide," and said: "I will leave it to you." Dana: *Recollections of the Civil War* (New York, 1898), p. 82.

[2] Dana says: "Grant came out to breakfast fresh as a rose, clean shirt
and all, quite himself. "Well, Mr. Dana," he observed, "I suppose we are
at Satartia now." Dana told him they were at Haynes's Bluff. Ibid.

supply of whiskey from on shore and was quite as much intoxicated as the day before. The same tactics were resorted to,
but I encountered less fierce opposition. On the return of the
escort, Grant ordered the boat to proceed to Chickasaw Bayou.

If we had started then we would have arrived at the Bayou
about the middle of the afternoon, when the landing would
have been alive with officers, men and trains from all parts of
the army. To be seen in his present condition would lead to
utter disgrace and ruin. Capt. McDougall was also alarmed,
as to the consequences to himself. He was now very willing
to take orders from me: First, not to start immediately, making the pretext of low fires, green wood, &c. Next, to not start
until I assented.

An hour or two was thus consumed. When Grant's impatience at last threatened to burst all restraints I could put
upon him, McDougall was directed to start, but to look out
for a safe sandbar or beach to stick on for awhile. This was
done. We finally arrived at Chickasaw Bayou about sundown
and ran into the landing alongside of a large steamboat used
by "Wash" Graham, as a headquarter sutler boat. Graham
kept open house to all officers and dispensed free liquors and
cigars generously.

I climbed over the guards; saw Graham; cautioned him
against allowing Grant to have any liquor because he had
been drinking heavily, and had not recovered from its effects;
received his promise that the General should not have a drop
of anything intoxicating on his boat; and then hurried back to
assist in getting the horses off the Diligence. This was soon
effected, but when ready to mount the general could not be
found.

Suspecting that he had gone aboard Graham's boat, I went

to its office on the bow, but no one had seen Grant. I started aft in search of him, and soon heard a general hum of conversation and laughter proceeding from a room opening out of the ladies' cabin. Pushing in among a crowd of officers, of all ranks, I found Graham in front of a table covered with bottled whiskey and baskets of champagne, and Grant in the act of swallowing a glass of whiskey. I was thoroughly indignant and may have shown rather scant ceremony in saying to him that the escort was waiting, and that it would be long after dark before we could reach headquarters. He was not very well pleased by my interruption, and urgency in starting.

He had taken on this trip for his own use a horse belonging to Col. Clark B. Lagon called "Kangaroo," from his habit of rearing on his hind-feet and making a plunging start whenever mounted. On this occasion Grant gave him the spur the moment he was in the saddle, and the horse darted away at full speed before anyone was ready to follow. The road was crooked and tortuous, following the firmest ground between sloughs and bayous, and was bridged over these in several places. Each bridge had one or more guards stationed at it, to prevent fast riding or driving over it; but Grant paid no attention to roads or sentries. He went at about full speed through camps and corrals, heading only for the bridges, and literally tore through and over everything in his way. The air was full of dust, ashes, and embers from camp-fires; and shouts and curses from those he rode down in his race.

Fortunately horse and rider escaped impalement from bayonets, and equally fortunate were not fired upon by the guards. I took after him as fast as I could go, but my horse was no match for "Kangaroo." By the time the escort was mounted Grant was out of sight in the gloaming. After crossing the last bayou bridge three-fourths of a mile from the landing, he abandoned his reckless gait, and when I caught up with him was riding in a walk.

I seized his bridle rein and urged the danger to himself and others in such racing, on such roads; told him the escort could not even keep in sight in the dust and dusk of the evening. He tried to snatch the rein from my hand, but in the scuffle I got the long flowing double-rein from over the horse's head and told him very firmly that he should ride as I directed. I secured his bridle rein to my own saddle and convinced him that I was master of the situation. His intoxication increased so in a few minutes that he became unsteady in the saddle. The escort was not in sight. Fearing discovery of his rank and situation, I turned obliquely to the left away from the road and took refuge in a thicket near the foot of the bluff. Here I helped him to dismount, secured our horses, stripped the saddle from "Kangaroo," and induced the General to lay down on the grass with the saddle for a pillow. He was soon asleep.

My next anxiety was to communicate with the escort. They were spread out over the bottom for a half mile circling about in search of the general, fully expecting to find him lifeless. One of the men at last came within hailing distance (John Walters if my memory is accurate) and answered my call. I ordered him to proceed directly to headquarters and report at once to Rawlins—and to no one else—and say to him that I wanted an ambulance with a careful driver, sent to me immediately—and that he (Walters) must guide them back to me as soon as it could be done. It was entirely dark by this time and I had no fear of discovery except from some straggling bummer, but I was prepared to cut off his shoulder-straps instantly if anyone approached. After an hour's sleep he arose and wanted to start to Camp. I took him by the arm, walked him back and forth, and kept up a lively rather one-sided conversation, till the ambulance arrived.

This became another source of contention. The general refused to get in it, and insisted on riding to camp on horseback. We compromised the question by my agreeing to ride in the ambulance also, and having our horses led by the orderly. On the way he confessed that I had been right, and that he had been wrong throughout, and told me to consider myself a staff officer, and to give any orders that were necessary in his name.

We reached headquarters about midnight, and found Rawlins and Col. John Riggin waiting for us at the driveway. I stepped out of the ambulance first, and was followed promptly by Grant. He shrugged his shoulders, pulled down his vest, "shook himself together," as one just rising from a nap, and seeing Rawlins and Riggin, bid them good-night in a natural tone and manner, and started to his tent as steadily as he ever walked in his life.

My surprise nearly amounted to stupefaction. I turned to Rawlins and said I was afraid that he would think I was the man who had been drunk.

But he replied in suppressed tones through his clinched teeth: "No, No. I know him, I know him. I want you to tell me the exact facts—and all of them—without any concealment. I have a right to know them, and I will know them." The whole appearance of the man indicated a fierceness that would have torn me into a thousand pieces had he considered me to blame.

So I began with Grant's transfer to the Diligence, stated his condition and my fruitless endeavors to prevent his getting liquor, and told him fully and truthfully of my usurpation of authority. I said to him that I knew it to be in violation of all military rights and rules—that I considered these in the outset and deliberately resolved to do as I had done, and to accept the personal consequences, whatever they might be. That Gen. Grant could send me out of the Department in disgrace—possibly would do so—but that I had treated him precisely as I would thank anyone for treating me, should I ever be found in a similar condition.

"He will not send you out of the department while I remain in it," was the reply to this. After asking me questions in detail, and having me repeat some of my statements, as if to fasten them in his memory, Rawlins thanked me warmly for what I had done; told me to dismiss all fear of disagreeable consequences to myself on that account; and bidding me "good night," walked away to his tent.

But in spite of these assurances I was somewhat in doubt as to the view of the matter Gen. Grant would take next day. I slept very little that night rather expecting to be summoned to his presence next day.[3] I purposely kept out of his way for twenty-four hours to spare him the mortification I supposed he might feel, or the necessity for any explanation or apology. The second day afterward I passed in and out of his presence as though nothing unusual had occurred. To my surprise he never made the most distant allusion to it then, or ever afterward.

But there was a perceptible change in his bearing towards me. I was always recognized and spoken to, as if I had been

---

[3] That morning Rawlins wrote Grant a letter, which began: "The great solicitude which I feel for the safety of this army leads me to mention what I hoped never again to do—the subject of your drinking. . . ." James H. Wilson: *The Life of John A. Rawlins* (New York, 1916), p. 128. Dana saw Rawlins's letter. But he never reported the incident to the War Department. James H. Wilson: *The Life of Charles A. Dana* (New York, 1907), p. 232.

regularly gazetted a member of his staff. My comfort and convenience was considered; a tent pitched and struck for me whenever and wherever I chose to occupy it; in all provisions for transportation and subsistence I was counted as a member of the staff; on several occasions he introduced me to others as a member of his personal staff; later on I often performed staff duty in carrying orders and dispatches; and was also later on furnished with orders to all guards and all picket guards, in all the armies of the United States, to pass me at any hour of the day or night, with horses and vehicles; to all Quartermasters of transportation to furnish me transportation on demand for myself, horses and servants; and to all Commissaries of subsistence to furnish me subsistence on demand for myself, horses and servants. (These orders, or passes, still exist among a few of my precious possessions.)

When in front of Richmond I might have visited Jefferson Davis daily, so far as our own troops were concerned, and often did pass through Weitzell's [Major General Godfrey Weitzel's] corps to the front to exchange Federal for Confederate newspapers. I could take possession of any vessel, from a tug to the largest government transport, allow no one but myself on board, and proceed wherever I pleased. I frequently used tugs or small dispatch boats, and on one or two occasions used fast steamboats between City Point, Fortress Monroe and Baltimore. On another occasion the regular packet from City Point was held at Fortress Monroe six hours to enable a fast dispatch boat to overtake it bearing my account of the celebrated "African Church meeting" in Richmond. At a time too when President Lincoln's permits to civilians to visit the Army of the Potomac were ruthlessly disregarded by order of Secretary Stanton, I constantly carried three or four passes, signed up by Gen. Grant, with blank spaces to fill with the names of any persons I wished to bring to the front.

From the date of this Yazoo-Vicksburg adventure until the end of the war, and during my semi-connection with Grant's headquarters in Washington City, ending in the fall of 1866, my standing with the general and his staff became stronger month by month. I constantly received flattering personal and professional favors and attentions shown to no one else in my position.

CHAPTER

Eight

. . . My confidence in the military ability of Gen. Grant had become so great by this time that I was unwilling to jeopardize his reputation in public opinion by adding anything to the rumors and stories in circulation concerning his inebriety. The circumstances I have just narrated were never spoken of by me to any one excepting to Rawlins, and a very few friends and relatives of Grant's to whom Rawlins first told the story and who afterwards came to me to thank me for my silence. My wife never heard a word of the affair till hostilities ceased, and we had all returned to civil life. My object in giving this full and detailed statement of the unfortunate occurrence at this late date, is to set at rest the conflicting statements which have at various times been published about Gen. Grant's habits. . . .

During the siege of Vicksburg Joseph B. McCullagh was correspondent of the Cincinnati *Commercial*, and had presumably sent some account of Grant's intemperance to Murat Halstead, editor and proprietor of that newspaper. Mr. Halstead had joined in the hue and cry against Grant from the outset, opposed his promotions, and labored incessantly to have him removed from every important command ever given him. In February 1863, he wrote in confidence to Salmon P. Chase, then a member of Mr. Lincoln's Cabinet, and afterwards Chief Justice of the United States as follows: ". . . Our noble army of the Mississippi, is being wasted by the foolish, drunken stupid Grant. He can't organize, or control or fight an army. I have no personal feeling about it but I know he is an ass. There is not among the whole list of retired Major Generals a man who is not Grant's superior. McClellan, Fremont, McDowell, Burnside, Franklin, even Pope or Sumner, would be an improvement on the present commander of the Mississippi."

Many such letters were written by Halstead as urgent reasons for Grant's removal, down nearly to the day of Vicksburg's surrender.[1] That glorious consummation condoned

---

[1] A letter from Halstead to Chase, dated April 1, 1863, and evidently copied by Chase and taken to President Lincoln, was revealed with the opening of the Robert Todd Lincoln Collection at the Library of Congress. The letter reads: "You do once in a while don't you, say a word to the President, or Stanton or Halleck, about the conduct of the War?

"Well, now, for God's sake say that Genl Grant, entrusted with our greatest army, is a jackass in the original package. He is a poor drunken imbecile. He is a poor stick sober, and he is most of the time more than half drunk, and much of the time idiotically drunk.

"About two weeks ago, he was so miserably drunk for twenty-four hours, that his staff kept him shut up in a state-room on the steamer where he makes his headquarters—because he was hopelessly foolish.

"I know exactly what I am writing about and the meaning of the language I use.

"Now are our Western heroes to be sacrificed by the ten thousand by this poor devil?

"Grant will fail miserably, hopelessly, eternally. You may look for and calculate his failure, in every position in which he may be placed, as a perfect certainty.

"Don't say I am grumbling. Alas! I know too well that I am but faintly outlining the truth. . . .

"Anybody would be an improvement on Grant. . . . If . . . Grant is allowed to bury 100,000 in the Mississippi swamps, we are gone up."

every fault in Grant's past career, and silenced, if it did not convince or placate, his defamers. Halstead concealed his dislike of Grant for years, and the full measure of his hostility was unknown to the public until some political accidents brought it to light.

After the death of Chief Justice Chase his daughter Kate Chase Sprague became the custodian of all her father's papers and correspondence. Halstead's letters were supposed to have been given by her to Senator Roscoe Concklin [Conkling], of New York, to avenge himself upon the writer. At all events publicity ensued. Their authenticity could not be denied. Halstead waited, watched and worked for some opportunity to retrieve his blunders about Grant in the past. It came in a strange way.

At the time of Rawlins' death one or two trunks filled with valuable papers and documents which always stood in his bed chamber, mysteriously disappeared. In one of these trunks was a copy of a letter sent by Rawlins to Grant, dated June 6, 1863, protesting in his usual vigorous manner against the General's drinking. This letter or a copy of it was furnished by Rawlins' family to Gen. [Henry] Boynton and was made the pretext for re-opening the old question of Grant's intemperance. Under the plea of doing tardy justice to Rawlins, there was an underdrift intended to disparage the personal character and military ability of Grant; and of justifying or defending the individuals who had been persistently and malignantly aspersing his character, while pretending the utmost friendship. Conspicuous in this list were Murat Halstead and Gen. Halleck.

Traducers of Gen. Grant had been driven from line after line of defense and now had but the single one left of showing that their former charges of his drinking to excess were true; that he did drink to the extent of jeopardizing the armies he commanded; that his successes were due to Rawlins; and that their criticisms, allegations and secret charges against him a quarter of a century before, were justified by the facts. They were exceedingly anxious to show that his military ability was quite ordinary, and that the glorious reputation he had achieved was due to the advice, support and maintenance given him by others, and to the control so notably exercised over him by Rawlins. . . .

Like thousands on thousands of such men, when he recovered from a season of dissipation, Grant resolved to never drink again. This resolution would be firmly adhered to for months at a time, and gave rise to the conflicting stories in circulation. One person would state that he had seen him drunk. Another would deny it; declare him to be a teetotaler, because he had ridden across the continent with him and never saw him drink a drop of any intoxicant; but had on the contrary seen him refuse numberless invitations to drink; and had sat down with him at banquets where he kept his glass upside down from beginning to end, and refused all entreaties to take a single sip.

The truth was Gen. Grant had an inordinate love for liquors. He was not an habitual drinker. He could not drink moderately. When at long intervals his appetite for strong drink caused him to accept the invitation of some old classmate, or army associate, to take "just one glass before parting," he invariably drank to excess unless some one was with him (whose control he would acknowledge) to lead him away from temptation. Both extremes of public rumor rested on some foundation in fact. Though absolutely refusing to drink on one day, or occasion, there was no certainty that he would not be inebriated on the next. . . .

In addition to the letters written to Grant by Rawlins at the time of the Satartia trip the whole subject was gone over in a private conversation between them in which Rawlins became impetuous and stormy. He recalled to mind Grant's repeated promises to never drink again; cited numerous instances in which he had violated them; and declared that if he (Grant) had no more regard for his own reputation, and for the lives of the men he commanded, than to continue such dissipation, that he (Rawlins) demanded the immediate acceptance of his resignation, for he would no longer be a party to further concealment but would retire from his official position while he could at least maintain his own self-respect.

To all this sharp invective Grant replied with the utmost good-humor; said that he had quit drinking; and so disarmed Rawlins by his confessions, his open sincerity, and promises of amendment, that the latter was induced to pass the matter over for that time. I had this report of the substance of that interview from Rawlins himself (and from Bowers) to a much more detailed extent, on the day of its occurrence.

So far as I know Gen. Grant did not touch any intoxicants afterward until his visit to Gen. Banks at New Orleans.[2] I was at Memphis and Cairo at that time and can only speak upon information obtained at Headquarters on my return, which was to the effect that his being thrown from his horse on his return from a review of Gen. Banks's troops, was solely due to his drinking. He narrowly escaped instant death, and did not recover from his injuries for several months. From this time on till our arrival at City Point, he was perfectly abstemious so far as I knew. But on several occasions during the summer, and prior to Jan. 1st 1865, he caused much solicitude in

---

[2] Grant's visit to Banks occurred in mid-August 1863.

the small circle of sincere friends who realized his danger, and had constituted themselves a body-guard to prevent his drinking.[3]

Rawlins quietly but relentlessly exercised his personal and official influence and authority. It came to be well understood that any staff officer who furnished Gen. Grant a single drink; or drank with him when away from headquarters; or in any way whatever connived at, or concealed, the general's drinking, would be summarily ordered to his proper command, or be disgraced, broken in rank, or run out of the service, if in his power to accomplish it. His authority was unquestioned. His control over Grant was fully recognized. More than one staff officer was barely given the option of resigning, or of being crushed by the iron hand of the great Chief of Staff.

No open drinking was allowed at headquarters and very little liquor was permitted to be brought there. If one of the staff had in some way come into possession of a bottle or demijohn of whiskey, and wished to share it with a caller or a friend, he took him into his tent, closed the flap, and drank with the utmost caution and secrecy. It can be safely asserted that no officer or civilian ever saw any open drinking at Gen. Grant's headquarters from Cairo to Appomattox. This was wholly and solely the result of Rawlins' uncompromising atti-

---

[3] On November 16, 1863 General Rawlins wrote from Chattanooga to Miss M. E. Hurlbut: ". . . Today however matters have changed and the necessity of my presence here made almost absolute, by the free use of intoxicating liquors at Head Quarters which last nights developments showed me had reached to the General Commanding. I am the only one here (his wife not being with him) who can stay it in that direction & prevent evil consequences resulting from it. I had hoped but it appears vainly his New Orleans experience would prevent him ever indulging again with his worst enemy. . . . [P.S.] What I have said about the General is strictly confidential." Original owned by the late Foreman M. Lebold of Chicago, Ill.

tude, and Grant's acquiescence in what he knew to be for his own good. But at intervals, when at other general headquarters, he could not resist the temptation to drink, and would return to his tent much the worse for his potations. On a few occasions his negro servant "Bill," supplied him with liquor. Rawlins ascertained the facts, strung "Bill" up by the thumbs for awhile, and threatened him with every conceivable punishment most horrifying to the "darky" imagination. "Bill" came to believe that Rawlins would actually murder him, or burn him alive if he ever caught him so offending again, and governed himself by the law of self-preservation.

Rawlins ablest coadjutor in restraining Gen. Grant from drinking was the latter's excellent wife, Julia Dent Grant. Everything seemed absolutely safe when she was present. Her quiet firm control of her husband seemed marvelous to those who had so often tried and failed. When the army had a period of repose and inaction, and Rawlins was nearly worn out by the eternal vigilance necessary to Grant's salvation, it was noticed that Mrs. Grant and family invariably visited headquarters for a few weeks, when "all went merry as a marriage bell." There was no dissipation—no fear of any—and all apprehensions on that score ceased until she took her departure.[4]

When the Citizens of Philadelphia presented to Grant an elegant residence in that city about 1865 or 6, it was finely furnished from cellar to attic, and filled with the choicest stock of eatables and potables that the markets afforded.[5] The wine cellar was generously provided with a large quantity of the finest wines and liquors which could be obtained.

---

[4] The late Lloyd Lewis, who was working on a multivolume biography of Grant at the time of his death, told me that he had concluded that Grant was such a devoted family man that loneliness for Mrs. Grant largely accounted for Grant's lapses from temperance.

[5] The house in Philadelphia was a gift from the Union League Club.

Soon after its formal presentation and acceptance, Mrs. Grant made a minute inspection of the premises and took an account of the stores. She was greatly disturbed by finding so many fine wines, brandies, whiskies, &c., and on her return to Washington City drove directly to Rawlins' house for his advice in the matter. Being a free gift she could not return it, and felt that it was dangerous to keep it. Dreading to act upon her own judgment in so delicate a matter she was anxious to be advised in the line of her own inclinations.

Rawlins listened patiently but made no recommendations. Mrs. Grant tried for some minutes to obtain his opinion by indirection, but was obliged to ask him plainly and pointedly what she ought to do under the circumstances. He finally replied: "Mrs. Grant, you ought not to ask me any such question," accenting the word "*me*" (alluding no doubt to the position he occupied and the seeming impropriety of his meddling with the housekeeping affairs of other people, and especially those of his superior officer). "You ought to know precisely what to do. Go to Philadelphia immediately. Send for some responsible broker, or commission dealer, in such commodities; have him dispose of the entire stock at once; and put the money in your pocket." My informant said this advice was acted on as soon as possible, and that Grant probably never even sampled the stock. . . .

To speak the whole truth concerning Gen. Grant's periodical fits of intemperance has required all the courage I could summon to my assistance. Unhappily (Unfortunately) for his reputation these were too widely known before his resignation from U.S. Army in 18[54] to be denied even by his friends, or excused by the public at large. But as he rose by successive promotions during his service in the Civil War they again became the subject of violent discussion throughout the country, and of anxious inquiry and consideration by state and national authorities. The nation first became proud of his military achievements, and then of his name and personal fame. He was soon surrounded by a halo of hero worship, and thenceforth was a mythical as well as a historical character. Rival parties claimed him, and all praised him. The war was half over before it was certainly known whether in political opinions he leaned most towards the democrats, republicans or abolitionists. . . .

Returning to the front of Vicksburg: Everything dragged along slowly so far as important results were concerned, for weeks after the assault of May 22d. Several approaches were made at different points by trenches under cover, and mines were prepared in the hope of blowing up some rebel intrenchments. . . .

By June 25th all was in readiness. The ditch had been widened to admit the passage of four men abreast. Picked men were in readiness to lead the assaulting column as soon as the mine was sprung. [Mortimer D.] Leggett's brigade was moved up as a reserve for these brave fellows in front, and [John D.] Stevenson was a little to the rear, to follow up any advantage which might be gained. All troops excepting sharpshooters and those selected for the assault were withdrawn.

The match was applied at 3:00 p.m. The burst was terrific. For a few seconds, which seemed minutes if not hours to those engaged and to all beholders, the air was filled with dirt, dust, stockades, gabions, timbers, one or two gun carriages, and an immense surging white cloud of smoke which fairly rose to the heavens, and gradually widened out and dissipated. The charge was gallantly made before the debris had entirely fallen, and was as gallantly resisted. The dirt, timber and heavier portions of the works, blown into the air, fell back not far from its original position, only leaving a yawning crater where the mine had been, which was rendered almost impassable by the confused mass. All the Union batteries opened fire at once. The enemy replied vigorously, and the most deafening cannonading of the war to that time ensued for nearly an hour. The Confederates rallied to the reconstruction of their works, timbers were thrown across the breach, dirt banked against these as fast as men could accomplish it, and despite the most heroic attempts we were unable to gain any tenable footing within the rebel works. . . .

McPherson undertook to fortify and hold the ground gained; but the hand to hand fighting on his narrow front placed him at such disadvantage, that our men were withdrawn during the night, and operations resumed their usual course. The loss in killed and wounded on both sides was large in proportion to the number actually engaged, but was small when compared with those of a great battle.

I was suddenly called to my home in Milwaukee the last of June by sickness and death in my family, and was not present at the surrender on July 4th and the triumphal entry of our army. . . .

CHAPTER

Nine

. . . On my return to Vicksburg about July 20th I found that Gen. Grant was occupying the house, grounds, and an adjacent timbered and watered pasture lot, belonging to Mrs. Lum, a very wealthy widow. Gen Pemberton had taken the same premises for his headquarters during his stay in the city, so that it was only a change of tenants so far as the owner was concerned. It was a very agreeable change however from the terrors of several months continuous bombardment, and from the horrors of starvation and destruction which attended the siege. She remained in a part of the house with one or two members of her family and had the satisfaction of collecting her rent in greenbacks instead of the worthless money of the Confederacy. . . .

Upon the fall of Vicksburg Gen. Sherman, by previous arrangement, turned upon Gen. Johnston next day and pursued him far beyond Jackson. The rebel general made a stand and some show of resistance at the latter place but was driven out precipitately as soon as Sherman could get his forces well to the front. Johnston was compelled however to leave a vast

amount of property and subsistence behind that would certainly have been taken with him or destroyed had his danger
been less imminent. He fired the city in many places in his
attempt to burn public stores.

On our occupation of Jackson in May, pains were taken to
leave all private, and much of the public property of the place
uninjured. No buildings were burned by us that did not contain Confederate property or were in some way in the use of
the Confederate government. Many even of these escaped.
But the behavior of Johnston, and the citizens of Jackson,
absolved Sherman from obligations in that direction, and his
troops were inclined to finish what Johnston had begun, and
reduce the place to smouldering ruins. But discipline restrained
them.

The head of Sherman's column reached Big Black on the
return trip, July 22d. He reported to Gen. Grant that the people of that part of Mississippi were the worst-whipped communities on the face of the earth. They were completely
humbled and begged for mercy on every hand. They acknowledged themselves thoroughly conquered; admitted their in-
ability to longer oppose the Federal government; expressed
their willingness to come into the Union again on any terms;
and begged of him in the name of everything held sacred to
oppress them no further.

Judge Starkie [William L. Sharkey, of the High Court of
Common Pleas], Mr. Miller, Mr. [Dr. W. Q.] Poindexter and
other prominent men of the state came forward and proposed
organizing a state government favorable to a reconstruction
of the Union on the best terms obtainable, pledging all the
influence they possessed against the rebellion and in favor of
the Federal government. The country between Vicksburg and
Jackson was completely devastated. No subsistence of any kind

remained. Every growing crop had been destroyed when possible. Wheat was burned in the barn and stack whenever
found. Provisions of every kind were brought away or destroyed. Livestock was slaughtered for use, or driven back on
foot. He asserted that nearly the entire population must leave,
be fed by our government, or starve. Thousands were already
applying for food to sustain life; and that such heart-rending
destitution had never been witnessed on the American Continent as in the region indicated. He had been compelled to
establish a temporary system of relief, and issue army rations
to the most needy. Gen. Johnston's army he said had been
subsisting almost wholly on green corn for several weeks, and
half his troops were probably unfit for duty. They were found
sick at almost every house, and lying languishing or dead in
hundreds of fence-corners. The utter impossibility of supplying his army with necessary food had been a sufficient reason
for Johnston's not falling upon Grant's rear and attempting to
raise the siege.

When last heard from Pemberton was a considerable distance east of Jackson and his army of nearly 30,000 paroled
soldiers which marched away with him had dwindled down
by sickness, death and desertion, to less than 5,000.

The wisdom of Grant's releasing them on parole was thus
early proven. Thousands of them declared they would never
fight again, and such of them as lived in the territory held by
us could never be forced to return. The lists of these paroled
prisoners which Rawlins carried with him to Washington,
filled a box three feet long, two feet in width, and two feet
deep. It was a very cheap way however of transporting over
30,000 prisoners.

The distress reported by Sherman appealed strongly to
Grant's sympathies. He approved Sherman's plan for relief

and ordered medicines and food issued to destitute families as well as to the sick and wounded, thinking, as he said: "that it was only fair that we should return to these people some of the articles we had taken while marching through the country.". . .

Before dismissing this subject I will quote from a letter of mine written in Vicksburg, August 1, 1863: "Vicksburg is ours, the Mississippi is opened, and people wait anxiously to see the practical results so long predicted. Many have looked forward to this consummation as the ending of the war. Almost all have vaguely hoped and believed that it must, in some way, amount to its virtual ending. To me nothing is plainer than that a majority of the people will be seriously disappointed. The war will still go on. Other armies, and still others, will be raised. Battles as bloody as any that preceded, have yet to be fought. When and how the peace so much desired by all, will be obtained, no man living can tell.

"By the capture of Vicksburg the Confederacy has received a terrible blow, but its armies are not disbanded. The people of many adjacent Counties are made penniless, homeless, and dependent on charity for bread; but I have no satisfactory evidence that any considerable number advocate unconditional submission. They all desire peace, but all (so far as I can ascertain) couple it with conditions.

"Gen. Sherman honestly believes that a strong Union sentiment exists. I as honestly disbelieve it. I have conversed with hundreds of families between here and Jackson, and have not found one citizen who could properly be termed a Union man. Many profess a conservatism which in the opinion of the administration at Washington, is treason. Very many more attempt no reserve or concealment, but openly proclaim their attachment to their own government, while drawing rations and supplies from ours. All are intensely pro-slavery in feeling, and curse the Yankees for 'stealing their niggers.'

"In one particular the people of Vicksburg and vicinity differ widely from all other communities the fortune of war has thrown us among. While cherishing the utmost bitterness and malignancy towards us, they nevertheless accept our favors and benefactions. They even come as cravens and sycophants to beg favors that were denied when insolently demanded. They lack honesty and sincerity in a markable degree.

"Elsewhere the citizens have submitted to our rule under protest (as a matter beyond their control) but have preserved their own self-respect, and often challenged ours. They were sometimes sullen and morose, but, if enemies, were openly and consistently so. Here no duplicity is too low; no cunning or treachery too base, to practice towards us. The people as a whole are the most ungrateful on the face of the earth. They should either act honorably, or refuse to receive their daily bread from our hands. Probably more than ten thousand rations are daily issued to rebel citizens on the score of humanity, to prevent starvation, and probably there are not ten of these but would glory in betraying us.". . .

Nothing was heard of the latent Unionism of Mississippi after Gen. Sherman returned to Big Black. The following is extracted from a letter written by me at Vicksburg, August 14, 1863. "Sherman unquestionably believed a real Union sentiment was developed by the tread of his victorious legions, and Gen. Grant seems to have entertained a similar opinion. Their means of obtaining correct information so far exceed mine that it may be deemed presumptuous to doubt. However, we hear nothing more of the movement for organizing a new state government. The 'prominent gentlemen' who advocated unconditional return to the Union when Gen. Sher-

man's cannon was thundering at their doors, have been as
dumb as oysters ever since. The crowds that continually
swarm hitherward from Black river come to *claim* rations,
protection, and other *rights* of citizenship; but are wonder-
fully reluctant to acknowledge or discharge the duties thereof.
None join our army; none contribute in word or deed to the
Federal Cause; all look upon us as enemies; and nearly all admit themselves to be our enemies, even when asking for, and
accepting, subsistence at our hands. Their manners are often
insufferably insolent and insulting. I must reiterate that after
long, close, and (I believe) impartial investigation, I can find
none whom I believe to be truly Union men or women, in this
entire region. If here, it has never been my fortune to meet
them.". . .

In August I was in Memphis on business, and upon attempting to send some public and private telegrams northward, was
surprised to learn that Gen. Hurlbut had forbidden the transmission of anything coming from me, or going to the Chicago
Times. Supposing it to have been a part of Hurlbut's suppression of the Chicago *Times* the previous winter which
had been promptly revoked by Gen. Grant, at my request;
and that the telegraphic prohibition had merely been overlooked, I walked directly to post headquarters and called upon
Adjutant [Henry] Binmore. He was a little red-headed English dude or Cockney. I introduced myself as modestly and
quietly as possible; and began apologetically to say that I
had no doubt but the general had overlooked or forgotten
this telegraphic interdiction. The little fellow flamed up in an
instant: "Not at all, sir; Not at all sir; nothing is ever overlooked or forgotten in this office." He inquired when I arrived,
in which direction I was going, and when I expected to leave.

On being informed that I was just from Vicksburg, and

would leave by packet that afternoon for Cairo, he said with insulting emphasis, that it was a very fortunate thing for me that I was on my way northward, out of that district as I would otherwise have been instantly arrested. I looked him in the eye for a moment; said very deliberately that I should return from Cairo on the same packet in a few days, when he would have ample time and opportunity for my arrest. He turned to an orderly and directed him to bring a file of soldiers. Without waiting for their arrival, I saluted and walked away unmolested. I have been uncertain ever since whether Binmore really intended to lock me up, or whether the order was given to bluff and intimidate me. I returned as stated, was in Memphis several times afterward while Hurlbut commanded there, but heard no more of the matter. I raised the telegraphic embargo immediately, and used the wires freely to show my authority to do so.

The sequel of this episode occurred the following winter. Binmore had been in the meantime dishonorably kicked out of Hurlbut's headquarters, and mustered out of the service. I collected a bundle of damaging facts in writing and held them for use at the proper time. That time came unexpectedly. I had been home on a short leave, and on my way back to the army stepped into the city editor's and reporters' room of the Chicago *Times*, to see an old acquaintance. While I was there Binmore came in with some "law reports" for the paper. He evidently recognized me; pretended to be in great haste; turned in his reports hurriedly; and started for the door. I called him by name, and requested him to wait a moment, as I wanted to speak to him. He stopped quite unwillingly, plead short time and hurried engagements, and started for the door again. But I placed myself squarely between him and the door, and asked if he knew me.

"Well no, no; couldn't say that he did. Might have met me somewhere, but really couldn't remember." I said my name was Cadwallader.

"Oh, ah, yes, yes; thought he had heard my name before; but really couldn't tell when or where."

I replied by saying that I called upon him in Memphis, at a certain time, upon official business; that I conducted myself by act and speech, in the most gentlemanly manner I was capable of; but that he had, without any cause whatever, insulted me grossly, like the dirty little cur that he was, and had even threatened me with imprisonment.

He began to bluster up—would allow no man to talk to him in that manner—made a push for the door—but finding that I barred his passage—seemed to be feeling for a weapon in his pocket. I took him by the collar, backed him against the wall, and threatened to break every bone in his body if he attempted any defense; and told him he should not leave the room until he heard me through. I then narrated his disgraceful conduct at Memphis in taking an "abandoned woman" from Chicago and introducing her to Mrs. Gen. Hurlbut as his wife, for which he came near being killed; his expulsion from service; his disreputable conduct at Cairo while there; and drew out of my pocket a number of unreceipted washbills, which he had failed to pay. When I exhausted my epithetic vocabulary I swung him to the door and literally kicked him out. The quarrel raised quite a commotion in the office, there being nearly twenty persons present when it began; the number was soon doubled by others rushing in from different parts of the building. I found Binmore was heartily despised by all who knew him but had been engaged on the *Times* as an expert stenographer. I apologized for commencing a personal quarrel on private premises, but was told no explanations were needed in that instance. I never saw him afterward. . . .

During the siege of Vicksburg, Mr. De Bow Randolph Keim, previously mentioned, found himself unable to obtain permission to remain at (or very near to) Gen. Grant's headquarters, and was sufficiently conscientious to state the fact candidly to Mr. Bennett of the *Herald*. . . . He came to me, wanting to employ me as his assistant. I explained to him that my independent position on the Chicago *Times* was far better than any temporary and subordinate one on any other paper; and that I could not do much for the *Herald* while holding my present place. He came again, not long after, saying that he must be temporarily absent, and had authority to employ me to write private letters to Mr. Bennett, which would never be published, about men, commands, and events in the Department of the Tennessee, giving such information as would be valuable to that great paper, though never put into type. To this I consented.

I had the utmost confidence in Grant's military ability—assured Mr. Bennett that he stood far above any other western general—that in my opinion he had no superior in the United States—and predicted that time would prove the truth of all I claimed for him. These letters were doubtless instrumental in securing for Gen. Grant before the year closed, the conspicuous support of the *Herald*—a support which was steadfastly given him at all times till the war ended, and never relaxed till he became President.

I wrote cautiously at first, having no personal acquaintance with Mr. Bennett, but did have a vivid recollection of the untoward consequences to Isham and others, who had incurred Grant's displeasure, by publishing news that should have been withheld. But Mr. Bennett was too sagacious to allow the slightest breach of confidence, in letter or in spirit. Anything inclosed to him personally, and marked private or confidential, was sacredly held as such until all restrictions were removed. . . .

By this time great uneasiness prevailed at Washington at Rosecrans' tardiness in moving towards Chattanooga. He was repeatedly urged to do so without further delay, but always plead incompleted preparations. At one time it was an insufficient force of cavalry; at another, lack of full supplies, complete equipments, &c., &c. He was finally informed that further delay would not be tolerated; that the temper of the country was such that it would not brook any longer delay; and the Ass't. Sec. of War, Charles A. Dana was dispatched to the Army of the Cumberland, presumably with authority to force an immediate advance. Then began Rosecrans' campaign which ended so disastrously at Chickamauga, Sept. 20, 1863.[1]

Early in September Grant was ordered to send reinforcements to Rosecrans to assist in the capture of Chattanooga, and Halleck suggested that some suitable corps commander be sent with them. Grant decided to send Sherman. The order for this reinforcement was telegraphed from Washington September 13th, and was repeated more urgently on the 17th. Grant says in his Memoirs that he received this order September 27th. I think it was one or two days earlier. I have before me as I write a private letter written by me, dated September 26th, on the Steamboat Liberty No. 2, when near Helena, Ark., on my way to Memphis, with the first reinforcements sent by Grant to Rosecrans. So prompt and ener-

---

[1] The Battle of Chickamauga, on September 19–20, 1863, resulted in the defeat and partial rout of General Rosecrans's army.

getic were Grant and Sherman, that one division of fifteen regiments was marched from its camps on Big Black, twelve miles east of Vicksburg; embarked on steamboats with its quartermaster, commissary and artillery trains complete; and was steaming up the river for Memphis in less than twelve hours after Grant received the order. Nothing equaling this occurred during the war, and is not recorded in any history I have seen.

At Memphis we received the first news of the battle of Chickamauga. Sherman's troops were sent by rail as far as Corinth and from there marched to Iuka, repairing the railroad as they went. Gen. Rosecrans had been so unjust to Grant and his troops in the past that I decided to send a special correspondent with them to see that newspaper justice was done them. This correspondent overtook me at Iuka, and I started back to Memphis on my way to Vicksburg (as I supposed), to rejoin Gen. Grant.

A ride around the environs of Iuka greatly increased my opinion of its military strength. The fortifications thrown up the year before by our troops were in good condition. The village stands on a series of ridges intersected by ravines, and the whole forms a sort of plateau, or basin, surrounded on all sides by high ground. On this elevation our earthworks were constructed, generally connected with rifle pits, and able to withstand the assault of a heavy force.

The battleground of the year before [2] lay two or three miles south-west of the village and bore but slight traces of the struggle. A stranger might have ridden across it repeatedly

---

[2] In the Battle of Iuka, on September 19 and 20, 1862, a Union force commanded by General William S. Rosecrans, operating under Grant, had decisively defeated a Confederate force commanded by General Sterling Price. The Union loss in killed, wounded, and missing was 782, that of the Confederates 1,516.

without seeing anything to attract especial attention. The young trees were thrifty, the foliage heavy, and an under-growth of scrub oak coming up vigorously. Persons familiar with the battle were generally interested and felt a half day well spent in riding over the ground. The large trees bore evidence of the storm of iron that once swept the field, and many scarred trunks will silently attest the locality for years to come. The dead were separated and buried together in rows, as far as practicable; but in a great many instances were covered where they fell. But this was not always sufficiently done. The dead were a vast multitude—the fatigue party a small one. Many were placed in shallow gulleys and gulches, and covered there. The first freshet washed them out, until every ravine became a Golgotha. To the honor of the ladies of Iuka it can be recorded that they repaired to the battlefield in small parties, with shovels and hoes, and consigned these bodies a second time to Mother Earth, there being no men left in the community to discharge this duty.

When I was there in October 1863, the grass was growing green on most of the graves, the birds sang sweetly in the woods as of yore, and but little was left to denote that the din and shock of battle had so recently woke the echoes for miles around. By October 13th trains were running regularly between Iuka and Memphis.

As I rode down the principal street of Memphis on the aft-ernoon of October 16th an acquaintance accosted me from the side-walk; inquired where I was going; and then informed me that Gen. Grant had passed up the river two days before; the headquarter flag was flying; and the bow of the boat covered with horses; and that no one knew where he was going.

I suspected the truth at once; left my horse at a sale-stable to be sold at once; ordered the equipments and price of the horse to be held for further directions; and in less than thirty minutes was steaming up the river on the four o'clock mail boat for Cairo. I arrived at the latter place Sunday afternoon, October 18th, and learned that Grant had taken the train for Indianapolis. No one knew his destination. Gen. Read [Hugh Thompson Reid], the post commandant, could give no further information. I took the Louisville evening train and soon procured daily papers stating that Gen. Grant met Secretary Stanton at Indianapolis, and that they had gone from there by special train to Louisville.

Foreseeing, from these meager facts, an arduous, busy campaign I proceeded directly to Cincinnati; procured a necessary winter outfit; arrived at Louisville Wednesday, noon; rode to Nashville Thursday; and remained there till the following Monday, in company of Capts. Peter Hudson and Orlando H. Ross, of the staff, who had been left behind for some purpose. . . .

[*At Nashville, Cadwallader learned that Grant had already left that place for Chattanooga, where he had been ordered to take command. Beleaguered by the Confederate General Braxton Bragg, the Union forces there were threatened with starvation and capture.*]

Monday, October 26th, I left Nashville with Capts. Hudson and Ross. At Bridgeport I could neither buy or borrow any horse able to carry me to Chattanooga. The mountain sides were covered with abandoned army mules in all stages of starvation. For fifty cents in fractional money a darkey caught and brought to me the best one he could lay hands on. He was uncommonly large, zebra striped, with good eyes, wind and limbs, in fair flesh, but with galled back and shoulders.

For another half dollar he got me a piece of a bridle; another tip brought a thrown-away McClellan saddle-tree, without stirrups, breastplate or crupper; still another obtained leather straps which would be used for these purposes; he finally in some manner got hold of two pairs of dilapidated cavalry pouches; so that at a cost of less than five dollars I found myself in possession of the best "mount" that could be purchased in Bridgeport for any price. I could get army blankets. Strapping several of these on the raw back of my mule; and filling one pair of cavalry pouches with shelled corn (which I suppose the darkey purloined) for the beast's support to Chattanooga, and the other pair with such articles of food for myself as could be had from officers and sutlers; I mounted and headed the procession of three, *en route* to the besieged city.

We traveled by the courier line over the mountains, most of the way, to avoid mud, and to shorten the distance. We stayed at night with a typical southern mountaineer whose nearest neighbor lived many miles away. He only visited "the Cities" as he termed Bridgeport and Chattanooga once or twice a year to exchange coonskins and other furs and hides for a coveted supply of coffee and a jug full of "mountain dew," when the home, or moonshine, article fell short. A grown daughter had never been out to civilization, and the wife and mother of the family had not been off the mountain for nine years.

They were all clad in the old fashioned homespun cotton and woollens; all went barefooted in warm weather, and wore moccasins of their own manufacture in the winter. They owned a few sheep, hogs, horses and cattle; raised cotton, flax and tobacco for family use; depended greatly on squirrels, pheasants and other game for fresh meat; and managed by pack animals to get salt enough to make some bacon every year. Of vegetables they never had many. Of cultivated fruits, none but what was yielded by a few old stunted peach trees. Sugar they never had unless they made it from the mountain sugar maple. Pumpkins they had, green or dried, all the year round. Wild plums, whortleberries, and black haws could be had in their season for the picking. Honey was sometimes abundant. We paid for shelter in the tumbledown log cabin, by furnishing coffee for ourselves and the whole family, night and morning. Their hospitality was only limited by their means. "And buirdly chiels, and clever hizzies, are bred in sic a way as this is."

Starting early Wednesday morning, October 28th, we reached Chattanooga in the afternoon, my mule leading the way gallantly, and actually enduring the strain of the journey better than the staff horses. There was no alternative but turning him out again, and I fear he shared the fate of his kind, and died from lingering starvation. Shooting him might have been merciful, but I could not bring myself to do it, and gave him the only chance in my power to live.

Gen. Rawlins and Col. Duff had established a mess for themselves in a small house near the one Gen. Grant had taken for his own use. They had been expecting me for several days, and had reserved a place for me in the mess, which I gladly accepted. On their arrival there they had been entertained a day or two at Gen. [George H.] Thomas' headquarters, till they could establish their own. They had nothing to eat for the first five or six days but bread, coffee and sugar. These articles were all good of their kind. Soon after my arrival we received a treat in the form of a barrel of "desiccated vegetables," composed of potatoes, cabbage, beets, turnips, carrots, parsnips, onions, and possibly some

others, which had been finely chopped when green, dried
in some kind of evaporator, and barreled. They were deli-
cious in several forms. We used them in soup and beef stew
mainly when we reached the beef "course" in high living.
I suppose it was not a regular army ration then or since, but
it certainly "filled a long felt want."

For days and weeks afterwards I often saw soldiers walking slowly along the main thoroughfare from the river to
the camps (over which all supplies had to be hauled) with
their eyes fixed on the ground as if searching for some lost
valuable, and stopping at times to gather from the dirt, dust
and sand of the street one or more grains of corn or oats
which had jolted out of wagons. When a handful had been
accumulated they were roasted and eaten voraciously. I saw
rations of corn in the ear, and the poorest toughest beef
ever slaughtered issued to entire brigades on alternate days
—never by any chance, beef and corn on the same day. The
ears of corn were carefully counted, and the beef as carefully weighed. "Only this and nothing more." I saw many
hundreds of mules lying where they had been chained to
trees, till they starved to death. Other hundreds lay chained
to abandoned wagons, dead. The poor brutes had in scores of
instances eaten nearly through the trunks of large pine trees,
and eaten all the soft parts of the running gears of the wagons within their reach. . . .

The day after my arrival I noticed a photographer's tent
near the Crutchfield House, which was surrounded by a
crowd of soldiers. The operator was selling photos from the
last negative ever taken of Gen. Grant (as he asserted) at
fifty cents each nearly as fast as he could make change. A
glance showed me that they were not photos of Grant from
any negative, but really those of some (to me) unknown gen-

eral officer. The rascal had sold many hundreds of them as genuine, life-like pictures of Gen. Grant. As very few soldiers in that army had ever seen Grant, the imposture was easy. I exposed the fraud promptly. The money was refunded to every purchaser present, and a file of soldiers sent to prevent his being thrown into the river by the swindled and infuriated men.

November 3d I concluded to make a personal inspection of our picket line for my own information. It was a drizzly, misty morning. I was enveloped in a roomy rubber overcoat reaching nearly to my ankles when mounted. My Brigadier's hat, cavalry boots, and horse equipments, caused me to be mistaken for the officer of the day, or some one of superior rank, and several times on the tour, as I neared a picket camp, the guard was called out, and the salute given, due to a general officer. There was no time for explanations—I could only acknowledge the salute, and pass on. The ride revealed a strong Confederate picket line, not more than two hundred yards distant from our own in many places. By tacit agreement no picket firing was practiced during the siege. Our pickets were instructed not to fire unless the rebels advanced beyond their place, or made some hostile demonstration. The rebels probably had similar instructions, for the pickets of both armies stood on their beats within hailing distance of each other continually, without firing. I received one or two salutes from single Confederate pickets who brought their muskets to the "present" as I passed; but whether it was intended as a compliment, or a mockery, I was not in position to inquire.[3]

---

[3] For the sake of continuity this paragraph and the one preceding it have been inserted here. In Cadwallader's manuscript they precede the first paragraph beginning on page 155 of this book.

CHAPTER

Ten

[*Within two weeks Grant had reopened the Union supply lines, and Cadwallader watched military developments closely as the new commander maneuvered his forces into position to raise the siege of Chattanooga.*]

. . . It is due to Gen. Rawlins, Chief of Staff, to state that upon this occasion, as upon that of all Grant's great campaigns, he is unquestionably entitled to one-half the praise, for the strategy. Tactical successes were due to others; but no general or broad plan of campaign, or pitched battle, was ever adopted by Gen. Grant without the unqualified assent and approval of Rawlins. The latter was his only military confidant and adviser, and often originated many of the most successful operations.

The position of the Union troops and the general plan of the great battle which everyone now saw was impending, may be summarized as follows: Sherman's forces lay opposite and above Chattanooga, concealed from the Confederates on Missionary Ridge and Lookout Mountain by a high range of hills covered with timber. Campfires were measur-

CHATTANOOGA AND VICINITY

ably prohibited, so that neither smoke in the day time nor fires by night, revealed their presence to the enemy.

Hooker [1] lay in the Wauhatchie Valley at the base of Lookout, with his forces so stationed as to fully protect Brown's Ferry, and our new lines of supply from Bridgeport by river and wagon roads. He was also in position to prevent any attempts on Bragg's part to turn that flank, as he could now be reinforced from Chattanooga in half the time that the Confederates would require to mass in his front, if they ever contemplated doing so.

Thomas was posted in Chattanooga with his right reaching down to the creek separating the valley from the upper or eastern base of Lookout, and his left extending more than two-thirds of the way to the upper end of Missionary Ridge. To the left of Thomas, Gen. [Oliver O.] Howard's eleventh corps had been pushed as far to the front as could be done without bringing on a general engagement, and held there in readiness to co-operate with Sherman as soon as the latter had forced the passage of the Tennessee above him. Our lines were circumscribed, and Chattanooga completely besieged.

Bragg held Missionary Ridge from end to end; was strongly intrenched on its crest; had a strong line of rifle-pits half way down the slope facing us; and another line of rifle-pits at the base, both of which were strongly manned, and seemed to completely command a half mile of open cotton fields across which our men must advance without any protection whatever, should an assault be ordered on that part of the front. A strong picket line, with reserves, was still in front of this

---

[1] General Joseph Hooker had been dispatched from the Army of the Potomac with parts of two army corps, consisting of some 20,000 men, to help raise the siege of Chattanooga.

open ground, protected by the cottonwood and underbrush which grew luxuriantly. In addition to this he was strongly intrenched on Lookout Mountain, and with heavy guns could actually throw solid shot into Chattanooga, and the right of Thomas' line.

It is necessary to a correct understanding of the part assigned to Gen. Sherman to state that there are two streams called Chickamauga emptying into the Tennessee river above Chattanooga. North Chickamauga rises in Tennessee, flowing into the river about eight miles above town. South Chickamauga rises in Georgia and runs into the Tennessee about four miles above the city. Sherman's advance lay on the North Chickamauga, awaiting orders. He had collected there one hundred and twenty-five ponton boats,[2] with a detachment of carefully selected men to man them with all material necessary for quick work when the time came.

On the afternoon of November 23d I carried to Gen. Sherman his last written orders to cross the Tennessee river and bring on the great battle. At one o'clock on the morning of Nov. 24th one hundred and sixteen ponton boats containing thirty men each, dropped silently from their moorings in the North Chickamauga, floated into and down the Tennessee to the places previously selected for laying two bridges. One of these was to be at a point directly opposite the upper end of Missionary Ridge (and where it would have struck the river bank had it been prolonged across the bottom) and the other was to be just above the mouth of the South Chickamauga. Both landings were effected without discovery, pickets thrown out, some of the pontons put into position and others sent to the north bank to ferry over additional men.

[2] Grant says 116.

The noise at last reached the dull ears of the Confederate pickets who were supposed to be guarding the river but these were substantially all captured before any alarm was given.

The full significance of Sherman's movement was not comprehended by Bragg till the middle of the forenoon. Not until the middle of the afternoon was he prepared for any serious fighting. In the meantime Sherman had posted some batteries of heavy guns on the heights of the north or west side of the river to cover and protect his landing. Union troops of all arms were poured across the river in surging masses; pushed well forward and set to intrenching.

By noon Sherman had eight to ten thousand of his old veterans in line of battle, and behind earthworks from which Bragg's whole army could not have driven them in any reasonable length of time. By half past three in the afternoon he occupied the heights at the upper end of the Ridge with his flanks well extended on each slope. His artillery was dragged to the top by brigades of soldiers, and every precaution taken to hold the ground he had taken. His cavalry had also been dispatched in the direction of Chickamauga Station to threaten Bragg's line of supplies, and long before night the last man of his entire army was on the south side of the Tennessee.

Late in the afternoon he encountered some opposition from the Confederate troops, and was given a foretaste of what the morrow had in store for him. The day had been dark and drizzly, obscuring or hiding his movements, which may have partly accounted for Bragg's slowness in taking the offensive. A heavy fog settled down at night and Sherman was left to hold the ground he had gained. During the night Gen. Howard forced a crossing of Citico Creek connecting with Sherman's right, as had been previously ordered.

On the morning of Nov. 23d Thomas moved his three corps from their fortifications into the open ground in front in such a slow and orderly manner that Bragg at first concluded they had marched out for "another Potomac review," as he termed it. He was soon undeceived. They were thrown into line of battle and each proceeded deliberately to drive in the rebel pickets, and carry by storm their outmost line of works lying half way between the Union forts and the foot of the Ridge. The loss, in this movement was not serious, but the advantages gained were great. The key to this line was a bold conical hill called Orchard Knob. The rebel fortifications on Orchard Knob were turned during the night by our men and made to face the other way. Our battle front was now about six miles long. . . .

Hooker's attack on Lookout commenced early on the morning of the 24th. He ascended the lower slope steadily for awhile then swung to the left and began to push his way around the face of the mountain next to the river. The ground was very rough everywhere and often precipitous. Bragg had evidently considered it impregnable from this quarter (or in this manner) and Hooker met very little resistance in the forenoon. It was a constant skirmish in which a vast amount of ammunition was uselessly expended on both sides. The alarm however was genuine and the batteries on Lookout were thundering all day. Their cannon could not be sufficiently depressed to play on Hooker's column. The musketry fire was unusually heavy from morning till night, which gave the affair the appearance of a hard fought battle.

A drizzling rain fell all day as previously mentioned. This

added to the smoke of musketry and cannon often enveloped all the troops in an impenetrable fog. Hooker's right wing extended up the mountain, above the lowering clouds, and it not unfrequently happened that the flash of muskets and guns would be distinctly visible in the purer air above. From this circumstance, it caught the name of the "Battle above the Clouds."

By dark Hooker had passed around the face of Lookout. His left reached to the creek almost connecting with Thomas' right. His right extended directly towards the summit of the mountain. He lay there all night well satisfied with his day's work. As his troops went into camp for the night, campfires were kindled rapidly and produced one of the most beautiful sights I ever witnessed.

I rode with Hooker's command a large part of the day, and on returning to headquarters was closely questioned by Gen. Rawlins as to the character of the fighting, the probable losses, and the certain results. I may have spoken of it rather nonchalantly, for Gen. Grant seemed somewhat surprised. When I gave it as my opinion that Hooker's list of killed would be less than one hundred, he asked how much of the ground I had traversed, and made the jocular remark attributed to him in "Richardson's History of U. S. Grant," that he feared I was a better newspaper man than soldier. The remark was made in the utmost kindness, but did mean to imply that I must be badly mistaken. So the laugh was on me at headquarters for two or three hours.

But before midnight Hooker telegraphed Grant that his losses in killed were very trifling indeed, more than indorsing all I had said. The tables were so effectually turned that more than one box of cigars was dumped into my arms, and a jolly supper followed. I wish to say once for all on this sub-

ject that no engagement of the war was so magnified in public as this so-called "Battle above the Clouds." In those days
it scarcely rose to the dignity of a battle. It was nothing but
a magnificent skirmish from beginning to end. Had any serious opposition been encountered by Hooker he never could
have made such progress that day.

Its results were all that could be hoped for, however, and
were precisely what Grant expected and desired. The defenses of Lookout Mountain were turned by Hooker's position at night. Bragg was not only compelled to abandon
them hastily during the night, leaving many heavy guns and
stores of ammunition to fall into our hands next day; but
he was also obliged to make a forced march far to the southward to avoid the capture of the entire force. These troops
were separated from his main army on Missionary Ridge,
and were not used during the remainder of that campaign.

The morning of Nov. 25th found the lines of the contending armies about as follows: Sherman strongly posted and
intrenched on the heights of Missionary Ridge above Chattanooga, his right flank connecting with Howard's corps which
reached to Thomas' left, and his cavalry far to the extreme
left threatening Chickamauga Station and Bragg's line of
supplies by the railroad. Thomas firmly established on the
advanced line he had taken on the 23d, with his headquarters near the center on Orchard Knob, about a mile and
a half from the Ridge, and [John M.] Palmer's corps forming his right reaching nearly to the creek at the foot of Lookout. Hooker lay across the creek below Palmer with his right
reaching up the mountain to the palisades.

Bragg occupied Missionary Ridge from end to end, every
rod of which had been fortified and protected in the highest
style of military art. The force compelled to evacuate Look-

out Mountain to avoid capture was hurrying back along the
mountain hoping to pass around Hooker's front and join
the main army on Missionary Ridge. It will be seen at a
glance that the relative positions and conditions of Grant
and Bragg had been wholly changed within two days. . . .

Bragg's strategical mistake of detaching [James] Longstreet (with his corps) on November 4th to join in the expected capture of Knoxville,[3] rendered his defeat certain by
the combinations of Gen. Grant. He might have deceived
a less wary opponent, or outgeneraled one of less ability.
Longstreet was lured on towards Knoxville daily, by a feeble
show of resistance at various points, until too far away to be
recalled in time for the great battle. . . .

The morning of Nov. 25th opened with a splendid sunrise,
and the atmosphere was uncommonly clear until obscured
by the smoke of battle in the afternoon. Gen. Hooker found
Lookout Mountain abandoned by the enemy and took possession of its heights as soon as a column of men could be
moved to the top. In pursuance of his general orders issued
days beforehand, his advance was thrown forward towards
Rossville, and he was expected to cross the creek in that
vicinity early in the forenoon, drive any detachments of
Confederate troops left there, back on their main line in
front of Thomas, unless he could succeed in separating,
capturing or destroying them. Failing in this he was to join
in the main attack on Missionary Ridge, or by extending his
right so as to cut off Bragg's line of retreat, attack him flank
and rear.

The enemy destroyed all bridges in Hooker's front before

---

[3] A Union force commanded by General Ambrose E. Burnside had
taken Knoxville; but the troops were far from a good base, and their
position was precarious.

retreating from Lookout, so that all his artillery and a considerable portion of his men were delayed about four hours
in crossing the creek. His advance however effected a crossing farther up stream, drove the Confederates before them
and were ready for their share of the day's fighting later in
the day. Hooker's attack on the lower end of the Ridge was
intended to commence the day's work. This was delayed for
the reasons stated till the middle of the afternoon. . . .

The signal for the combined attack of the whole Union
army was to be the discharge of six cannon, fired in rapid
succession from Orchard Knob. These shots rang out at ten
minutes past four, p.m., and instantly the earth seemed to
be alive with the armed hosts which sprang from their cover
as though they had been belched forth from subterraneous
recesses. The air was filled with every conceivable projectile
known to modern warfare. The rattling of musketry, screech-
ing of shell, and the roar and thunder of heavy field and
siege artillery, was beyond the power of description, and for
intervals of time rendered conversation impossible. Grant and
Staff, Thomas and Staff, and many other general officers
were on Orchard Knob, as general headquarters for the day.
From there the semicircular sweep of the entire Union line
from the river above to the river below Chattanooga was
distinctly visible, as well as the corresponding heights of Missionary Ridge.

We could overlook the belt of cottonwood timber next in
front of our line (nearly a half mile in width), see the open
cotton fields across which our troops must advance to reach
the strongly prepared line of rifle-pits at the foot of the
Ridge, could see plainer even than all others the second line
of rifle-pits half way up the face of the Ridge (for the sun-
light fell directly upon them), and could see the frowning

earthworks bristling with heavy ordnance on the crest of the Ridge, and back of these could often catch glimpses of rebel battle flags, troops in line or movement, and Confederate officers scanning us through their field-glasses, or galloping back and forth, apparently carrying orders.

As the echoes of the signal guns died away the Union army filed out through selected and prepared places and took their position in line of battle with the mechanical precision of clockwork. Some hurry and excitement there necessarily was. The men whooping, yelling and hurrahing; the officers giving orders in stentorian voices; bugles sounding commands on the flanks in the distance; and the whole presenting to eye and ear, an experience never to be encountered twice in one life time.

No battle ever fought on this continent afforded such opportunity. The day and the ground conspired to give an unbroken view of the whole field, and probably no great battle ever fought on the American continent, equaled it in this regard. With bands playing, flags flying, soldiers cheering and yelling, our men three lines deep in perfect alignment, poured out through the young cottonwood timber, swept the rebel skirmishers out of the underbrush into the open cotton field, and pursued them on the run under a severe musketry fire to the first line of rifle-pits. The sudden and intrepid Union assault greatly surprised the Confederates. They could not fire upon it without shooting down their fleeing men. Almost before they realized the extent of the movement their lower chain of rifle-pits was captured, and the Stars and Stripes were flying over the trenches triumphantly.

The original intention had been to call a halt of our troops in these trenches until the whole line could be reformed, and directions given for the perilous ascent before them. But the old veterans of so much campaigning, had learned greatly from experience, and become somewhat a law to themselves. They were not much given to waiting for orders from officers who knew but little, if any, more than themselves. In their own language: "When they saw a good thing, they knew it, and took it."

Seeing themselves supported right and left, they had scarcely made a show of halting in the rifle-pits till the color bearers, non-commissioned officers and men began to swarm up the foot of the Ridge cheering and encouraging each other. It became a foot and hand struggle to see who should first reach the second line of rifle-pits half way up the Ridge. Sometimes the advanced line of climbers seemed ragged and irregular and grave fears were entertained by Thomas and others that it could not sustain itself, but would be shot down or captured before supports could reach it.

The propriety of commanding a halt from headquarters was seriously discussed for a few minutes. But Grant could not find it in his heart to dampen the enthusiasm of his men, and said: "Let us wait a few minutes and see what the boys will do. They are not so badly scattered as they seem to be. We see much more bare ground between them on the hillside than we would if they were on a level with us. We shall soon see. The boys feel pretty good. Let them alone awhile."

Word was sent right and left that the lower trenches were carried, and an immediate assault ordered upon the crest of the Ridge, and every intervening obstacle. "Take the Ridge if you can! Take the Ridge if you can!" were the orders sent out by Aides in every direction. Slowly at first, but steadily, our skirmishers advanced, soon followed by a more substantial body of troops till the face of the Ridge was cleared of every rebel defender, and the boys in blue reached the summit. . . .

Lieut. Col. James H. Wilson, then engineer on the staff, and myself, mounted the earthworks [on Orchard Knob] as our troops filed out, and remained there till the victory was won on the Ridge, when all mounted and started in pursuit. We were stormed at, scolded, threatened, and repeatedly ordered down; but the fascination of the great battle wholly overcame all prudential considerations. There is nothing on earth approaching it in sublimity. My own experience and observation is probably that of most men similarly situated. Personal danger was forgotten till the excitement was over.

As previously mentioned Hooker's attack was intended to commence the day's fighting. But his delay of fully four hours in rebuilding bridges, put Sherman in a critical condition. He was contending gallantly, and thus far successfully against great odds. Bragg had a double row of intrenchments across the Ridge which Sherman must carry by storm, or before any further advance could be made there. These could only be reached by ascending a steep declivity, under a concentrated fire. Two attempts were made to carry them by assault, each of which failed, entailing heavy loss. I had been standing by the side of Gen. Grant in silence for several minutes and we both witnessed Sherman's second discomfiture. He dropped his glass, turned to me and said: "Driving our boys quite lively, aren't they?"

"Yes, driving them back badly," I replied.

"Do you see the signal flag beyond and a little to the right," he inquired.

I answered that "I did."

"That's where Sherman is posted; he'll soon make it all right," was the quiet, self-assured reply of Grant, and our glasses were turned to other parts of the line for several minutes. Grant's confidence in Sherman had come to be unbounded. Under given conditions he knew precisely how far he could depend upon him. In this instance his temporary repulses never caused a moment's uneasiness, or doubt as to his final success, in the mind of his superior officer. In less than an hour Sherman swept away the hindrances on his front, and was rolling Bragg's line back on itself along the Ridge in great confusion. Attacked and defeated on both flanks and in front before sundown, a hurried retreat under cover of night and darkness was the only alternative left to the vainglorious Confederate commander who had only a few days before notified Gen. Grant that he expected to capture Chattanooga, and by inference the whole Union Army, immediately.

There was one singular occurrence when the advance of Thomas was made from Orchard Knob that provoked comment at the time, and was never explained that I know of. Gen. Gordon Granger commanded the Fourth Corps. He was on Orchard Knob with one of the batteries, sighting the guns with all the enthusiasm of a boy, and shouting with the men whenever a shot had done execution. He had apparently forgotten his soldiers who lay in the rear, ready for the assault. Finally Rawlins inquired of Grant: "Why are not those men moving on the rifle pits. I don't believe they have been ordered forward."

Grant—"Oh yes, I think the order must have been given. Gen. [Absalom] Baird,⁴ why is not your division in motion?"

Baird—"We have received no such orders, sir."

Grant—"Gen. Thomas, why are not these troops advancing?"

---

⁴ Grant states that he made this inquiry of Gen. Thomas A. Wood.

Thomas—"I don't know. Gen. Granger has been directed to move them forward."

Grant—"Gen. Granger, why are your men waiting?"

Granger—"I have had no orders to advance."

Grant—"If you will leave that battery to its captain, and take command of your corps, it will be better for all of us."

Granger obeyed promptly and rushed into the fight like a wild Irishman. This delay I witnessed. Part of the conversation I heard. The balance I had upon information. Rawlins had no confidence in Granger, and Grant soon after lost all the respect for him that he ever entertained.

When Grant attended the army on the 26th and 27th in pursuing and driving Bragg's demoralized "outfit," he dispatched a staff officer to Thomas to start Granger instantly for the relief of Burnside at Knoxville. When he returned to Chattanooga on the 29th he was surprised to learn that Granger had not yet started, although Burnside's necessities were known to be extreme. On page 92, second volume of his Memoirs, Gen. Grant says: "Finding that Granger had not only not started, but was very reluctant to go, he having decided for himself that it was a very bad move to make, I sent word to Gen. Sherman of the situation, and directed him to march to the relief of Knoxville." This was substantially the last heard of Gordon Granger. When Grant became Lieut. General he carefully kept such officers in the background.

I also think it was the beginning of Grant's comparative lack of confidence in Gen. Thomas which was occasionally manifested afterward. This was not so much a distrust of his soldierly qualifications and reliability in defensive operations, as a fear that when he was left to act on his own responsibility he would be too slow in assuming the offensive. I think this estimate of Gen. Thomas will be considered just

by future historians. He was unquestionably one of the greatest subordinate commanders the war produced, but he
never distinguished himself unqualifiedly in any independent
command. In the latter sphere of action he fell so far below
Sherman or Sheridan, or Wilson, as to make comparison unfriendly, and to class him with McPherson, Logan, Howard,
Slocum and others. . . .[5]

On the evening of Nov. 24th I wrote a full account of the
battle of Lookout Mountain and took it to Major [William]
McMichael, on Gen. Thomas' Staff then acting as telegraphic
censor, for approval, and transmission by the military telegraph line to Louisville, to be forwarded from there in the
ordinary way to the New York *Herald*. Major McMichael
demurred to some portions of the dispatch and finally declined to approve it on the ground that the line was already
overloaded with military dispatches, and that mine could
only be sent at the expense of more important matter.

To have failed in transmitting news of the day's fighting
to the *Times* and *Herald* might have caused me to lose my
place as their correspondent. I returned hastily to Gen. Grant
for assistance. Without reading it, or making the slightest
inquiry as to its character, he took my manuscript and wrote
across the folded back of the last sheet: "Send the within." I
never visited Gen. Thomas' quarters afterwards. I no longer
needed favors, but was rather in position to extend them to
others.

---

[5] Cadwallader's opinion of Thomas is scarcely valid in view of
Thomas's virtual annihilation of the Confederate army sent against him
when he later commanded at Nashville.

C H A P T E R

Eleven

IT was well understood on the morning of Nov. 25th, that the fighting would be forced to a finish before night. It was certain that not one tenth part of the newspaper correspondence could be telegraphed that night from Chattanooga. It might be two or three days before the wires could be freed from military use long enough to transmit it all. The nearest railroad station was Stevenson, sixty-five miles distant, by the only safe road.

I decided to leave Chattanooga at the close of the day's battle; make the night ride to Stevenson in time to catch the six o'clock morning train of the 26th from there to Nashville; and do all the writing I could on the cars. The road crossed the Tennessee river at Chattanooga on a ponton, passed behind Moccasin Point to Brown's Ferry where it recrossed the river on another ponton bridge, thence up the Wauhatchie Valley a few miles, around by Whitesides, down the river through Nickajack and Shell Mound to Bridgeport, where the river was again crossed, and then by a dirt road to Stevenson, which ran nearly parallel to the railroad. I was satisfied that no other correspondent would attempt a journey beset with so many difficulties; and if successful I would be many hours in advance of all competitors.

In anticipation of the night ride my thorough-bred mare was carefully groomed and fed all day. Several assistants were on the field under orders to hand in full notes of the day's work to me not later than six o'clock in the evening. I intended starting promptly at eight p.m., without allowing any rival to know of my departure. But some of my plans mis-carried—one of my assistants did not return on time— and at the last minute Lieut. H. N. Towner, Adjutant to Col. Duff, sent for me. He had been shot in the shoulder about sundown, rupturing the subclavial artery, from which there was a possibility of his bleeding to death. Just as I was bending over him as he lay pale and exhausted on his cot, taking what I thought might be a final leave, he looked me in the face with a faint smile and said: "How about that two dollars?" He had been claiming that I had backed his opponent to that amount in a recent game of poker. It was a grim exhibition of humor, but of course such a patient would recover.

At ten o'clock I was in the saddle with sixty-five miles of exceedingly bad roads before me which must be covered in eight consecutive hours, or all results of the undertaking would be lost. The Wauhatchie Valley was over knee deep in mud for three or four miles. The pickets on the road at Nickajack were found asleep and I passed in and out of that post without disturbing their slumbers. The outpost at Shell Mound ordered: "Halt, who comes there?" To my answer, "A friend," he replied: "Dismount friend, and advance."

I tried to explain to him that I was from Gen. Grant's headquarters and a bearer of military dispatches, which was strictly true. But a musket brought to the shoulder at full cock, with a peremptory command to dismount, was not to be lightly disregarded. The officer of the guard was called, and accompanied me to post headquarters. The Colonel commanding sent a mounted orderly to set me on the road outside the lines, so that but little time was lost.

The bridge at Bridgeport, including its approaches and defenses, was over a mile in length, and strongly guarded day and night. As I dismounted the officer appeared to whom I explained who I was, and the object of my mission, and its haste; and requested him to walk with me across the bridge so that I could give him news of the fighting on Missionary Ridge, and the flight of Bragg's army, without any loss of time. The bridge was lined with soldiers and sentries who overheard enough of my conversation to know that a great victory had been won, and commenced shouting and yelling the news to others. In a few minutes time thousands of men were yelling themselves hoarse. I mounted and rode away without any interruption. For all that officer learned to the contrary, I might have been Jefferson Davis. I left a dispatch at the telegraph office which was sent by orders of Gen. Grant.

It was now past three o'clock a.m., and I had twelve miles to ride over a road cut to pieces with heavy artillery, converted into deep mudholes by recent rains, with a crust of frozen mud and ice covering all, but not strong enough to bear the weight of myself and mare. Added to this I failed to find the direct road leading out of Bridgeport. But at this juncture I met a belated orderly who had been out carrying dispatches, and compelled him to start me on my way. An added inducement in form of a greenback, kept him as my guide till we came in sight of Stevenson. Five miles back my mare lost a foreshoe. The frozen ground soon broke her hoof to pieces, and she galloped into town in a pitiable plight; but as full of game and spirit as when I mounted at Chattanooga.

The bell was ringing, the whistle blowing, and the train within three minutes of pulling out, as I swung from my saddle on to the rear platform of the hindmost car in the train, with my bridle rein in my hand. One of Gen. Grant's couriers returning from Nashville saw me dashing up on horseback, and came elbowing through the crowd to where I was. To him I intrusted my gallant little mare, with orders in Gen. Grant's name to remain in Stevenson until he could ship her by car to Nashville.

I was many hours in advance of all other correspondents and had reasonable expectation of making a decided "newspaper beat." But at Anderson we encountered a wrecked freight train which obstructed the track for four hours. At Wartrace another wrecked train delayed us sixteen hours. When in sight of Nashville our own engine gave out, and I was obliged to walk three or four miles to the city. The delays on the way had, however, been turned to the best possible account. I had written and corrected a very full account of what had transpired. I proceeded at once to Gen. R. S. Granger, post commandant at Nashville; had him approve them—hurried to the telegraph office and filed them before dark for transmittal; and went to Donneganna's Restaurant in the same building, and leisurely ordered the first full meal I had eaten for several days. My fatigue was extreme and I was on the sidewalk congratulating myself upon my own success, and the possibility of rest and sleep, when I saw Mr. W. F. G. Shanks, correspondent-in-chief of the New York *Herald* in the Department of the Cumberland, coming up the street on a half run, and nearly breathless.

His experience on the trip from Chattanooga to Nashville was ludicrous beyond description. He left the former place in the forenoon of Nov. 26th—the day after my departure—reached Bridgeport by steamboat; and there found a dummy engine standing on the track which had just brought Gen. Logan from Nashville. For one hundred dollars in greenbacks he induced the engineer to fire up and carry him to Nashville without allowing anyone else aboard. As the locomotive was slowly pulling out Shanks saw a dirty greasy looking civilian swing carelessly on the tender, and supposed him to be an assistant engineer or fireman, and paid but little attention to him. The engineer also saw him climb on directly under Shanks' observation, and took it for granted that he was going with his knowledge and consent.

Shanks, with the instinct of a trained correspondent, forced an explanation at the end of a two hours ride, when it transpired that the nondescript passenger was Mr. Woodward, the correspondent of the Cincinnati *Times,* and that Shanks as a matter of fact was actually paying one hundred dollars to transport him to Nashville. The engine was stopped, and everything short of personal violence resorted to, to get him off the locomotive. Expostulations and threats were in vain. He stuck to "the machine," and in turn threatened Shanks and the engineer with exposure and punishment, if he was not allowed to come on with them to Nashville. At the depot, Shanks got away from him and came running up the street in advance.

I was called into play at once to intercept and delay Woodward, while Shanks hastened to get his budget of telegraphic correspondence approved and deposited in the telegraph office. Woodward soon came along in a leisurely manner and was glad to meet me. I took him into the restaurant

and ordered an elaborate supper for two, composed of such
dishes as would consume the most time in preparation; occasionally ordered an extra dish for which we would have to
wait, and consumed easily more than an hour's time before
we had finished supper.

Woodward then drew out his manuscript to start to the
telegraph office. Some comparisons were instituted between
his descriptions and mine, and more time consumed. But
he finally climbed the stairs to the office and was there informed that no telegrams could be dispatched without the
approval of Gen. Granger. This alarmed him and he soon
came back to me for advice. I assured him that Gen. Granger's approval was the first thing to secure. He trudged off
to headquarters, but found them closed for the night. He
returned a second time to me. We then took a hack and
visited all the hotels, and most of the public places in the
city, without finding Granger. Between eleven and twelve
at night Woodward found him at the theater, but he was
displeased at such untimely and unofficial importunity and
refused to be troubled with the business.

Woodward then repaired to the St. Cloud Hotel and went
to bed after having the clerk register him by name and room,
to be called for the early morning train to Louisville. For an
additional five dollar greenback, Shanks bribed the negro
porter to erase Woodward's name from the list to be called
up in the morning, and he was consequently left over another
day in Nashville.

Knowing the crowded condition of the telegraph line, I
spent most of the evening in the office, watching the transmission of business and hoping to get off at least a part of
my voluminous correspondence. At midnight I had an elegant
hot supper sent up to every employee, and stimulated them

to renewed efforts in my behalf. At two o'clock all seemed hopeless. I might possibly get my dispatches as far as Louisville, but the operator there wired us that he already had more matter in hand than he could transmit by daylight. I replied instantly, that should any opportunity present itself, I wanted a commencement made on my dispatches—that I had deposited ten dollars to his credit in the Nashville office as a retainer for his services till four o'clock in the morning, and hoped he would do all in his power to accommodate me. Within half an hour he wired that it was started at Louisville; and at 3:30, that the last word had just been transmitted. Shanks' dispatches followed mine, but were not in time for the morning papers.

The next day Shanks and myself proceeded to Louisville, writing steadily all the way, and telegraphed our matter promptly from that city. Woodward's failure to transmit his accounts cost him his place, and my success led to many subsequent promotions in the New York *Herald* service.

After exhausting my note-book and drawing upon my recollection of events connected with the great campaign, and its culminating battles, of Lookout Mountain and Missionary Ridge, I spent a few weeks with family and friends in Milwaukee, and rejoined headquarters at Nashville in January 1864. I had consigned my little mare to Col. Ely S. Parker, A.A.G. on Grant's Staff, and found her in excellent condition for subsequent service.

While at home I procured a list of all Wisconsin regiments and batteries in the department of the Cumberland, and visited each of them in their encampments so far as possible. The infantry commands were in excellent shape, but . . . [the 8th Wisconsin] battery, which served with such distinction in the battle of Chickamauga, that an elegant shaft has recently been erected on the field of battle by order of the Wisconsin legislature to commemorate its services and position in that great contest, was in a most pitiable condition. Many of its horses were lost in battle; many others actually starved to death before supplies could be forwarded to it, or the battery withdrawn to Stevenson; and the officers and privates had been strained and overworked till they also were nearly broken down. The men were drawn up in line to receive me, and I extended to them the private and public thanks of the officers and citizens of Wisconsin for their heroic defense of their State and National flags, from their first engagement down to that day.

It was an occasion of much congratulation. This battery [1] had stood the brunt of many fights—was always called upon for arduous duty—and sometimes felt that their services and hardships had not been duly appreciated by state or nation. But my message to them cleared all this away. It was soon newly refitted and equipped. Capt. Henry E. Stiles, its first senior Lieutenant, was made captain immediately; led it into many bloody battles; and finally marched it triumphantly into Milwaukee in the summer of 1865, when it was ordered home for "muster out" after the close of the war. . . .

I also visited all the Nashville hospitals; carried messages and monies to many of the inmates; and contributed in a small way to the alleviation of mental and physical suffering. At this time postage stamps were as difficult to obtain by soldiers as dollars. I always carried a few dollars' worth of these for gratuitous distribution among the sick and wounded men.

Years afterward an amusing incident resulted. I was walking a street in Milwaukee when a seedy and altogether dis-

---

[1] Cadwallader refers here to the 8th Wisconsin Battery. It fought at Corinth, Chaplin Hills, Murfreesboro, and around Chattanooga.

reputable looking individual accosted me, and after staring me in the face awhile, asked me if I did not visit the Nashville hospitals in the winter of 1864. Upon my answering affirmatively, his face brightened up, and he soon called me by name. He next jerked a greasy fifty-cent fractional currency piece from his vest pocket and said he owed me that much money. I protested that he did not to my recollection, and refused to take it. But he said I gave him that amount in postage stamps when he was stretched on his back in the Nashville hospital, and now was the time to pay it.

No remonstrances availed. It was a point of honor, and he was sufficiently obstinate, if not intoxicated, to have made it the grounds of a personal quarrel. I accepted the money, but wronged the man in my heart for some time afterward. I believed that he only made this pretense of honesty, to obtain a heavier advance from me in the future. To the honor of our common humanity I gladly record that although he had abundant opportunity to do so, he never requested another favor, but remained friendly and respectful as long as I knew him.

On my return to Nashville I first realized the horrors that followed the battles at Chattanooga. They had been dimly set forth by cautious correspondents, and often suppressed by military authority. The accommodations for the wounded and sick at the front were so woefully deficient, that entire trains of boxcars were filled with them and dispatched to the convalescent hospitals northward. Surgeons and detailed soldiers for nurses, went with each train. But the men died by hundreds in transit. December proved an unusually cold month, and scores upon scores of weak, bloodless, sick and wounded, succumbed to the exposure, and were taken from the cars at Nashville frozen as stiff as dressed hogs in midwinter. It may have [been] unavoidable but was none the less horrible.

The winter was one of comparative military inactivity. I made several trips to the front revisiting battlefields, calling at military camps and gaining all possible information as to present and future affairs. On one of these trips while in Huntsville, Alabama, then Gen. Logan's headquarters, I made the acquaintance of several excellent families in the place. When at the depot to return to Nashville I met four ladies from some of the families I had visited. They had obtained permits from Gen. Logan to go to Nashville for the purchase of necessary dry goods and family supplies, and were glad to have me for a traveling companion. We took the train to Stevenson, where a change had to be made to a through freight train to Nashville.

The rear car was what is known as a caboose, containing some benches, a stove and several bunks, or sleeping berths, ranged above each other, as in ocean steamers. I assisted the ladies at Stevenson, saw them in the proper car of the right train, and then stood around outside in conversation with army friends and acquaintances. I promised the ladies to come aboard the car they were in, and ride with them to Nashville. But the train started unexpectedly and I had barely time to jump into the special pay-car assigned to Major [William R.] Gibson, and his clerks, then on their return from Chattanooga where they had been paying off a portion of the troops at that place.

I intended going back to the caboose at the first stop our train made, but we sped on, and on. Night overtook us. We were all tired and sleepy and finally lay down on buffalo robes and blankets and were wrapped in forgetfulness. It afterward appeared that our train had stopped at Anderson for a supply of water, and while standing there was run into by another section which followed closely in our rear.

We were awakened by the crash; the pay-car was crushed all to pieces, and its inmates tumbled down on the track amid the debris of broken boards and scantling, robes, blankets, paymaster's iron chests and everything the car contained. Scrambling to our feet and finding ourselves with unbroken bones, we set to work securing the paymaster's chests. By the time this was done, the uproar at the rear, attracted our attention and reminded me of my promise to the women from Huntsville.

On rushing there we found the car in flames and scores of men vainly endeavoring to rescue those inside. An Iowa surgeon was the only man in the car. The locomotive of the train following ours had plunged into the caboose, upsetting the stove which soon fired the car, and as was supposed, instantly killed one of the women who was asleep in a berth. The collision had so twisted and wrenched the frame-work of the caboose, that the large sliding doors at each side were immovable. Before axes and other tools could be obtained to tear the caboose to pieces, it was a mass of roaring flames. The surgeon was shouting for help, and blistering his hands, in trying to extinguish the women's burning clothing.

The only opening in the caboose was a hole about eighteen inches square, near the roof, at the forward end. The gallant hero inside next tried to lift the women up to that hole, and get them out in that way. He soon found this to be impossible, and then managed to crawl out himself, and tried to stand on the iron ladder fastened to the outside of the caboose, and pull the women out one by one. He succeeded in getting two out alive, both of whom died before morning.

The third woman was too large and heavy to be drawn through the aperture and was soon suffocated and cremated. The fourth woman, as stated, was presumably killed by the collision as none inside saw her after the accident. The surgeon was so badly injured that his life was barely saved. I was the only person who knew the names or residences of the women, and remained in Anderson till the arrival of their relatives from Huntsville, in answer to my telegram conveying the horrible message of death.

The winter dragged uneventfully along. My health was seriously impaired, and that of my family in Milwaukee had become alarming. My brother-in-law, Mr. [Edward A.] Paul, needed my assistance on the Daily he had purchased in expectation of our joint proprietorship. Gen. Grant was to be created Lieut. General, and go east. Everything conspired to decide me to leave the field and return to home, and civil pursuits in life. I accordingly left headquarters, where my stay had been so pleasant for eighteen months, leaving my friends in expectation of my return after a period of rest at home, but scarcely thinking I should ever rejoin them again. I transmitted a statement of account to the *Herald;* notified the manager that I would draw on the office for the balance due me; did so within a week afterward; was paid my account in full, and considered myself out of its service.

Nearly a month elapsed before I heard a word from the *Herald.* Then I received a short letter from the manager saying that military affairs were active and engrossing in the army of the Potomac, and my presence would soon be necessary. I replied, in surprise, that I supposed I had severed my connections with the *Herald,* reminded him of my former letter to that effect, &c., &c. Nothing further was heard from the office for about two weeks when I received a telegram from Mr. Frederick [Frederic] Hudson, manager, requesting me to come to New York immediately.

This was a still greater surprise. In the light of our correspondence I concluded that Mr. Hudson probably intended to give me some temporary work in the office, so taking a small valise I started to the metropolis fully expecting to be in Milwaukee again within a fortnight. But I afterwards learned that Mr. W. F. G. Shanks had been recommending me strongly to Mr. Hudson as a suitable person to be in charge of all correspondence from the Army of the Potomac, or to keep as a "roving" correspondent with Gen. Grant.[2]

I arrived in New York at 12:20, p.m., April 27th 1864. In the afternoon I had my first interview with Mr. Hudson. He said, smilingly, that he had not attached much importance to my letters, feeling certain that a short stay at home would recuperate me for another campaign, and believing that with my past stirring experiences, I could never sit quietly at home till the war was ended. He asked if I did not believe in Gen. Grant's ability to capture the City of Richmond and put down the rebellion; if I did not wish to witness that consummation, and be a part of it; if it was a question of situation or salary, that caused my hesitation?

My private letters to Mr. Bennett for more than a year were filled with expressions of unqualified confidence in Gen. Grant, as Mr. Hudson well knew. He at length frankly admitted that the *Herald* needed my services at headquarters—that he had sent two or three capable and discreet correspondents there, but none of them had been able to gain any recognition de-

---

[2] Promoted to the rank of lieutenant-general in command of all the Federal armies on March 3, 1864, Grant had established his headquarters near Culpeper Court House, Va.

serving mention. He then showed me a letter just received from Mr. Finley Anderson (afterward A.A.G. on General Hancock's Staff with the rank of Colonel) asking to be transferred from Gen. Grant's headquarters to some other place, as he could be of very little service to the paper where he was. He finally said he preferred to give me an independent position at present, with the understanding that I was to remain with Gen. Grant, transmit my dispatches in my own way and time, subject to no orders from any one but himself or Mr. Bennett, and proposed a larger weekly salary than I had ever received, and all my expenses to be paid in addition. I accepted the offer, and left by the evening train for Washington City.

Mr. [Frank G.] Chapman, the *Herald* correspondent-in-chief for the Army of the Potomac, was directed to supply me with a suitable horse and equipments if he had them; otherwise I was to procure a satisfactory mount in my own way, and put its cost in my expense account. I found Mr. Chapman in Washington when he should have been at the front. A few days prior to the first day of May, orders were issued by Mr. Stanton, Secretary of War, forbidding all passage between Washington and the Army of the Potomac, which was rightly construed to mean that a forward movement of that army was imminent and that every possible precaution would be taken to prevent detailed information being carried through our lines by spies or disaffected citizens. This order caught Chapman away from his post of duty without the knowledge or consent of the *Herald*. The goodly fellowship of many scores of army officers caught in the same predicament was poor consolation. He was unable to obtain permission to go to the front, for many days into May.

My only acquaintance in the War Department was Mr.

Dana, then absent. No influential civilian could obtain the favor for me. I tried to see Sec. Stanton, but could not gain access to him. Major [Henry] Pelouze [of the Adjutant General's Department] devoted himself for hours, to the attempt of getting my case before Mr. Stanton. Mr. Stanton's telegraphic censor refused to allow me to telegraph to Gen. Grant.

Gen. Pirie finally ventured to telegraph my request to Gen. Grant to order me to be sent to the front. When Col. Bowers read this telegram at Culpeper Court House where headquarters were established there was a laugh at my expense; but the order was promptly transmitted. I left by next morning's train, but had to run the gauntlet of guards at the depot, at Long Bridge and at Alexandria. The provost officers were divided in opinion as to the meaning of the telegram. Some favored its literal translation and thought I should be sent under a strong guard as a military prisoner, to which I cheerfully assented. But the conclusion was to allow me to proceed alone. I reached headquarters late in the afternoon and was warmly welcomed.

CHAPTER

Twelve

I TOOK with me from Washington City, a good army saddle, pouches, and horse equipments, in addition to my blankets. It was the evening of May 2d, and the whole army was astir with preparations for the movement ordered for May 4th. The next day I bought a fine sorrel horse of Col. Wm. L. Duff, Chief of Artillery, which he was afraid to ride, for two hundred and fifty dollars in gold; visited the cavalry outposts; learned all I could about the proposed line of march; the topography of the country; and felt myself in readiness for hard field work.

The day and night of May 3d was probably the busiest period I witnessed during the war. Officers and clerks at all general headquarters worked without intermission. Quartermaster and Commissary departments were taxed to the utmost. Ordnance and ammunition supplies had to be provided for every exigency. Cartridge boxes, haversacks and caissons were all filled, fires were burning day and night for many miles in all directions, troops and trains were taking their assigned positions, staff officers and orderlies were galloping

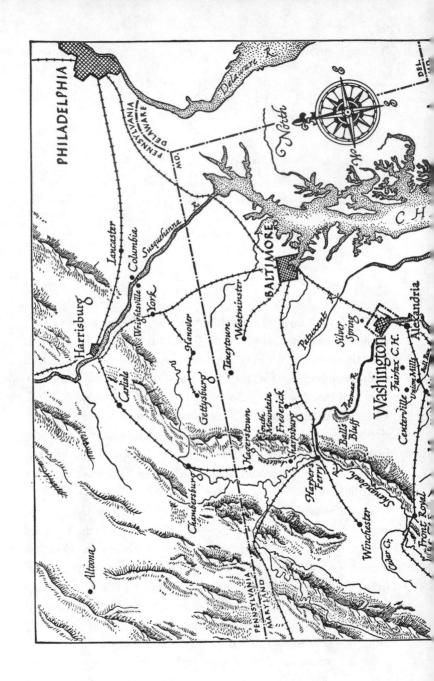

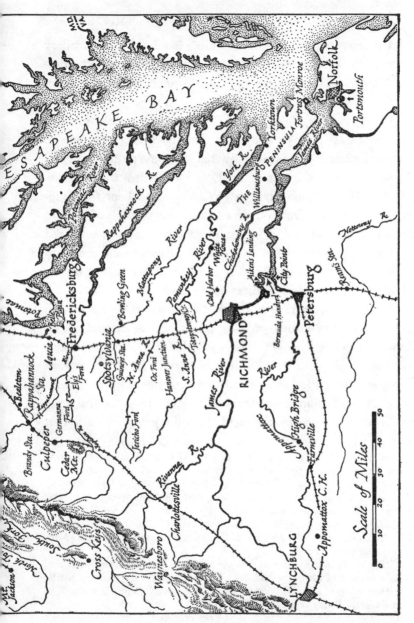

THE EASTERN THEATER OF OPERATIONS

in hot haste carrying orders, whilst the rumble of artillery wheels, the rattling and clanking of mule teams and the shouting, song, and laughter of thousands of men, were "faint from farther distance borne.". . .[1]

All things being in readiness, on the morning of May 4th, the tents were struck at daylight, and the whole army was in motion soon after sunrise, by the various routes assigned them, leading to Germanna and Ely's fords across the Rapidan. [Col. J. H.] Wilson's division of Cavalry had kept the country well patrolled from our front to the north bank of the latter stream, for several days. It now took the advance prepared to force a passage of the river, and had with it all necessary appliances for laying ponton bridges at each crossing by the time the infantry and artillery should arrive.

The sun arose serene and beautiful, and its rays soon fell on our deserted camps—on long trains of wagons and ambulances, winding among the hills—on dense columns of troops on the march, with the shimmer of their bright bayonets resembling the glitter of frost on hedgerows in winter. The air was soft and balmy, and the bright emerald grass springing forth on the southern slopes of the hills gave evidence that

---

[1] On the night of May 3, Cadwallader informed Hudson: "The army moves in the morning. Gen. Meade's H'd Qrs. break up at 5 o'clock. Gen. Grant's during the day. Our troops will force a passage of the Rapidan tomorrow. Immediate, and obstinate fighting is apprehended. Burnside is in the rear as a reserve corps, and can be thrown to the right, left or center, as demanded.

"Mr. Chapman came as far as Meade's Hd. Qrs. today. . . . Saw Mr. N. Davidson & Mr. Hendricks this evening. Both are prepared for any emergency. . . .

"No private telegrams will be permitted to pass between here and Washington until further orders—which means, until 3 days after a battle. We shall have to depend on mail and messengers." James Gordon Bennett Papers, Library of Congress.

On May 5, Cadwallader told one of his reporters, L. A. Whitely, that he would send out his reports via Grant's private mailbag. Bennett Papers.

spring had really come. The songs of birds as they caroled in the rosy beams of the morning sun, blended strangely with the roll of drums, the gay laugh and shout of the soldier, and the shrill blast of trumpet and bugle. Never since its organization had the Army of the Potomac been in better spirits, or more eager to meet the enemy; and never did an army seem to be in better condition for marching or fighting. . . .

Before dark on the 4th all the troops, excepting the 9th corps, had crossed the river, and by the evening of the 5th, the various trains numbering over four thousand wagons, were safely on the south side of the Rapidan. Gen. Rufus Ingalls was the Quartermaster General of the Army of the Potomac, and one of the ablest officers in that line of service the world ever produced. The various army corps had adopted badges as corps designations. These were conspicuously sewed on to each side of all wagon covers, in scarlet cloth, so that the corps (and the brigades and divisions of each corps) to which each wagon belonged, could be known at sight almost as far as the wagon could be seen. Had these wagons been placed in a single line, at the intervals required on the march, they would have reached from the Rapidan to Petersburg, and probably beyond. Ten days' rations with a supply of forage and ammunition were taken in these wagons. Beef cattle were driven with these trains, and butchered daily as they were needed. . . .

Grant's headquarters the night of Wednesday, May 4th, was on a knoll on the south bank of the Rapidan, only a few hundred yards from Germanna ford. Troops and trains were hurrying past us all night, and by sunrise next morning the federal army was fairly in position for the great drama which commenced before noon.

It is well to understand that in this campaign Grant decided to operate without any well defined base, as he did in that of Vicksburg. On leaving Culpeper he abandoned his railroad connection with Washington City. He kept in position to make a new base at Fredericksburg if it became necessary or convenient; and transports were loaded with needful supplies at the capital and ordered down the Potomac, in readiness to move up the Rappahannock, or any other navigable stream, as future exigencies might demand. Rations and ammunition were taken with the army, to last till one battle at least had been fought, and the strength of the enemy ascertained. . . .

On taking the positions assigned them, each corps began the hasty construction of field breastworks in front of its first line of battle, and soon had them capable of offering formidable resistance. The face of the country, and character of the growing timber, was found to be the most unfavorable imaginable for offensive operations. The roads were very narrow and tortuous; bounded on both sides with a dense growth of young pine, chinkapin and scrubby oak that rendered the forests in many places almost impenetrable. The pines were low-limbed and scraggy, and the chinkapins the stiffest and bristliest of their species. An advance in line of battle was nearly impossible. Artillery could not be brought into action at all. A few places on the road where there was a small break in the timber were the only places possible for planting batteries. Over three hundred of our cannon lay idle during the whole of this day's fighting.

The position was admirable for defense, and was selected by Lee instantly on learning that Grant had outmaneuvered him, and gained a crossing of the river without a battle. Many of the ravines were deep and impassable, but a majority of them were not so precipitous but what infantry could cross.

The main obstacles the Union troops had to contend against were the thick growth of scrubby timber and the undergrowth of hazelbrush. These prevented the proper handling and alignment of our men, and concealed the enemy's presence, and the disposition of his forces. . . .

[*Cadwallader's account of the bloody but indecisive Battle of the Wilderness, May 5–7, 1864, adds nothing to what is known about it, except that he questions Grant's statement that by the 7th Lee had withdrawn within his entrenchments and that nothing but skirmishing took place on that date.*]

Gen. Grant's statement that there was no battle on May 7th was no doubt intended to be understood in a comparative sense. Compared with the fighting on the 5th and 6th, all that was done on the 7th scarcely deserved mention. Yet there are those who will testify that some ugly work was done by both armies on Saturday, May 7th. I think it was on the morning of this day that I saw the New Jersey "Butterfly" cavalry regiment driven in upon our lines, from Germanna Ford, utterly broken up and demoralized. It was nothing but a mob of armed men on horseback who seemed much more likely to cut off their own horses' heads with their sabres, in their panicky flight, than to inflict any injury on their opponents. When Lee had succeeded in getting past [General John] Sedgwick's right, Friday evening, his infantry marched to, and actually occupied the road, by which we had marched from Germanna Ford to the Wilderness. It was this force which so utterly routed the N. Jersey Cavalry regiment. At other places during the forenoon of Saturday there was considerable uncomfortable fighting, although it seems not to have risen to the dignity of a battle in Grant's estimation. . . .

The Union losses at the Wilderness could not have been less than fifteen thousand, and probably reached twenty thou-

sand.[2] I have no official records at hand and base this estimate
on recollection, and on the fact that at noon of Saturday,
May 7th, I had transcripts from the books of all field hospitals
to that date, giving the name, state, regiment and rank of
every wounded man received. The number of these was between eight and nine thousand. The killed, the slightly
wounded, the dead and the prisoners, would almost certainly
be that many more. The Confederate loss probably did not
exceed one-half of ours.[3] We often fought, knowing our losses
were two or three to one; but had to wage the battle on Lee's
terms, or leave the field. . . .

On the afternoon of the first day of battle, Thursday
May 5th, when the first batch of Confederate prisoners were
marched to the rear, surrounded by a cordon of Provost
Guards, I obtained permission of Col. Johnson, commanding
the guard, to go among them and gather such information as
I could. There was great anxiety to know at headquarters
whether or not Longstreet had arrived with reinforcements for
Lee. I had what was supposed to be a complete roster of the
Confederate army. By learning from any Confederate soldier
the state he was from, and the number of his regiment, I could
instantly tell his brigade, division and corps. I was not long
in learning that Longstreet's corps had arrived.

Gen. Marcellus [Marsena] R. Patrick was Provost Marshal
General of the Army of the Potomac. He then was (and so
remained till the day of his death) in my opinion, the finest
existing fossil of the Cenozoic age. From his position on an

---

[2] Official figures put the Union losses at 17,886. *War of the Rebellion:
. . . Official Records of the Union and Confederate Armies,* Vol. XXXVI,
pt. I, p. 133. The *Official Records* are referred to hereafter as *O. R.*

[3] Frederick Phisterer: *Statistical Record of the Armies of the United
States* (New York, 1883), put the Confederate loss at 11,400.

eminence near at hand, he discovered me among the prisoners, and sent one of his staff to put me under arrest. As I neared the august presence of the old martinet, he was pompously strutting back and forth for a few yards, looking as black as a thunder cloud. He finally roared out:

"Who are you, sir?" I modestly gave him my name.

"What were you doing among those prisoners, sir?" was his next interrogatory.

"Trying to learn to what commands they belonged," I softly replied.

"Who gave you permission to go inside of the guard line?" he thundered out.

I answered that Col. Johnson's permission had been obtained. Gen. Patrick seemed at first inclined to dispute my word, but finally sent for Col. Johnson. Upon his admitting that he gave me the permission I asked for, Patrick promptly put him under arrest. Col. Johnson attempted to explain that I had an order in my possession directing "all the guards, and all the picket guards, in all the armies of the United States, to pass me by day or night, with horses or vehicles." But Patrick either did not, or would not hear him. Turning to me again he said:

"Young man, I think you have not long been in this army," to which I quickly responded:

"Thank God, I have not."

This produced a fearful explosion of anger. He finally strutted up close to me and wanted to know by whose authority I was there.

I handed him my pass and credentials from Gen. Grant. He deliberately put them in his pocket; refused to return them to me; and ordered up a file of soldiers to march me to the "bull-pen."

Luckily for me, Col. W. L. Duff just then came in sight, to whom I called in my extremity. Duff was a tall, dark-haired, severe looking officer when on duty. On hearing my statement he rose in his stirrups till he seemed to be going to the tree-tops, and turning to Gen. Patrick with a lowering look, and a glittering eye, said:

"Do you know me, sir?" Patrick replied, with a salute:

"You are Col. Duff, of General Grant's staff."

"Release this man instantly, and return his papers," were Col. Duff's only words as he rode away leaving Patrick speechless with rage and mortification.

I was not long in learning that this incident made Gen. Patrick my implacable enemy. He, and his subordinates, were systematic in subjecting me to annoyances. My horses were thereafter only safe from wrongful seizure, when inside the line of Gen. Grant's stable guard. My correspondents and messengers were often hindered and dismounted—sometimes stopped at the gang-planks of steamboats, and kept there till the boat departed. But time at last made all things even, as will be shown later on. . . .

[*During the night Cadwallader and all others at headquarters were awakened by a surprise attack on General Warren's corps.*]

. . . After everyone at headquarters had retired for the second time, to get some rest and sleep if possible before daylight, I sat down by a smouldering fire in front of Grant's tent, and found myself distressingly wide-awake. Unpleasant thoughts ran riot through my mind. We had waged two days of murderous battle, and had but little to show for it. Judged by comparative losses, it had been disastrous to the Union cause. We had been compelled by Gen. Lee to fight him on a field of his own choosing, with the certainty of losing at least two men to his one, until he could be dislodged and driven from his vantage ground. We had scarcely gained a rod of the battlefield at the close of a two days' contest. And now had come the crowning stroke of rebel audacity in furiously storming the center of our line, and achieving temporary success.

For minutes that seemed hours, for the first and only time, during my intimate and confidential relations with Gen. Grant, I began to question the grounds of my faith in him, so long entertained, and so unqualifiedly expressed. Could it be possible that I had followed Gen. Grant through the Tallahatchie Expedition; the operations against Vicksburg; the campaign at Chattanooga; and finally to the dark and tangled thickets of the Wilderness; to record his defeat and overthrow, as had been recorded of every commander of the Army of the Potomac? But my faith in the man rose superior to all these calamitous surroundings, and I still believed in his transcendent military genius, despite this momentary weakness of fear and unbelief.

About the time I had arrived at this comforting conclusion, I happened to look obliquely to the right, and there sat Gen. Grant in an army chair on the other side of the slowly dying embers. His hat was drawn down over his face, the high collar of an old blue army overcoat turned up above his ears, one leg crossed over the other knee, eyes on the ashes in front, causing me to think him half asleep. My gloomy thoughts of but a few minutes were instantly chased away by my study of the figure before me. His nervous changing of one leg over the other showed he was not asleep. His whole attitude showed him to be in a brown study.

In a short time, however, he straightened up in the chair and finding that I was not asleep, commenced a pleasant chatty conversation upon indifferent subjects. Neither of us alluded to what was uppermost in our mind for more than a half hour. I then remarked that if we were to get any sleep that night, it was time we were in our tents; and that it was a duty in his case to get all the rest he could. He smilingly assented, spoke of the sharp work Gen. Lee had been giving us for a couple of days, and entered his tent. It was the grandest mental sunburst of my life. I had suddenly emerged from the slough of despond, to the solid bed-rock of unwavering faith. . . .

C H A P T E R

Thirteen

. . . While the army lay on the railroad between Culpeper and Washington, Mr. Frank G. Chapman, correspondent-in-chief for the New York *Herald* put up lock-boxes at every station, into which all *Herald* correspondents were directed to drop their letters and dispatches for the office. Special messengers ran in and out daily by rail, gathered the contents of these boxes and delivered them to Col. L. A. Whitely, the Washington correspondent of the *Herald,* to be telegraphed or forwarded by mail as their importance demanded.

But when the army cut loose from its railroad communication this was all ended. Chapman and the messengers were caught in the capital, and unable to get to the front. One or two days' fighting had taken place at the Wilderness, before Chapman arrived. He probably came through with Mr. Dana. He was so ignorant of details, and so crest-fallen at the exposure of being caught away from his post of duty at so critical a time, that he came to me for information, and on the plea of being too sick to do the work in person, besought me to act in his place, and take charge of all *Herald* correspondence from the field, as he ought to have done himself. My arrangement with the paper made me wholly independent, and I refused to assume any additional responsibilities.

But some perplexing conditions surrounded me. One day's marching, and two of fighting, had taken place, and I had not been able to transmit a line of news to Washington City or New York. The Confederate cavalry held undisputed control of a wide strip of country in our rear. Gen. Grant had been too much occupied with the rebels on his front to pay any attention to these marauders in the rear, and the War Office had no information from his army from Wednesday May 4th, when it left Culpeper, till the Sunday and Monday following. Realizing that no dependence could be placed on Chapman, I tried to hire men to carry dispatches from me to Washington. Several promised to make the attempt, but all backed out when it came to starting. I offered to furnish any messenger a horse, saddle and bridle, and pay him two hundred dollars in cash—one half on starting, and the balance on delivery of a single large envelope, filled with my correspondence, to Col. Whitely in Washington. All my negotiations fell through, and men refused to incur the risk for any price.

On Saturday morning, May 7th, I sent word to every *Herald* correspondent with the army, that if they would deliver their dispatches to me at headquarters by noon of that day, I would make an effort to get them off, if I had to start myself. I was unwilling to ask any one to do what I was afraid to undertake in person, and I realized fully the dreadful suspense, and consuming desire for news, which prevailed in every northern hamlet and home. Most of the men came to headquarters promptly, and thanked me sincerely for what I intended doing.

So filling two cavalry pouches with correspondence, and

many private letters, I mounted at three o'clock p.m., and started for Washington with full reports of the battle, and with the most complete list of casualties I ever obtained. At the last minute Mr. J. C. Fitzpatrick, *Herald* correspondent with Burnside's corps, concluded to accompany me. To avoid Lee's troops, on the Germanna Ford road as we supposed, we took the road to Ely's Ford, which crossed the Rapidan six or eight miles further down, intending to proceed thence to Rappahannock Station, and from there to Washington by rail. It was understood at the time that a large number of slightly wounded and sick were to be sent back to the Washington hospitals, under a strong cavalry escort. When near Ely's Ford we were overtaken by Mr. Edward Crapsey, correspondent of the Philadelphia *Inquirer*. He had heard in some way of our starting to Washington, and determined to overtake and accompany us.

At Ely's Ford we learned that no trains were in readiness, so we decided to push on alone. The distance to Rappahannock Station was estimated to be over thirty miles by the route we designed to travel. This we supposed we could easily traverse by midnight, and if no train was likely to leave there at an early hour next morning, we could ride to Washington on horseback before Sunday night. We had less hesitation in undertaking this night ride from knowing about three hundred of our cavalry had crossed at the Ford, an hour before, going in the same direction. Night found us a couple of miles on our way from the river crossing. There was no moonlight and the road was narrow, crooked, gloomy and forbidding. Young pines arched densely over the road—the track was several inches deep with dust made by [Winfield Scott] Hancock's troops on their way to the Wilderness—and our horses made no noise unless they struck a foot against a stone. Thoughts

of rebs, robbers and Libby prison were suggested by everything animate and inanimate.

At a turn in the road we discovered a squad of infantry
approaching from the opposite direction. The order to "halt,
and advance singly," was obeyed, and they proved to be Union
soldiers, pushing ahead to rejoin their command. We breathed
freer on learning who they were, and sincerely hope they did
the same.

We had not advanced five hundred yards from that place
(almost as the dusky forms of the Union soldiers disappeared)
when five mounted men plunged into the road from the thicket
that skirted it, in our front and rear, and the click of revolvers
were at our ears in an instant. "Surrender." "Give up your
arms." "Speak and you die," in suppressed excited tone of
voice, were the persuasive words that greeted us. We were
surprised, surrounded, defenseless. Compliance with their expressed commands became a "military necessity." In less time
than it has taken to describe it, a dozen strong arms seemed
to have seized us. We were jerked violently from our horses,
dragged into a thicket at the roadside, thrown sprawling on
the ground, and found the cold steel of revolver barrels
jammed against our heads. It was "pitch dark" by this time
and nothing but the shadowy outlines of our captors could
be discerned. This darkness served me one good purpose,
however, for under its cover I was able to fling one of my
two cavalry pouches into the brush without discovery. The
other was found when my horse was afterward examined.

We lay there in silence for a minute or two when I commenced some explanations. But these were not well received.
From the staff equipments on my horse, and especially the
holsters at the pommel of my saddle, they jumped to the conclusion that I was a Colonel riding at the head of a regi-

ment, which would soon run into their cul-de-sac. As soon as
they were undeceived in this particular, conversation became
general, but in very low tones. We were allowed to rise from
the ground and were searched for arms and valuables. The
clothing, and cheap outfits of Fitzpatrick and Crapsey, made
their representations somewhat credible. They claimed, truthfully to be unarmed civilians and army correspondents, and
were apparently believed. But they viewed my case differently from the outset and treated me accordingly. I too, was
dressed in a civil suit, without anything on my person to denote rank or service, but no statements would convince them
that I was lower in rank than Colonel.

After what seemed to us a long time we were taken by our
captors back to the plains of the Rappahannock by the road
we had intended to travel. While lying on the ground I managed to slip a roll of "greenbacks" into a watch pocket opening
at the waistband of my pants, and to get a valuable watch into
an inside vest pocket, without attracting attention. Neither
were discovered in at least two, if not three, personal exam-
inations, made by the rebels. The watch I succeeded in bringing home; but the "greenbacks" were put where I was con-
fident they would do the most good, later on.

On reaching some open land we were dismounted and
searched the second time for papers and valuables. No fires
were lighted. The glimmering starlight and an occasional lu-
cifer match, had to suffice. I again undertook to convince our
captors that we were only newspaper correspondents; never
recognized in our own army as belonging to it, or being part
of it; and stated that I had been captured before, had never
been detained more than an hour or two, and expected to be
promptly released again. I urged them to take us to a suitable place, examine our credentials, and allow us to proceed

unmolested on our way to Washington. But my proposition found small favor in their eyes.

During this halt the Confederate captain in command wished to place us under parole to not attempt an escape. As spokesman for the captives I refused to make any promises. This probably strengthened their distrust of me, for an old, knee-sprung, brown horse, desperately thin in flesh, was led up for me to mount instead of my own, when we were ready to start. I objected—said the old stumbling "crowbait" would break my neck on the first hill he attempted to descend —claimed the right to ride my own horse, &c., &c. But all to no effect. I was peremptorily ordered to mount. Seeing no better way out of the dilemma, I offered to take a parole to not escape till sunrise next morning; if allowed to ride my own horse. To this they assented with the remark that "before sunrise they would have me where it would make no difference whether I tried to escape or not." So I took the parole, mounted my own horse, was placed near the center of the column in march, guarded by non-commissioned officers who were instructed in my hearing to shoot me down without further orders, if I made the slightest attempt to get away.

We expected to be hurried past the left flank of the Union army that night—perhaps taken to Fredericksburg. But neither was done, and I have never been able to account for the slow, undecided, dilatory march of that night. We went through dark forests, across deep ravines, by deserted farms, through family door-yards, by blind paths, often with no path at all, till the roar of falling water proclaimed the presence of some mill dam on the Rappahannock. At times when we approached some out-of-the-way cabin during the night, the company would halt—an officer would ride to the door—hold a whispered conversation with some inmate—return to the troops and resume the march. We forded the Rappahannock at an obscure place well known to these partisans, far from house or road. But we rode on very cautiously and slowly, in silence, through dismal forests and waters, till the stunted pines on every hand seemed the spectres of departing hopes.

We were finally dismounted at the house of Mr. Stringfellow, near Cold Spring, all horses unsaddled and fed, our papers and letters opened and examined by the light of a kitchen fire and a piece of candle. The officer in command was now confirmed in his opinion that I was a general officer, probably on the staff of Gen. Grant, and next to Grant in importance. The character of the letters and papers found in the Cavalry pouch which I had been unable to throw away or destroy, gave strong evidence in favor of this presumption. Several of the letters were written and signed in the well-known names of Grant's military family. The list of wounded carried into our field hospitals, embracing between eight and nine thousand names, with rank, regiment and state of each, bore the stamp of authority, and would only be entrusted to some confidential person, as carrier. Their vigilance over me was at once redoubled. We were put into a large room on the second floor, an armed guard placed at the door, a sentry placed under each window opening from the bedroom into the dooryard, where they stood guard over us till daylight. Three wide old fashioned feather beds stood in the room, in which we slept till morning. The guards were as lynx-eyed and vigilant, as though we were modern Atlases, with the whole weight of the bogus Confederacy on our shoulders.

At sunrise we were ordered out of bed, and I was taken under guard to the house of Mr. Sears, near at hand, for breakfast. The balance remained to honor the hospitality of Mr. Stringfellow. Of my breakfast too little in praise cannot be said; but it had the redeeming feature of being graciously presented. The lady regretted—as what genuine housekeeper does not—that she had nothing better to offer me. Her husband—an old gray headed man—was a prisoner in Washington, she said. I always suspected that she wished me to escape, and had an unspoken hope that I might in some way render him a service. The exigencies of my business prevented me from making any inquiries into his case; but he or any member of his family (or relative or friend) may draw on me at sight for a better breakfast than I there received.

An hour later the Captain announced his intention of taking us to Fredericksburg and turning us over to Gen. Fitz Hugh [Fitzhugh] Lee. Libby Prison with all its recounted and uncounted horrors seemed gaping to receive us. When near Fredericksburg a genuine "bushwhacker," came from a hiding place by the roadside, stopped the Confederates and gave them information of some sort, which seemed to make them wary and apprehensive. I suspected its nature for I knew that Sheridan had received orders to drive Fitzhugh Lee out of Fredericksburg at any cost. The whole army would support him, if necessary. It was to be a base for federal supplies. All this I had kept to myself, hoping I should be taken to that vicinity and in some way regain my liberty.

The videttes thrown out in front after the interview with the "bushwhacker," were soon fired upon, and fell back on the head of the column. The captain who thought they had encountered nothing worse than a band of bumming stragglers from the Union army, threw out flankers, and dashed up the road in fine form. It was Sheridan's pickets and that halted them.

In the meantime we had been sent to the rear in charge of an orderly sergeant. I soon convinced him as to the real situation and assured him that if he remained where we then stood, for fifteen minutes he would be my prisoner instead of my being his. I advised him to take the best horse in the outfit, return up the Rappahannock and ride entirely around both armies to the westward, as the only way of escape open to him. The serious skirmish in front was hidden from our view by timber and brush, but the carbine and musketry was distinctly heard. I then drew from my watchfob, the roll of "greenbacks" previously mentioned, thrust them into his hands, and plunged into the laurel brush near at hand closely followed by Fitzpatrick and Crapsey. The "sergeant" seemed confused and undecided at first; but I intended to make a break for liberty at the risk of being shot, for there was but little choice between Libby prison, and sudden death. I never looked back—don't know whether he made a pretense of firing on us, or not—I only know he did not fire, and we escaped, leaving horses and outfits behind.

We ran a short quarter of a mile I suppose through the tangled thickets of laurel, when we stopped for a breathing spell, and clambered into the bushy tops of some young holly trees, so as to not be readily discovered and retaken by any of the retreating rebel cavalry. We remained there till all firing and hurrahing ceased—till the sound of the routed Confederates died away as they fled back on the road they came—when we abandoned the tree tops for terra-firma and held our first council of war. Should we advance boldly up to the line on which we heard the skirmishing, trusting to Sheridan's being in possession of Fredericksburg; or should we turn our faces toward the Potomac, and work our way to Washington? It was decided to take no chances, as recapture was about equivalent to death.

Then arose another trouble. In which direction from us was

the Potomac river? It was very little past noon—the sun shone brilliantly—and the reader will say that any intelligent man would know that if we traveled with Fredericksburg at our backs we would be facing the Potomac. But no persuasion could convince either of my comrades of this fact. The midday sun cut no figure. They were bound to travel in some other direction. When arguments and demonstrations failed, I bid them goodbye and started off alone. They soon hallooed for me to wait, said they would follow my guidance for awhile at least, and so we proceeded onward. Knowing ourselves to be in a hostile country we avoided all roads, skirted all farms and open ground, and when we crossed a dusty road, did so walking backwards, hoping should anyone see our tracks they would be misled in this way.

Our route was nearly north. By keeping as near in the same direction as possible, we had to cross all the gulches, ravines and small brooks in the dividing range, which made it an afternoon of climbing up and down. Of the toil and fatigue of the trip but little need be said. The day was excessively hot. We had nothing to eat, and depended on brook-water for subsistence. Night came upon us without any special adventure except the persistent barking of a dog that discovered us in a pawpaw thicket, and followed us for over a mile, barking and yelping continuously. After a short rest at dark we scrambled on in single file, with the north star for our guide, till nearly midnight. We found an open valley ahead of us apparently a mile in width, extending as far as we could see to the right and left, and on the opposite mountain slope were what appeared to be the camp-fires of a large body of troops. I knew they could not be federal troops; and did not believe it possible for any Confederate force to be in that quarter. But apparent facts were against my theorizing, and there was nothing to do but wait for daylight to clear up the mystery.

We slept restlessly till morning. I was disturbed for some time by a tree frog which kept up its croaking but a few feet above my head, and vainly tried to catch it for a breakfast broil. Soon after sunrise, Monday 9th, the fog was lifted from the valley, and "the sun of Austerliz" sprang to our lips simultaneously. Before us lay the beautiful valley of Potomac Creek. To our right, a mile distant, was the trestled railroad bridge on the railroad from the mouth of Aquia Creek to Fredericksburg. The camp-fires of the night before, on the opposite slopes of hills, proved to be nothing more than woods on fire.

At a log cabin on the other side of the valley and somewhat to our left, we saw two horses standing under an apple tree, saddled for mounting. As we were crossing the valley obliquely toward the railroad, two men in butternut clothing came out of the cabin, and on seeing us, mounted their horses and rode up a ravine in their rear. I had taken the precaution to get a stick about the length of a gun-barrel which I put under my rubber poncho, crosswise, to convey the impression that we were armed. We bore to the right, struck the northern end of the railroad bridge where it entered a deep semicircular cut, and followed the track till it emerged on level ground. This we approached cautiously fearing the two men seen might be waylaying us somewhere.

Our conjectures were right ones. Not two hundred yards in advance they sat on their horses with carbines ready for instant firing, and plainly intending to pick us off at sight. We fell back unobserved, but frightened. Advance was impossible; retreat, or escape very nearly so. While debating what course to pursue, we heard men talking in the cut to our rear. They soon came up to us and proved to be slightly wounded Union soldiers on their way to Washington hospitals. They were all armed, and tried to steal a march on the two Confederate cavalry men; but the latter were too cunning, and escaped. From there to the Potomac river was uneventful.

We reached the mouth of Aquia Creek about nine o'clock, A.M. and found there over three hundred wounded Union soldiers waiting for transportation to Washington. They had walked all the distance from the Wilderness battle-field, by way of Fredericksburg, and had been compelled to fight their way part of the time. The citizens of the latter city subjected them to every possible indignity as they passed through, and they came near firing the town in revenge.

As vessels feared decoys, they rarely answered signals from the Virginia shore of the river, and we found the soldiers engaged in building rafts from the half-burned plank and timber left from the destruction of our government storehouses when Hooker abandoned the line of the Rappahannock the summer before. We correspondents also fell to work and by noon had a raft or float barely capable of bearing up three persons. My recollection is that the Potomac is nearly five miles wide between the mouth of Aquia Creek and Point Tobacco, on the Maryland shore; but we pushed and paddled into the sluggish current of the river, hoping to get across before dark.

The government transport Rebecca Barton, commanded by Capt. Baker, came up the river about two o'clock in the afternoon, found the stream full of rafts, took all on board, and placed all the eatables and potables at the disposal of the wounded and hungry men.

A more exhausted, foot-sore and hungry trio could not have been found when we were picked up by Capt. Baker's yawl.

To a detachment of the Ninth Virginia Cavalry, commanded by Capt. Curtis,[1] I have always had a debt to cancel. Our treatment had been heartless and abusive. They all appeared to have a special grudge against me. They were especially severe and insulting in my case, and stood ready to shoot or hang me on the slightest provocation. But I lived to be in at the death of the Confederacy.

When our boat tied up at the Seventh street wharf, Washington, we took a carriage to Willard's Hotel. My first order was to have a hot bath prepared, and my second one to have a bell-boy placed at my sole disposal for a few hours. I remained in the hot bath a long time—sent for new clothing and underclothing—informed Col. Whiteley of my arrival—soaked some of the soreness and stiffness out of my bones and joints—and towards the last of my stay in the bathroom, held a levee (as I dressed) of dozens, scores, and possibly hundreds of people, who had heard of my arrival, and to whom I brought the first authentic information from the Army of the Potomac. The lobbies of the hotel were crowded to hear the news, which had to be repeated by proprietors and clerks, for my duties called me elsewhere. For a couple of hours at least, Gen. Grant himself, was never more besieged or stared at than I was.

Up to date—Monday evening, May 9th—the *Herald* had not received a line from any one of its many special correspondents with the Army of the Potomac. All other papers, however, were in the same predicament.[2] But this fact did not

---

[1] The only person of this name on the roll of the 9th Virginia Cavalry is 2nd Lieutenant A. M. Curtis.

[2] Cadwallader is mistaken in this statement. Henry Wing, a nineteen-year-old reporter for the *New York Tribune*, after a journey similar to Cadwallader's on which he twice escaped from John S. Mosby's cavalry and was then taken for a spy by the Union authorities, had been brought

console Mr. Bennett, nor Mr. Hudson, greatly. I soon received a telegram congratulating me on my escape, and requesting me to wire the longest and best account possible in such difficult circumstances. I went into the back room of *Herald* headquarters on Fourteenth Street opposite Willard's Hotel, locked out every one but the janitor, denied myself to all friends, and commenced writing at the top of my speed. My dispatch was carried to the telegraph office a few pages at a time, and was in type in New York City in a few minutes afterward.

For awhile all went well, but towards midnight fatigue and loss of sleep overcame me. A hot lunch was ordered and eaten. A bottle of whiskey was sent for and half of it drank. But nothing revived me. I have a dreamy consciousness of sitting for interminable hours trying to write, but going to sleep—of waking nervously, seizing my pencil, and scrawling a few more pages—of being told it was four o'clock in the morning and that nothing further could be transmitted—of receiving a telegram late at night, directing me to take the morning train for New York, and report at the *Herald* office—of going to a room at the Hotel after leaving orders to be called in time for the first train to New York—of being dragged out of bed and sent in a carriage to the depot at six o'clock—and of one of the longest and most wearisome rides of my life to the metropolis next day. The weather was hot, the road dusty,

---

to the War Department on orders from Stanton himself. Convinced at last of Wing's identity and overjoyed at his encouraging report, Stanton allowed him to wire dispatches to his paper, then took him to the White House. Lincoln was so delighted at the news Wing brought that he threw his arms around the boy and kissed him. Wing's report of the battle appeared in the *Tribune* on May 7. Ida Tarbell: "Lincoln Kissed Him," *Collier's*, Vol. LXXIX (January 15, 1927); Bernard A. Weisberger: *Reporters for the Union* (Boston, 1953), pp. 218, 290–1. See also, *O. R.*, Series I, Vol. XXXVII, pt. I, p. 404.

the cars crowded, everybody importuning me for news, and no one considerate enough to allow me such rest as I could get on my way.

A supper at the Astor House revived me a little. An interview with Mr. Hudson gave me some additional life and courage. He commiserated my condition so sincerely, and told me of his and Mr. Bennett's rejoicing at my escape so fully, and thanked me so amply for doing what I had to serve the paper, that I would have walked into a fiery furnace to render them further service. I commenced writing again. Mr. Hudson took me into his private room, gave up his desk to my use, ordered the colored janitor to stay within sound of my bell, and to bring me anything I could eat or drink as long as I remained. On leaving after midnight he complimented me on the progress I had made—apologized by allowing me to do an hour's work that night—told me to go to the Astor House and stay there until fully restored—and then call upon him, as he had several matters of consequence to discuss. Great hearted, chivalrous, magnanimous, Fred Hudson! I cannot write of him, even at this distant time, with dry eyes. He was to Mr. James Gordon Bennett, Senior, what Rawlins was to Grant, which exhausts human praise.

I went to bed at the Astor House, intending to sleep all the next day. But I rolled and tumbled all night, too nervous to sleep. The first stir in the morning roused me past further sleep. I rose; tried, ineffectually, to eat an early breakfast; read the morning papers; entered the dining room a second time hoping to swallow some light food; ordered a bottle of wine to provoke an appetite; but everything failed. I was bordering on insanity for forty-eight hours, and needed opiates more than food; but did not realize my condition. At the end of that time—possibly sooner—I saw Mr. Hudson. He informed me that Mr. Bennett had resolved to remove Mr. Chapman from his place as correspondent-in-chief for the Army of the Potomac, and to put me in his place. Armed with orders for Chapman to turn over to me all *Herald* horses, vehicles, tents and other property in his possession, I started for Washington City. All correspondents were instructed to report to me, and act under my orders, as absolutely as under those received from the office. Mr. Chapman complied with the best grace he could assume; was banished to Cairo, Ill.; and never regained his former standing in the *Herald* office.

Mr. Bennett wished me to purchase the best horse to be had for my own use—urging me to not allow Gen. Grant to ride a better one, if I could prevent it—wanted me to keep open a "Herald Headquarters" that should equal any in the field—to set a dinner daily to which I would not be ashamed to have distinguished officials sit down, and to exercise generous hospitality to all visitors. I was to include the cost of all this in my expense accounts, and the *Herald* would foot the bills.

A fairly good ambulance and team was turned over to me by Chapman. I laid in a stock of provisions, procured a professional cook from Willard's hotel, and started to the front, by way of Belle Plain and Fredericksburg. Owing to my unsettled condition I was not able to carry out my instructions as to keeping open house at *Herald* headquarters until we arrived at City Point. . . .

CHAPTER

Fourteen

ON going east I had no acquaintance with army correspondents there, knew but few of the general officers, and felt that I must have some well-tried and well-trained men in the field. I had full authority to employ and discharge them, as well as to fix their compensation; and was not long in gathering around me a corps of correspondents vastly superior to those of all other papers combined, many of whom have never had any superiors, and possibly no equals, in that line of work in any armies of the world. No man was retained in the *Herald* service who hesitated, or neglected, to accompany his division or corps wherever it went, and to share the dangers and hardships of officers and men. This was necessary to gain the respect of the troops, which was a prerequisite to usefulness in obtaining army news.

Two or three of these, of whom I only remember Mr. [L. W.] Buckingham—were instantly killed in battle. Nearly a dozen were wounded, of whom I can only name at this time, Anderson, [John A.] Brady, [S. T.] Wilson and myself. Five were in rebel prisons at one time, as the price of personal courage and newspaper enterprise. Two of the five were imprisoned for a year. Others for shorter terms. Still others escaped on their way to southern prisons; as I did twice. The term: "*Herald* Correspondent," became a synonym for bravery and daring.

And this may be a proper place to state that the pay of every captured correspondent was continued till he was released and reported at the *Herald* office in person; and to this was often added large amounts to cover expenses during that time. Good service to the *Herald* insured good pay, rapid promotion, and a personal treatment by Mr. Bennett and Mr. Hudson, beyond computation in dollars and cents. It was not surprising, therefore, that the *Herald* gathered around it, the ablest men in the country, any one of whom would risk his life in collecting valuable information, and transmitting it to the office in advance of all competitors.

Of the marching and fighting from the Wilderness to Spotsylvania I shall attempt no detailed information, as I was not present. It is well known, however, that Grant's order to Meade on the morning of May 6th, was carried out to the letter. The different corps moved by the routes specifically named in the order, and met no serious impediment till they had passed the line of Todd's Tavern, where they emerged from the Wilderness and entered the open country between there and Spotsylvania. Gen. Lee had fallen back precipitately to the cover of the strong earthworks and abatis previously constructed, only leaving sufficient cavalry and infantry outside to harass and obstruct our advance.

By the morning of the 9th, the place was invested on the north and west, and a deadly struggle commenced.

I was not on the ground till Friday, May 13, too late to witness the operations of that day. But I soon learned at headquarters that the glorious news of Union successes on the 12th was not overestimated. . . .

The following extracts from a letter to my wife, on Steamboat "Highland Light," May 16th, 1864, show the mental and physical strain I was again undergoing: "I feel as though the experiences of a year had been crowded into the last three weeks. . . . The excitement of the Wilderness—the capture and escape on my way to Washington—the work in Washington and New York—the immediate return to the front with the responsibility of looking after more than a dozen (to me unknown) correspondents, with their horses and outfits—the anxiety to perfect arrangements by which these men shall best cooperate in securing and transmitting news—the hard work, hard riding, and lack of rest and sleep for days together —conspire to make the time seem longer than it has actually been.

"I left Washington Friday at 5:00 p.m. by boat for Belle Plain and arrived there at midnight, accompanied by Capt. Smith, of Halleck's staff, bearing dispatches to Grant. Got an escort of twenty men at 2:00 A.M. Saturday—rode to Fredericksburg for breakfast, and to headquarters at Spotsylvania by noon—could get no passes for *Herald* men detained in Washington—had to ride back to make other arrangements— got to Belle Plain Sunday, and to Washington at midnight— sent dispatches to New York—took Fitzpatrick with me and started back immediately—found two of my messengers at Belle Plain who had got there 'somehow'—pushed to the front as fast as my horse could carry me.

"I cannot get my messengers to and from Washington as I desire—no trouble at this end of the line—but when a correspondent or messenger goes to Washington, Stanton will not allow him to return—three are there now who belong here—

[Leonard A.] Hendricks, [J. C.] Fitzpatrick and [Francis C.] Long are my only assistants at present, with Trembly for a messenger, to and from Belle Plain, where N. Davidson is stationed to receive and transmit news—expect to have a regular and sufficient corps of messengers in a few days—have applied to the Sec. of War for their passes—if he refuses must depend on Gen. Grant—the hardest fighting is yet to do, which means the hardest work for me, and all *Herald* men.". . .

There were two prominent generals in front of Richmond whom I instinctively distrusted—[Gouverneur K.] Warren and [Benjamin F.] Butler. I was not long in learning that my distrust was fully shared by Gen. Rawlins. This emboldened me often to speak as I felt, concerning them both, in Grant's presence. My comments were often made to others, in Grant's hearing, rather than being pointedly addressed to himself. But I never succeeded in drawing from him any unfavorable remark about either of them, for many months. His features would relax into a faint smile; or he would take his cigar from his lips and look at me intently; but the twinkle of his eye implied assent, and I was never checked or rebuked. Towards the close of the war he spoke more freely of them. Butler he never liked. Warren forfeited the high estimation in which Grant once held him. He was egotistical. His caution was excessive. His distrust of every one's judgment which ran counter to his own was universal. He lacked many qualities of a great commander. . . .

Grant decided at the end of the second day of battle at Spotsylvania that it could not be taken by assault, or regular approaches, without a loss of life far beyond its value. Lee's army was his objective point, and he knew that this wary general would withdraw in time to save the bulk of his forces. He decided to flank him out of his defenses, instead of fighting against such odds, by moving on Richmond. But the lack of supplies, and the terrible condition of roads, delayed this, for several days. The rain finally ceased, the sun shone out, the mud began to dry, and orders were given for another start. . . .

At one o'clock on the 21st, Hancock's corps broke camp on the left of our line, and took the road to Bowling Green, by way of Mattapossax church and Guiney's station. . . . Warren left his position at six o'clock A.M., and pushed on in Hancock's rear all day. . . . Grant's headquarters were at Guiney's station that night. Warren near by. Hancock to the left and in front. . . . Guiney's station will be memorable from "Stonewall" Jackson having died there. We were shown the house in which he drew his last breath—a small wooden building (or outbuilding) standing near a large, fine brick mansion, occupied by a widow, who claimed to be compensated for the loss of her husband, by having been able to contribute in making comfortable, the dying moments of the great Confederate general.

At noon of May 23d, our army was well closed up and marching on parallel roads towards Hanover Junction. By night Hancock reached the North Anna at a wooden bridge near where the railroad crossed it; and Warren had passed over the river at Jericho Ford (higher up) and had an unsuccessful engagement with the enemy. On the morning of May 24th Hancock crossed to the south side of the river; [Horatio G.] Wright passed over at Jericho early the same day and took position on the right of Warren.

Lee now had his entire army south of the North Anna, in by far the strongest defensive position I had thus far seen. His center commanded Ox Ford, with the two wings so thrown back as to nearly form a right angle, and conforming to the

course of the river in his front. He could reinforce quickly
from one wing to the other on a short line, whereas our semi-
circular lines confronting him were at least five miles in length.

To make a direct attack on formidable works thus situated
would have insured such a slaughter of our troops, as no reasonable success could justify. Orders were given to turn Lee's
right once more by moving down to the vicinity of Hanover
Town. . . .

So much has been said and written of the wide-spread deso-
lation the war caused in Virginia, that it may not be out of
place to state some facts which came under my observation.
From Spotsylvania to North Anna we marched through a section of country abounding in large farms, with elegant residences and commodious outbuildings. Many of these plantations were under a high state of cultivation. The soil was
rather light and sandy in the lowlands along the watercourses,
and seemed nearly worthless on the ridges and highlands that
intervened. Yet even the latter were sown and planted, and
promised to yield a handsome reward for the labor. Fields
of waving grain, stretched away from the roads for miles.
Wheat stood thin on the ground, but was well advanced for
the season. But little rye, oats or clover was seen, but a large
acreage of corn was planted. The fencing was better than expected. Every farmhouse had an extensive kitchen garden
well filled with growing esculents, and the people in general
did not have the starved and destitute appearance of those in
parts of Tennessee, Mississippi, Alabama and Georgia where
I had previously campaigned. Ice houses and ice plentiful.
Old corn fodder at every house not on some main road. Live-
stock and poultry were abundant, the scarcity of mules and
horses only being apparent. The finest natural leaf Virginia
tobacco abounded, and our soldiers no longer had to pay two

dollars a plug for it. Each had his pockets and pouches crammed with it, and hundreds had bundles of it dangling to their muskets as they trudged along. . . .

While the army lay in front of Lee on the North Anna I took a half day's rest—the first since rejoining headquarters at Spotsylvania. I had ridden and worked almost incessantly day and night, through storms and mud. Here for the first time since leaving Washington, I informed myself concerning the operations of the other armies. . . .

While here I made the acquaintance of such *Herald* correspondents as I had not previously seen since my appointment as chief of the corps. All of them expressed their gratification at Chapman's removal, and promised to follow my directions to the letter. Mr. N. Davidson was assigned to the collection of news at Fredericksburg and Belle Plain on the Potomac; to the forwarding speedily to Washington of all dispatches sent to him from the army in front; and messengers bearing our correspondence exclusively, were passing between us daily. But Davidson's ambition to make a reputation for himself soon induced him to open our dispatches, and revamp them into letters under his own name, at the cost of the correspondents in front. Complaints, and proofs, accumulated until I was compelled to make a change. The messenger line was continued, but made independent of any intermediate person.

While spending my day of comparative idleness, I rode to a large plantation house near by, owned by a Mr. Tyler, hoping to learn something in the way of news, and also to test the "southern hospitality" of which so much has been said. The place was abandoned by all excepting Mrs. Tyler, a rather young woman; an elderly woman as her companion; and the household negro servants. My reception by the ladies, bordered on positive incivility. I was made to feel unmistakably that I was an enemy, and that my presence was exceedingly distasteful.

Before I left Generals Grant and Meade rode up with their staff officers. Superior rank made the women more complaisant. Then occurred an incident related by Gen. Grant, and often told at Burnside's expense. Seeing Grant and Meade on the porch as the 9th corps marched past, Burnside dismounted for a few minutes, and after some polite salutations remarked to the old lady, in his off-hand jocular manner, that he "supposed they had never seen so many live Yankees before." The reply was instantaneous: "Oh yes, I have; many more." Burnside naturally inquired: "Where?" "In Richmond," she sarcastically replied, alluding of course to Union prisoners. Burnside was prepared to turn the conversation! . . .

[*Swinging southward across the Pamunkey River, Grant found Lee strongly posted at Cold Harbor. On June 3, he hurled his army forward in one of the most desperate assaults of the war, and within a few hours had lost 10,000 men. A lull in the fighting followed.*]

Taking advantage of a few days of foreseen inaction after our last assault on Cold Harbor I made a hurried trip to Washington and back by steamer. During my absence a circumstance transpired that caused considerable comment. It seems that Mr. Edward Crapsey, correspondent of the Philadelphia *Inquirer,* made some remarks about Gen. Meade in his published accounts about the battle of the Wilderness, to which Meade, and staff, took great exceptions. I cannot give the exact language, but its substance was, that at the end of the second day's fighting there, Gen. Meade was in favor of withdrawing the Union army back to the north bank of the Rapidan; and that this would have been done, had Meade been in supreme control, instead of Grant. . . .

[*On June 7, when Meade learned that Crapsey had rejoined the army after an absence in the North, he ordered that the correspondent be arrested, marched through the camp wearing a placard marked "Libeller of the Press," and then put outside the army lines and forbidden to return.*]

Perhaps nothing in this campaign was so pleasing and so gratifying to the whole nature of the man, as the execution of this order was to the brutal, tyrannical nature of Marsena R. Patrick, Provost Marshal-General. That the order was executed far beyond its letter need not be said to those who knew this "Squeers" of the military profession. To its letter was added every indignity and insult, which Patrick could devise. Crapsey was mounted and tied on the sorriest looking mule to be found, with his face to the mule's tail; when preceded by a drum corps beating the "Rogues March," he was literally paraded for hours through the ranks of the army. . . . Previous to this Patrick caused Gen. Meade's order to be read to every regiment he could reach, and the affair was treated with as much importance as if it had been the announcement of the collapse of the rebellion.[1]

I arrived at headquarters late in the afternoon, hot, dusty and fatigued by my ride from the White House, but repaired immediately to the Adjutant's office to enquire about affairs in my absence. Col. Bowers handed me a copy of Meade's Crapsey order, without a word of approval, disapproval, or explanation. From other officers I learned the particulars of the occurrence.

After supper we all assembled under the marquee in front of Gen. Grant's tent to smoke and chat, as we often did, when circumstances permitted. It was not long until some member

---

[1] Dispatches relating to this incident will be found in *O. R.*, Series I, Vol. XXXVI, pt. I, pp. 92–3.

of the staff commenced telling me the story of Crapsey's disgraceful punishment and banishment from the army. Another
pointedly inquired of me, what I thought of it. I was indignant, but calm and deliberate in speech, and replied that I
was not in position to decide impartially—that I had not seen
the statement which so greatly offended Gen. Meade—but I
was inclined to think Gen. Meade would live to regret the
manner in which he had treated the matter—that if his charges
against Crapsey were true, he would have been justified in
expelling him from the army—that perhaps some moderate
form of punishment would not have been out of place—but
that by the common opinion of nearly all mankind, any punishment which tended to degrade the offender, or was inflicted with that purpose and intention, would be condemned.
That in this case the world would be quick to believe that
Meade had abused his military power, to wreak his personal
vengeance on an obscure friendless civilian; and that it was
likely the general would get the worst of it in the end.

It was plain to be seen that the Staff were divided in opinion. It was equally plain that they were divided on the line of
the regular and volunteer service. [Horace] Porter, [Orville E.]
Babcock and I think [Cyrus Bellou] Comstock were sticklers
for military authority. Duff, [William Reuben] Rowley, Bowers and others manifested their feelings by ominous shrugs
of the shoulders rather than by words. West Point training
was quite apparent. When our conversation, and discussion
of the subject had about closed, Rawlins spoke in his sonorous
bass voice and said, with the prefix of an oath: "Gentlemen,
Cadwallader is always right. His democratic education can
always be depended on." With a laugh all around at the reason
given by the chief-of-staff for the correctness of my conclu-

sions, the conversation took another turn, and the affair was not mentioned again by any of them, for several months.

It is due to Crapsey to say that he always denied having confessed to the falsity of his charge against Gen. Meade. It may be that when Patrick had him in hand, he made some qualified statement, hoping by extenuation to escape the impending ignominy. He was not made of the stuff required for a modern martyr. But this is my own conjecture.

The consequences of Meade's act extended farther than he expected. Every newspaper correspondent in the Army of the Potomac, and in Washington City, had first an implied, and afterward an expressed understanding, to ignore Gen. Meade in every possible way and manner. The publishers shared their feelings to a considerable extent, and it was soon noticed that Gen. Meade's name never appeared in any army correspondence if it could be omitted. If he issued an official or general order of such importance as to require publication, it would be printed without signature, prefaced with the remark: "The following order has just been issued," &c. From that time till the next spring, Gen. Meade was quite as much unknown, by any correspondence from the army, as any dead hero of antiquity.

He was not slow to observe this, and first treated the neglect contemptuously. But at length it became irritating—then serious, but irremediable. The dignity of a major-general forbade complaints, and his individual pride prevented any acknowledgements. But some of his staff, who must rise or fall with their chief in public estimation, made some overtures towards a reconcilation. But nothing was accomplished. I had protested—mildly—against this conspiracy, for it was a conspiracy, on the ground that the position was entitled to more respect, if the man was not. I finally wrote privately to the *Herald*, recalling and recounting all the facts, and stating that I thought it had been carried far enough. Mr. Hudson replied, saying that he felt as I did, and hoped I would treat Gen. Meade with the consideration his military services and present position deserved. This was during the winter of 1864–5, and circumstances soon enabled me to "abandon the blockade" against him, without solicitation from myself, or any friend of his. Of this I will speak more in detail further on.

Previous to this, an incident occurred, which I omitted to mention in its proper place, affecting a newspaper correspond-ent of far greater pretensions than Crapsey. He was then known as plain William Swinton, correspondent of the New York *Times*. He afterwards bloomed out into a "historian"; wrote a book on the "Decisive Battles of the War"; [2] and later on became compiler of school text-books of more or less value. He was with the Army of the Potomac when commanded by Burnside, and remained with it under Hooker, until the latter sent him out of the department for his many misdemeanors. So far as I know, he never ventured within the army lines while Meade was in command; but as soon as Grant was made Lieutenant-General, he commenced intriguing to obtain stand-ing at his headquarters.

He was not permitted by the Washington authorities to join the army as an accredited correspondent, but concluded to steal his way there by false representations, and ply himself in his old vocation. He succeeded somehow in fastening on to Hon. Elihu B. Washburne, member of Congress, from the Galena, Illinois district (Grant's home) to the extent of being allowed

---

[2] *The Twelve Decisive Battles of the War* (New York: Dick & Fitz-gerald; 1867.) Better known is Swinton's *Campaigns of the Army of the Potomac* (New York: C. B. Richardson; 1866.)

to come with him to headquarters at the opening of the Wilderness campaign, under the pretext of gathering material for a history of the war. He assured Washburne that he was not a newspaper correspondent, but a literary gentleman of leisure, and was introduced as such to Gen. Grant. He no doubt expected to receive the general's hospitality and be invited to remain at headquarters during Washburne's stay there. But Grant and Rawlins, always exceedingly careful in such cases, omitted to do more than treat him politely, and left him to shift for himself.

I think he stopped with Capt. [Julius W.] Mason, commanding the headquarter cavalry escort, and was hanging around for a week or more. He would, no doubt, have been permitted to accompany the army in the capacity of a correspondent under the usual restrictions imposed upon all, had he truthfully stated his occupation, for none of us at that time knew his character and past reputation. But as the Confederates were then receiving full files of leading northern newspapers with about as much regularity as they ever did, some restraint was obliged to be put upon the character of the information sent from the front, or it would have been in the power of any unprincipled one of the number, to fill the part of a privileged spy for the enemy, inside of our own lines.

The first night after crossing the Rapidan, Gen. Grant gave the officer of the night at headquarters his instructions, verbally, about midnight. Three or four days afterwards he was surprised to read a verbatim report of these instructions in one of the Richmond papers. A night or two after this first suspicious occurrence, Swinton was caught hiding in the shade of a large stump, playing "eavesdropper," and trying to overhear a private conversation between Grant and Meade, when they were secluded, as they supposed, from all listeners in the privacy of Grant's tent, and Swinton was summarily dragged from his concealment, but allowed to leave without further punishment, than the shame of his exposure.

We heard but little more of Swinton until we arrived at Cold Harbor, when about the time Meade was having his trouble with Crapsey, Meade came to Grant's headquarters to tell him that Burnside had arrested Swinton for some of his past offenses, and had ordered him to be shot that afternoon! Grant thought this would be unwarranted, and ordered him released on the condition that he should be expelled from the Army of the Potomac, and not allowed to return. If Burnside had not been over-ridden, he would certainly have had his order executed. It seems Swinton had been with the army under Burnside and Hooker, and had indulged in so much detraction and defamation concerning the officers and men in both those campaigns, that Hooker expelled him from the army lines; but this had not appeased Burnside's growing animosity.

The sequel may as well be stated here as elsewhere. Notwithstanding all this, Swinton somehow got to the front again soon after we reached City Point; went into hiding with Capt. Mason; and began a voluminous correspondence "from Gen. Grant's Headquarters, City Point." His first letter attracted attention, of course, and I was instructed to learn its author if possible. I found Swinton easily, but before he could be arrested, he took "French leave," and was not seen again till the war ended. I doubt if Gen. Grant ever knew of Swinton's being at City Point. The matter was kept quiet, at Capt. Mason's tearful entreaty. . . .

Swinton was an Englishman by birth and education, with many of the vices and few of the virtues of his countrymen. He was tall and lanky in build; cold blooded, conceited and prejudiced to a surprising extent. He had such inordinate in-

dividual and national self-esteem, as to think it pitiable ignorance in any one to deny English superiority in all things.
When added to this it was found, that so far as he had sympathy for any person, or any cause, he was heartily in sympathy with the Southern Confederacy; and that the thick-
skinned imperviousness to argument, ridicule or reason, so
often found in his class, was colossal—monumental—it was
matter of small wonder that he was universally hated and
despised by all who knew him.

I was very much disturbed by the fact revealed at the
Wilderness that some person enjoying headquarter confidence,
was betraying it to Richmond newspapers. "Who could it be?"
was the first thought in every mind. There were very few
persons who could possibly have overheard and communicated the conversation. I was in the list of those who had the
opportunity to do so. Whilst I had no fear of the older members of Gen. Grant's military family, brought with him from
the west, doing me the injustice of suspecting my complicity
with it, there was a large number of new men on the staff,
who had never seen me till within a few days. I was very uneasy until all doubts were cleared up by Swinton being caught
in the act.

CHAPTER

Fifteen

GEN. GRANT having decided to transfer his army to the James River, preparations began at once. . . . On Tuesday morning, June 14th, Warren crossed [the Chickahominy] at Long Bridge, with Hancock following him. Burnside and Wright crossed at Jones' Bridge four miles below Long Bridge. The advance of the army reached the James before night, and commenced laying pontons immediately. The crossing was effected near Charles City Court House on the north side, and Fort Powhattan on the south side of the James.

Generals Grant and Meade broke camp near Cold Harbor at 3:00 p.m., Sunday, June 12th, and settled for the night at Summit Station. At six o'clock both were in the saddle, on their way to James River. On Tuesday afternoon, June 14th, Grant telegraphed from Bermuda Landing to Secretary Stanton, that the army was then crossing the river below, and that our movement from Cold Harbor had been made with great celerity and without loss.

Now was soon to commence the fiercest fighting of the war. Like the classic heroes of old Grant had been saying, by his movements, to Lee, for months: "If you are the general you claim to be, come out and fight me"; and Lee had replied, in like manner: "If you are the general you are represented to be, compel me to come out and fight you." In the end the latter was done. . . .

I reached Charles City Court House June 14th, before noon; pitched my tent on an eminence overlooking the place, and the James river for miles in both directions. Seeing the regimental colors of the "36th," [1] not far away, I walked down to them, and found officers and men in a pitiable condition. They came to the front raw troops, without military discipline or training; were immediately pushed into the forefront of battle; participated in the fights at North Anna, and Totopotomoy, with severe loss; and were in the charge on the rebel works at Cold Harbor. Out of two hundred and forty men of the Thirty-Sixth, which led this charge, one hundred and forty were killed, wounded and missing; and among these their gallant colonel [Frank A. Haskell].

This "green" regiment had been marching or fighting every day for more than two weeks preceding their arrival at Charles City Court House, and not an officer in the regiment had been able to make a change of clothing in all that time. They were literally incrusted in mud, dirt, dust, perspiration and blood—unwashed, unkempt, unfed, for rations had not always reached them as needed. Col. [John A.] Savage was lying on the ground, a picture of suffering, emaciation and exhaustion, never to be forgotten.

I had just received a fresh supply of rations and mess stores from Washington, so I took Savage to my tent, and ordered my negro cook, George to prepare the best dinner our commissariat afforded. Savage occupied my cot; and was fortified by

---

[1] The recently enlisted 36th Wisconsin Infantry.

a judicious admixture of spiritus frumenti and condensed milk, sweetened and spiced to taste, known in army circles by the complimentary name of "milk punch."

George was not long in announcing dinner, when we sat down to a royal meal for the times and circumstances. I remember many of the dishes as distinctly as if I had eaten them yesterday. We had potatoes, tomatoes and onions; canned fruits of many kinds; excellent fresh light bread; standard imported sauces and pickles; good fresh butter, a little of which I had transported with great difficulty without melting; a large genuine full cream cheese; bologna sausage, dried and corn beef, canned; oysters and lobsters, ditto; an elegant fruit pudding; and pies far surpassing any "your mother" ever made —as they seemed to us—for George had been a professional cook at "Willards," and was certainly surpassed by none, in the Army of the Potomac. The regimental officers were not overlooked. I could not entertain the whole command, but I sent basketsfull to their headquarters.

After the post-prandial cigars, I left Savage in my cot for an hour's sleep. I then filled his pockets with cigars, his canteen with whiskey, and took what proved to be my last earthly parting from him.

At two o'clock, p.m., June 18th in front of Petersburg another advance was ordered on the enemy's main intrenchment in front of the Second Corps, to which the 36th was attached. Col. Savage stepped in front of the colors, shouting: "Three cheers for the honor of Wisconsin; forward my brave men," at the same time springing over the slight works behind which they had been lying. Within two minutes he fell, mortally wounded.

Word was sent to me at City Point. I rode in hot haste to his regiment only to learn that he had been borne from the field and conveyed to the hospital on the Appomattox River a couple of miles above City Point. I rode there at full speed to learn that he had been carried aboard the hospital steamboat just starting for Annapolis, which was just then passing down the river beyond the reach of communication. But his injuries were not thought to be fatal, and I hoped for the best.

Two weeks afterward I registered at Barnum's Hotel, Baltimore, next under the signature: "Mrs. John A. Savage, and husband." I expressed my gratification to the clerk that he was so soon able to be taken to his home in Milwaukee; when the clerk stared at me dubiously for a moment, and said: "He's going home in a box." I afterwards learned that his wound was not necessarily a fatal one, but that he had succumbed because of his debilitated and exhausted physical condition, born of his thirty days' hardships and exposures, since entering the ranks in front of Spotsylvania.

By a singular misconception of his character nearly half of his regiment at first distrusted his courage. But the officers and men underwent a baptism of fire from Spotsylvania to Charles City Court House; and were bound together by links of steel, and the tempest and storm of battle, until each understood the other. When Col. Haskell was killed, and Lieutenant-Colonel Savage succeeded to the command, he rose to the requirements of his position; almost courted death in his exhibitions of personal bravery; and died the idol of his men. But the regiment never recovered from the loss of these two leading officers. It was so decimated in numbers, as to never be entitled to another field officer; but on account of its heroic services, was permitted to retain its organization till the end of the war, under command of its senior captains.

. . . I remained at Charles City Court House, while Gen. Grant ran up by boat to Bermuda Landing for a conference with Gen. Butler. The view from the front of my tent was among the most imposing I ever witnessed. As soon as the work of laying ponton bridges commenced, all navigation temporarily stopped. Vessels and transports of every description, loaded with army supplies, cast anchor and floated idly on the placid bosom of the James so far downward as the eye could reach, and still they kept coming. Many hundreds accumulated while the army was crossing. The troops were thrown across as rapidly as they could be moved, day and night, till all were safely landed on the south side of the river. As fast as they crossed by organizations, they pushed onward towards Petersburg with the hope of assisting to capture that place before Gen. Lee could send troops for its defense. . . .

[*The attack on Petersburg on June 15 was bungled, and Confederate reinforcements, arriving just in time, repulsed subsequent attacks with heavy losses. So Grant settled down to a siege. His army was now posted east and south of Richmond, and, with a numerical superiority of almost two to one, he pushed his lines steadily westward, forcing Lee to extend his thinner lines, until the two armies faced one another along a thirty-five-mile front.*]

I was beset with great difficulties in gathering and transmitting news to the *Herald* from such an extended field of operations; and when I succeeded in getting dispatches back to Washington City, they were often withheld for days at a time by order of Mr. Stanton, until they had lost much of their interest. In many cases paragraphs, and whole pages had to be stricken out before he would allow them to be telegraphed from the capital.

At the end of the first week's battling in front of Petersburg, Mr. Finley Anderson, correspondent with the second corps, wrote a carefully prepared account of the whole, and placed

the Union losses at about fifteen thousand,[2] if I remember
rightly. But instead of sending it to me, he rode to City Point to
consult me in person as to the propriety of some of his statements, and especially regarding his estimate of our losses. We
both knew Stanton's disposition to withhold all truthful accounts of reverses and losses. If Union forces were defeated, he
never allowed a candid admission of the fact to be made. If
Union losses were clearly above ten thousand (for instance)
one-third or one-half that many was the limit he would allow to
be made at first. The truth might be dribbled out little by little,
when, as he claimed, the public mind was better prepared
for it.

Mr. Anderson was one of the best trained correspondents
of the war. He was deliberate and conservative. Besides this,
his attachment to Gen. Hancock, and the second corps, was
such as to incline him to minimize its losses as far as he con-
scientiously could. At this conference we agreed as to all the
facts. I finally decided to cut his estimate down to eight thousand, and to soften and qualify many expressions. To my surprise Secretary Stanton would not allow this, only half truthful account, to be telegraphed, and cut out several pages from
Anderson's dispatches and my own.

Feeling that this could not be longer endured if any method
of correction could be devised, I proceeded to Washington
and vainly sought an interview with Mr. Stanton. I was persistently referred to a young officer whom he had made military censor of all army intelligence telegraphed from Washington. This young man would barely answer me civilly, and
peremptorily refused to discuss the matter, or listen to reasons
or explanations. On my saying that the *Herald* would no longer

---

[2] The official figure was 10,586 killed, wounded, and missing.

submit to such interference except on compulsion, he wanted to know, superciliously: "What I proposed to do about it?" To this, I vouchsafed no reply.

Within an hour I engaged three intelligent men, familiar with army life, to act as messengers in carrying New York *Herald* dispatches from City Point to Baltimore. The next day I employed two others, to receive these dispatches from the hands of the first bearers, on their arrival at Baltimore, and deliver them personally at the New York *Herald* office, daily. I had previously learned that by leaving City Point on the ten o'clock forenoon mailboat for Washington; and changing from that on its arrival at Fortress Monroe about 6:00 p.m. the same day, to the Baltimore and Chesapeake Packet line, close connection could be made next morning at Baltimore with the through morning train from Washington to New York; and all correspondence could be delivered at the *Herald* office early the same evening, by my own messengers, free from military censorship by mail or telegraph; and appear in the same issue of the *Herald* as if telegraphed from Washington.

It took three days for a messenger to make the round trip from City Point to Baltimore, so one was dispatched every morning. On arriving at Baltimore by boat he hurried to the railroad depot; delivered his sealed package to the messenger found there in waiting for him; took a receipt for its delivery, intact; and returned to me, with his receipt, by the next boat. The messenger from Baltimore made the run to New York one day and returned the next. Thus five messengers gave me daily connection with the office. We could write as freely and voluminously as we pleased. Postmaster-general Montgomery Blair could not withhold them at his pleasure; nor could Secretary Stanton tamper with them as caprice or spleen dictated. As each correspondent was required to affix his name at the head of all his letters and dispatches, personal responsibility insured carefulness, and the liberty thus secured never degenerated into unwarrantable or untruthful license.

The question of cost was the only consideration in my own mind. The messengers were paid twenty-five dollars per week for their services and eighteen dollars per week for expenses. They sometimes obtained transportation free, no doubt; although they were strictly forbidden to accept any such favors. At the end of a week Mr. Hudson wrote me that the messenger line worked to a charm—not a single failure had occurred—and the most gratifying feature of all was that it cost less than telegraphing from Washington. This special feature of the *Herald* service, was continued without serious interruption till the end of the war.

I procured from headquarters a pass for each messenger signed by order of Gen. Grant, and besides these was kept supplied with several others having blank spaces in which I could write the name of any person in emergency cases. The only stipulation required of me concerning these passes was that the messengers should confine themselves strictly to their duties, and not become purveyors on return trips of liquors, or other contrabands of war. For their good behavior I became personally responsible; and discharged one of the men for bringing a single bottle of whiskey to one of his friends at City Point.

Later on I was allowed to use these blank passes by furnishing one to any friend whom I wished to accommodate. This privilege was sparingly used, and never abused. I was repeatedly offered from three to five hundred dollars to pass a man to the front. The full significance of this trust can only be understood by stating that Secretary Stanton ignored all passes except those of Gen. Grant. All provost guards were ordered to disregard, take up, and destroy all others which might be presented. President Lincoln's passes were carefully scrutinized, *viséd* by the War Department, and sometimes revoked.

On my return to City Point by steamboat from Washington, the upper deck was covered with officers and men returning from furloughs or convalescent hospitals; and I became engaged in conversation with a group of them concerning our losses at Petersburg, and the action of Secretary Stanton in suppressing the news in this case, as he had in many others.

I commented freely, and probably severely, upon what I considered his unwarrantable interference with the freedom of the press. I pronounced it wrong and un-American—asserted the army correspondents then in the field to be better judges of what was proper for publication, than Mr. Stanton had shown himself to be; I claimed that the people of the country had a right to know the exact facts concerning any and all of our armies, where a publication of such facts did not foreshadow future movements—that if we were defeated in battle the nation demanded to know it—if we had lost an army, all that the loyal north required, was a statement of how many additional soldiers were needed to make all losses good and they would respond with alacrity—that withholding news; and publishing official bulletins, known to be false; was cruel and cowardly. I admit this to have been strong language within army lines; but I was still hot with resentment at the indignities heaped upon me by one of Mr. Stanton's attaches.

A tall dignified general officer sat within thirty or forty feet of me apparently heedless of this conversation. But within less than thirty minutes after our arrival at City Point he reported it fully to Charles A. Dana, First Asst. Sec. of War, who was

still at Grant's headquarters. I then learned it was Gen.
Thomas J. [T.] Eckert,[3] second Asst. Sec. of War, who had
overheard and repeated to Mr. Dana, my rather violent language on the steamboat.

Mr. Dana went to Gen. Rawlins' tent immediately in great
rage (as I was informed) and repeated it all to him. He declared it an outrage, and said any person guilty of using such
language concerning the Sec. of War, or any branch of the
government, was a disloyal and dangerous individual, and
should be promptly sent out of the department. Not receiving
any immediate reply from Rawlins, Dana again ran over some
of my most aggravating expressions, and seemed to expect
Rawlins to be as angry as he was himself.

But in a minute or two Gen. Rawlins began in a slow drawl-
ing manner peculiar to his moods of introspection, to say:
"Ye-e-s, rather severe speech. Cadwallader is sometimes rather
plain spoken. Bu-u-t, he's a pretty good fellow, an-n-d,—"

Dana was shrewd enough to perceive instantly, that I had
a staunch friend in Rawlins, and that nothing which he could
do or say would change headquarter opinion of me. He rose
and bowed himself out abruptly, commenced packing his
valise as soon as he reached his tent, left City Point by the
first boat, and was never at Gen. Grant's headquarters afterwards.

Rawlins, Bowers, and others soon informed [me] of the
occurrence, and I was very much disturbed at first by the
possibility of my indiscreet language creating bad feeling between Gen. Grant and the Secretary of War. They both advised me to pay no attention to the matter, and leave its after
treatment to Gen. Grant and themselves, should occasion de-

---

[3] Col. Eckert was not brevetted brigadiar general until March 13,
1865. He was general superintendent of the military telegraph.

mand it. A few martinets on the staff evidently thought my
conduct outrageous, and predicted that Stanton would revenge himself in the end. I never heard of it again in any
official way.

From what has been previously said concerning Mr. Dana's
official visits (and long stay) at Gen. Grant's headquarters,
the reader must have seen that his presence was very distasteful to the members of the staff. 1 shared their dislike fully, at
the time; and could not separate him from his official chief,
Mr. Stanton, whom I heartily detested. The passage of time
has modified my opinions by removing prejudices, until I
freely confess that Mr. Dana was substantially right; and that
my remarks concerning Mr. Stanton were indiscreet, ill-advised, and well nigh indefensible, when the time, the place,
and the surroundings were considered. My after intercourse
with Mr. Dana convinced me that I had misjudged him; and
that he was an able, far-seeing public official, and greatly
superior in most respects, to Mr. Stanton. Mr. Dana was also
an innate gentleman—Mr. Stanton was not.

On this trip from Washington, another incident occurred of
an entirely different character. A Massachusetts captain was
on board returning to his regiment. He was pale, emaciated,
bloodless and nerveless. He told me he was now on his return,
for a third time, from a convalescent hospital to which he had
been sent from the field to recover from wounds received in
battle. He had been shot almost to death, three separate times,
and had on each occasion been disabled for months, and consigned to a convalescent hospital. He had been torn almost
to pieces by minnie balls, but had thus far recovered. He
admitted that he was in sufficient physical strength to be
ordered to his company, but said that he dreaded it for the
first time in his life.

He had been so dangerously wounded each time, and had
suffered so terribly in the hospital before recovering, was so
broken down nervously that he didn't know whether he could
ever face the fire of the enemy again. He was afraid that if
ever again subjected to the test of battle, he would take to
his heels and run away. He distrusted his own courage for the
first time in his life, and was afraid he might disgrace himself
in the presence of the enemy. Still he was going heroically
to the front again, to do the best he could. His unassuming
heroism, in confessing his lack of courage, was very affecting.
I never knew his after record. He was a moral hero of the
grandest type; and should have been promoted, and honorably
discharged from the service, for physical disability. . . .

After the failure of our first attacks on Petersburg, which
practically ended about the 20th of June, there ensued a period
of comparative quiet. Our operations were confined to
strengthening our lines of intrenchment, so as to make them
impregnable against any sudden assaults of the enemy, and
extending our left flank south of the city to gain possession of
the Weldon railroad. Some severe engagements attended
these efforts which were confined to one or two corps, and
the gain was scarcely equal to the loss incurred. Sheridan had been previously sent, as mentioned, to destroy the
railroads north and west of Richmond, after which he was
to join Gen. [David] Hunter towards the head of the Shenandoah Valley and co-operate with him in the hoped for
capture of Lynchburg. But Hunter's failure, and defeat,
which compelled him to retreat through Western Virginia,[4]
obliged Sheridan to fall back to the White House, and sub-

[4] Lee sent Jubal A. Early to counter Hunter's movement against
Lynchburg, and after some skirmishing, Hunter, owing to a lack of ammunition, retreated to the Ohio by way of the Kanawha Valley.

sequently to move south of the James and out upon our left flank. . . .

Hunter's line of retreat left the entire Shenandoah Valley open once more to Confederate occupancy. Gen. Early saw his opportunity and pushed rapidly towards Harper's Ferry, meeting no obstruction worth mentioning on his way, and was emboldened to cross the Potomac into Maryland and threaten Washington City, which was uncovered and defenseless. There was great alarm at the capital. [James B.] Rickett's division of Wright's corps was sent by boat to Baltimore to assist Gen. Lew. Wallace commanding that district, in repelling Early's invasion, and to hold him in check at least, until other troops could be sent from the Army of the Potomac. Wallace met Early's advance at Monocacy; made as gallant a fight as possible with his inadequate forces; was defeated and driven back; but accomplished a great deal by delaying Early one full day, and giving the balance of Wright's corps time to reach Washington.

Knowing the gravity of the situation I left City Point twenty-four hours in advance of the Sixth Corps. On arriving at Washington about ten o'clock in the forenoon of July 11th, I mounted at the wharf and rode rapidly to the right of the Federal line of forts constructed for the defense of the city, and then turning to the left followed a chain of them reaching to the Potomac river. They were all in a deplorable condition. The armament was insufficient, the ordnance supplies limited, and all of them so weakly manned as to make any protracted resistance impossible. This chain of forts was about six miles out from the heart of the city. When I reached Fort Stevens, on the Crystal Springs [Silver Spring] road, Early's army was emerging from the timber and going into position in plain view from where I sat on horseback. A regular line of battle was extended to the right and left, running across farms, through orchards and dooryards, and batteries planting their guns to open on our fortifications.

The men stacked arms up and down the line as far as I could see, built fires, cooked and ate their dinners deliberately, and then commenced plunging shot and shell into our forts and earthworks. Our guns replied with as much vigor as possible, and a spirited cannonading was continued till night. Their troops were about a mile distant from Fort Stevens, across open plantations, affording a fine view of all that was done. A rebel battery was planted in the dooryard of my brother-in-law's house—Capt. Edward A. Paul—then with [Gen. William W.] Averill's Cavalry. The family remained in the house without injury, till Early's hosts retreated. The house was often struck by missiles, but no inmate was killed.

I have always wondered at Early's inaction throughout the day, and never had any sufficient explanation of his reasons. Our lines in his front could have been carried at any point, with the loss of a few hundred men. Washington was never more helpless. Several wide turnpikes led directly to it. Any such cavalry commander as Sheridan, Wilson, [Wade] Hampton or [J. E. B.] Stuart, could have ridden through all its broad avenues, sabred everyone found in the streets, and before nightfall could have burned down the White House, the Capitol and all public buildings. It has been stated that Early supposed it was fairly protected by federal troops. But this is a very poor excuse. As an army commander, it was his business to inform himself in such cases. His spies and Provost Marshals could have given him all these facts. Yet he spent the day supinely; and when he was about ready (in his own mind) to swoop down upon it, he found it strongly and sufficiently reinforced. Wright's corps arrived during the night of the 11th, and confronted Early next morning inside our forts. Thus ended the most imminent danger Washington was subjected to during the war.

Early's bold raiders pushed northward to the vicinity of Baltimore. His cavalry tore up the railroad track to a small extent between Washington and the Relay House, and between Baltimore and Havre de Grace. Telegraph wires were cut, and a few days of great alarm and excitement followed. It being important that lines of communication be kept open between myself and New York, I got to Baltimore with difficulty, and chartered a tug to take me to Elkton at the head of the Bay. Private conveyance from there soon took me to the nearest railroad telegraph station. Leaving a mass of manuscript with the operator, I chartered a hand-car to Havre de Grace, and proceeded on towards Baltimore, telegraphing whenever I could. But the Confederates were soon in full retreat and the last great raid ended.

Gen. Grant says, page 306, second volume of his Memoirs: "If Early had been but one day earlier he might have entered the Capitol before the arrival of the reinforcements."

I say from a knowledge of the situation superior to that of Gen. Grant, for I was present and personally inspected the whole field, that he might have entered the capital at any time before midnight of June 11th (I think that the hour of Wright's arrival) without having the march of his columns delayed a half hour, and without any loss of men worth a moment's consideration, when playing for such a stake.

Among the surprises to me on first reading Gen. Grant's Memoirs was the strong praise given to Gen. Lew. Wallace, for the battle of the Monocacy. In common with all the members of his old staff, I knew the esteem—or rather lack of esteem—in which Wallace had ever been held for his conduct at the battle of Shiloh.[5] Every member of Grant's staff at Shiloh were hot and outspoken whenever the subject was introduced. I have heard Gens. McPherson, [William R.] Rowley, [William S.] Hillyer, Rawlins, and others rehearse the affair many times, in Grant's presence. He always assented to their criticisms of Wallace's behavior. More conclusive than all this, he never intrusted him with any important command. But finding him commanding at Baltimore, he continued him, and gave him great credit for his conduct. I might have concluded that when Grant was so near the end of his own life, his resentments were softened, and that he desired to make amends for any possible injustice in the past, had it not been for one or two other surprises, more startling than this, to which I hope to allude in the future. . . .

---

[5] Wallace's delay in bringing up his division had almost proved fatal for the Union Army. Wallace pleaded a misunderstanding concerning the route he was to take.

CHAPTER

Sixteen

GEN. GRANT'S headquarters were established at City Point on the evening of June 15th and a few tents pitched for the officers. My own tent was under the umbrageous branches of a large mulberry tree which afforded protection from the blistering sunshine, until it had to be removed to conform to the general camp arrangement. By night of the 16th all was regularly laid out and adjusted. Headquarters proper were in the form of a parallelogram, with the two ends, and the north side closely filled with tents. The south side was open. The west end extended to the bluff bank of the Appomattox, perhaps fifty to sixty feet in height.

The cavalry escort camp was in the rear, reaching nearly to the bank of the James; the Infantry for fatigue duty was east of headquarters, and next east of this was a plateau soon covered with tents, shanties, restaurants and sutlers. The place was beautiful for situation, easily policed and drained, and was occupied continuously from the date of our landing there till after the surrender at Appomattox Court House, April, 1865. The landing on the James below the mouth of the Appomattox was extended a long distance, and from that time forward presented a scene of indescribable bustle and activity. From the lower end of the landing the south-side railroad ran out to Petersburg, and thence westward to Lynchburg.

From the 17th to the 20th the James was covered with vessels and transports which had followed the army with supplies, and with them came swarms of civilians—employees of the Sanitary and Christian Commissions—sutlers—pretended volunteer nurses—and greedy sight-seers who managed to get there to gratify their morbid curiosity. They swarmed around the wharves, filled up the narrow avenues at the landing between the six-mule teams which stood there by the acre, plunged frantically across the road in front of your horse wherever you rode, plied everybody with ridiculous questions about "the military situation," invaded the privacy of every tent, stood around every mess-table till invited to eat unless driven away, and wandered around at nearly all hours.

They congregated especially in the vicinity of headquarters, standing in rows just outside of the guard-line, staring at Gen. Grant and staff, pointing out the different members of the latter to each other, and seizing upon every unfortunate darky belonging to headquarters who came within their reach, and asking all manner of impertinent questions: "Does Gen. Grant smoke? Where does he sleep and eat? Does he drink? Are you sure he is not a drinking man? Where's his wife? What became of his son that was with him at Vicksburg? Which is Gen. Grant? What? Not that little man?" And so on by the hour. For several days headquarters resembled a menagerie.

On June 21st about one o'clook p.m., a long, gaunt bony looking man with a queer admixture of the comical and the doleful in his countenance that reminded one of a professional undertaker cracking a dry joke, undertook to reach the general's tent by scrambling through a hedge and coming in alone. He was stopped by a hostler and told to "keep out of here." The man in black replied that he thought Gen. Grant would allow him inside. The guard finally called out: "No sanitary folks allowed inside." [1] After some parleying the man was obliged to give his name, and said he was Abraham Lincoln, President of the United States, seeking an interview with Gen. Grant! The guard saluted, and allowed him to pass. Grant recognized him as he stepped under the large "fly" in front of his tent, rose and shook hands with him cordially, and then introduced him to such members of the staff as were present and unacquainted.

It transpired that the President had just arrived on the "City of Baltimore," and was accompanied by his son "Tad"; Asst. Sec. of the Navy, [Gustavus Vasa] Fox; Mr. Chadwick, proprietor of the Willard Hotel, as purveyor for the party; and the Marine Band. The conversation took a wide, free-and-easy range until dinner was announced. The President was duly seated, ate much as other mortals, managed to ring in three capital jokes during the meal, and kept everybody on the lookout for others, till the party rose.

He was naturally desirous of riding to the front, so at four o'clock horses were brought up. Mr. Lincoln was mounted on Grant's thorough-bred "Cincinnatus," the general on "Egypt," and "Tad," on Grant's black pacing pony "Jeff Davis." Accompanied by a large proportion of the staff, and a cavalry escort, the party rode to Gen. Wright's headquarters, where Gen. Meade and staff met them. The location commanded as good a view of Petersburg as could then be had from our lines. Maps were examined, the position of the army explained, its

---

[1] The reference is to personnel of the U.S. Sanitary Commission.

future operations discussed, the steeples and spires of the city observed as well as the dust and smoke would allow, national airs were played by the bands, the enemy's works on the opposite side of the Appomattox inspected, and after a stay of an hour and a half the party started on its return to headquarters.

On the way out many persons recognized Mr. Lincoln. The news soon spread, and on the return ride, the road was lined with weather-beaten veterans, anxious to catch a glimpse of "Old Abe." One cavalry private had known him in Illinois. Mr. Lincoln shook him by the hand, as an old familiar acquaintance, to the infinite admiration of all bystanders.

The noticeable feature of the ride was the passing a brigade of negro troops. They were lounging by the roadside, and when he approached came rushing by hundreds screaming, yelling, shouting: "Hurrah for the Liberator; Hurrah for the President," and were wild with excitement and delight. It was a genuine spontaneous outburst of love and affection for the man they looked upon as their deliverer from bondage. The President uncovered as he rode through their ranks, and bowed on every hand to his sable worshipers. After a nine o'clock p.m. tea, the visitors went to their staterooms on the vessel. They all visited Gen. Butler and the Army of the James next day, and started for Washington in the afternoon.[2]

In the west the headquarter staff was divided into several messes, according to the inclinations of the officers. On arriving at City Point Gen. Grant decided to embrace them all in his own mess. About this time on one of my trips to Baltimore, I was summoned to New York. Mr. Bennett wished to confer

---

[2] Lincoln's visit to Grant's headquarters at this time is confirmed by his letter of June 24 to Mrs. Lincoln, who was at Boston: "All well, and very warm. Tad and I have been to Gen. Grant's army. Returned yesterday safe and sound. A. Lincoln." *The Collected Works of Abraham Lincoln*, Roy P. Basler, ed. (New Brunswick, 1953), VII, 406.

with me on a number of matters, and among them that of im-
pressing me with the importance of running an independent
mess of my own, and entertaining liberally, as advertisement
for the *Herald*.

I thereafter kept "open house." My dinners equalled those of
Gen. Grant, and were free from restraints which often attended his. We could discuss men and measures as we pleased,
whilst such conversations would have been indecorous in the
general's presence. My preparations consisted in procuring
ample supplies of eatables and potables; a professional cook;
a tent for his kitchen; one large hospital tent for a reception
room, and another opening out of it for a dining room; an
old plantation house servant to always be in attendance on any
one who called; and white jackets and aprons for him, for
Cook George, and for Albert my hostler. These three were excellent table servants.

There was an understanding that all visiting civilians to
Gen. Grant, whom for any reason he thought best to not invite to his own mess, would be sent to me to entertain, if I
chose to do so. And they came by legions. Among them also
came furloughed and convalescent officers by dozens on their
way to or from their commands. I remember having Gen.
Thomas F. Meagher, the Irish exile and patriot, Gen. Henry J.
Hunt, chief of Artillery of the Army of the Potomac, Gen.
T. E. G. Ransom, Gen. John A. Logan, and others whom I
have not space to name, who remained my guests for a week
at a time, and several of them at the same time.

My ambulance would convey a party wherever it wished to
go, if that mode of conveyance was preferred. I kept four saddle horses and equipments; and could mount two or three
friends for a day at any time. Cigars of excellent quality,
stood open and free to all guests, or callers. In those times of

army deprivations, *Herald* headquarters soon became well known and famous.

Perhaps some staff officer from the front who had been riding all night would deliver his dispatches to Adjutant Bowers in the morning. Instead of being allowed to return to his camp miles away, tired, sleepy, muddy and hungry, I walked him to my tent, directed George to get up an elegant hot breakfast in haste, set one darky to brushing him off, another to blacking his boots, saw that his horse was watered and fed, seated him at a breakfast which was ample and inviting, stretched him on a cot with a good cigar after breakfast, and started him off in good humor. The *Herald* was paid many times over for the expense thus incurred, by the good will it secured. Officers would ride miles out of their way, when possible, to furnish me information.

Chadwick always stayed with me, when at the front, and declared, honestly enough no doubt, that he never had better meals in his life—that nothing in Willard's Hotel equalled them—so much has change, circumstance and environment to do with appetite. I furnished good enough food; but fresh air, hard riding and hunger, supplied a relish and sauce not found on Hotel tables.

Among my visitors from the north those days was Judge Levi Hubbell and James Ludington of Milwaukee. . . . Hubbell and Ludington could not rest till they had gone to the front, visited some Wisconsin officers and regiments, and actually seen something of war. We rode out on horseback one morning to the Petersburg intrenchments. At one place the Union and Confederate lines were within a quarter of a mile of each other, and sharp-shooting across some open ground was deadly. I explained all dangerous situations fully, and when we reached this open place I stopped, and ordered them to follow me at full speed across the narrow glade ahead of us; and as they valued their lives, to make no halt in the open ground.

Ludington and myself rode across safely. When Hubbell had ridden halfway he could not resist the temptation to have a good look at the rebel intrenchments, so he stopped, leveled his field-glasses at them, and finally joined us unhurt. Minnie balls whistled around him without hitting him, and he naively enquired of me what it was that made such a peculiar noise. I think my explanation frightened him.

For some time after arriving at City Point, and before the establishment of the *Herald* messenger line, my difficulties were great in transmitting dispatches. Under date of June 20th I wrote to my wife: "My habits may interest you. I rise about six o'clock, breakfast immediately, write what I can, look up a special messenger to carry correspondence to Washington, and get ready to supervise the dispatches which two messengers will bring to me from the front by 8:00 or 8:30, at farthest. These messengers breakfast here; loll around and sleep if they can till after dinner when they start back to each wing of the army; learn precisely where to call for correspondence that night; sleep in some camp till three or four in the morning; ride from one correspondent to another, collecting everything written up to that hour; and come to me again. . . . Hendricks is with the 5th corps; [J. C.] Fitzpatrick with the 9th; [John A.] Brady with the 18th; [Oscar G.] Sawyer with the 6th; Anderson with the 2d; [William H.] Merriam with the 10th; [Charles H.] Hannam at Butler's headquarters of [August V.] Kautz cavalry; Long with Wilson's cavalry; N. Davidson with Sheridan's cavalry—nine in all at present (besides messengers) but soon to be increased considerably in numbers.

"At ten o'clock every morning the mail boat leaves for Washington. I dare not send by mail and trust its frequent delays, nor the government's common detentions. Securing special messengers consumes half my time and accounts for my writing so little myself. Besides this I have to look after the horses and outfits of all these men. I am expending for the *Herald* nearly two thousand dollars per month, on an average, independent of the men's salaries with a certainty of greatly increasing this figure very soon.

"None but *Herald* men are recognized to the extent of being invited to share officers' quarters, messes, &c., on this campaign. Many correspondents are unable to get enough to eat and are leaving in disgust. Those who remain (excepting *Herald* men) roam about; have no regular stopping place; beg a meal here and there; and sleep under trees in the open air. An hour or two before the mail boat leaves they gather around it, like flies around a molasses barrel, and are the most unwashed, unkempt specimens of humanity on the globe. Yet many of these possess considerable capacity in mere letter-writing, but are totally deficient in address, or tact. They can't make friends; are never invited anywhere; and generally snubbed everywhere. The fault is their own. They should dress decently, behave like gentlemen, resent bad treatment, never crowd in where they are not wanted."

The *Herald* messenger line worked to perfection when fairly started, but the other metropolitan dailies were a month in finding out by what machinery its wonders were performed. The *Tribune, Times* and *World* of New York, and the Philadelphia *Inquirer* then banded themselves together to establish a similar line of communication between their offices and City Point, at joint expense. They sent a representative to headquarters to make arrangements. The first step was to

procure passes for their messengers, if possible. Gen. Grant
was not disposed to issue them at first, and Gen. Rawlins consulted me on the matter. I advised that no favoritism be
shown, and that the passes be issued if called for. I next saw
Gen. Ingalls and soon convinced him that the passage of so
many civilians on government steamers between City Point,
and Washington and Baltimore, was becoming unbearable;
and that the only way to stop it was to make it very expensive.

An order was immediately issued charging an exorbitant
price between these points to all except officers and soldiers
in the service. Meals and staterooms were to be one dollar
each in addition to passage money; and no civilian should
under any circumstances be furnished either, until every one
in the government service had first been accommodated. This
so increased the expense of the undertaking that these papers
became discouraged and abandoned the design. The *Herald*
messengers paid these extra charges cheerfully for a month
or two—possibly a longer time. When the affair was somewhat
forgotten, Ingalls revoked his order, and rates were restored
to the old figures. Gen. Grant was relieved from a disagreeable duty or predicament; and could not be charged with
favoritism to any one.

Gen. Patrick had been in the meantime advancing step by
step in the way of petty annoyances leveled at me; but embracing all the men I employed. Under cover of his official
duties as Provost Marshal-General, he could manage to make
the life of every newspaper correspondent a burden to him and
his friends. They were all civilians and could only remain
within army lines by military permission. This individual privilege carried with it by implication the right to pass from one
part of the army to another as their vocation demanded; and
to obtain from some source, subsistence for themselves and

their animals. All horses within the limits of our occupation were supposed to belong to the government.

Patrick instructed his subordinates to seize all unbranded animals, and branded ones in the possession of any civilian. It soon came about that if a *Herald* correspondent hitched his horse and passed out of sight for a short time, the animal would be seized, run into some government corral, and the owner subjected to the trouble and annoyance of finding it, and establishing his claim to it. Emboldened by a few successes of that kind he concluded to seize one or two of mine at the first opportunity. Being informed of this, I placed them all inside the guard line which always surrounded Gen. Grant's stables.

Headed off in this direction Patrick devised another plan to make me trouble. Under the plea that officers and privates were often passing to and from City Point on passes issued by those having no authority to grant them, he made an order that no person should be allowed to leave by boat, without first submitting their permission to do so, to his official inspection. If satisfactory to him, he either endorsed his approval on the back of it, or issued a special pass prepared in his own office. All holders of permits or passes were required to present them at Patrick's headquarters before they boarded the steamboat. Armed guards under a commissioned officer were stationed at the gang-plank to enforce this order, and another officer patroled the boat to see that none came aboard surreptitiously.

The result at first was that men were sent to Patrick's headquarters by dozens every morning; and stood in line waiting to have their passes *viséd*, in turn, by the single official assigned to that duty, until the boat has cast off and started down the river. Many were thus detained for twenty-four hours, whose right to go, without hindrance, should have been unquestioned. The *Herald* messenger was thus once detained; missed the boat; and reported the circumstances to me. I thought it time to make a test case, and leave to Gen. Grant the duty of enforcing his own orders.

The next morning I accompanied the messenger to the mail-boat. He presented his pass, attempted to go on board, but was pulled back by a Lieutenant, at the bayonet points of the guards, who stood with muskets crossed over the gang-plank. I stepped to the officer, and demanded that the messenger's pass be respected. He replied that Gen. Patrick was his superior officer and had stationed him there with absolute instructions to perform a specific duty; that he recognized the pass to be genuinely issued by order of Gen. Grant; but this did not absolve him from Gen. Patrick's later instructions.

I then stepped in advance of the Lieutenant, pushed the crossed muskets from over the gang-plank, put my messenger on board, and directed the Lieutenant to report my action to Patrick. There was some show of resistance for a moment, but I threatened to put everyone under arrest immediately who disputed my authority. I had no further trouble of that kind at City Point, and the Lieutenant asked me to protect him, if possible, from Gen. Patrick.

I then carried this little individual war into Africa, by having an inspection of the Post ordered. As inspector-general on the staff, General Fred. T. Dent performed this duty, and made such a report to headquarters as came near causing Patrick to be removed, and sent to his command.

Within a few days word was brought to me that the same thing was being done at Fortress Monroe. Major [Captain] John Cassel [Cassels], provost-marshal of that district, was putting holders of passes to the same inconvenience and delay.

In addition to this he sent an officer and a file of soldiers on every boat to seize and take up all passes that did not bear the stamp of his own office. I sent word to him that I would be in his office at a certain time, to settle the matter. He replied that if I came to his office on any such errand he would send me out of the department in irons. I was there at the appointed day and hour, but the doughty Major was prudently absent. His interference ended at that; but he was relieved from command almost immediately thereafter.

My affair with Cassels had a sequel years afterwards which may as well be related here. I was living in Milwaukee. Cassels was by Gen. Butler's influence made governor of the Milwaukee Soldiers' Home. I expected trouble with him on his arrival. Our first meeting was squarely face to face on the north side of Wisconsin street, between East Water and Main, one forenoon. Seeing that a meeting was unavoidable, he came up smiling, held out his hand, and said: "Cadwallader, I thought you served me a mean trick at Fortress Monroe; but that was a long time ago. Suppose we call it a stand-off." And so it was ever after. . . .

CHAPTER

Seventeen

. . . On June 25th work was commenced on the Petersburg mine, which obtained great celebrity at the time. It commenced in a ravine in front of the Ninth corps, and fell properly under Burnside's oversight. It was dug under great difficulties, such as lack of suitable mining tools, and the excavation was completed on July 23d. Two [four] days more were consumed in charging it with powder. . . . Orders were given for its explosion at a little after three o'clock on the morning of July 30th, but the fuse was not actually fired until after four o'clock. Then owing to splices and other imperfections in the fuse it failed to go off. Two volunteers followed the line of fuse in to the faulty place at which it had gone out, relighted it, and a few minutes before five o'clock, the whole mine exploded with a thundering roar that shook the earth and the heavens.

So far as the mine was concerned, it proved a great success. So far as results are considered it was a stupendous failure. Its cost in labor and money had been heavy. Its cost in killed, wounded and missing was set down at four thousand and three.[1] The enemy's loss in men was trifling. His loss in ground nothing. His prestige in successfully resisting the attack was deservedly great.

The entire failure of this enterprise keenly disappointed Gen. Grant. He should have known better, however, than to have trusted any necessary preparations to such an incompetent officer as Burnside had proved himself to be long before that. For this he deserves great blame. The selection of Gen. [James H.] Ledlie to lead the assault, was as bad as could have been made. He did not even accompany his men, but remained behind in a safe place, and was written down coward by all from that time forth.

It is needless to describe the carnage that reigned in and around the crater formed by the explosion; nor the death that was in the air to all who attempted retreat or escape from it. In fact its horrors were far beyond any description which could be made in cold blood years afterward. Seeing that it was a failure Burnside was ordered about nine in the forenoon to extricate his troops as he best could, as soon as he could, and return to his old lines. . . .

Mine explosions are rarely successful. They are subject to too many accidents and miscarriages. They can only be resorted to when the lines of the opposing forces are in close proximity. An observant enemy generally suspects the intention, and prepares for it, in great measure, by counter-mining and extra precautions. The precise point of danger may be a matter of conjecture; but able engineers can always determine certain limits within which such attempts must be made,

---

[1] The Union losses were all incurred in the attack following the explosion of the mine, and in the Confederate counterattack in the crater and at other near-by points where the Union troops took refuge. But the Confederate loss of 1,500 can scarcely be called trifling.

if at all. If the explosion should meet the expectation of its projectors, its final results depend upon the action instantly taken in the offensive. On the other hand there is in most cases, perhaps, an indefinable dread of such explosions out of all proportion to their real dangers.

I witnessed the three principal affairs of that kind during the war: That . . . at Vicksburg; this one on Burnside's front; and the Dutch Gap canal fiasco. Each of these was expensive in labor, material and loss of life. None of them resulted in any good to the federal troops. The Burnside mine was pronounced by Gen. Grant to have been a positive benefit to the enemy.

The scenic effects often surpass all powers of description. We stood, or sat, around in groups, on an eminence overlooking the field, for nearly two hours, waiting in painful silence, for the grand denouement in front of Petersburg. I happened to be looking directly at it when the enormous mass of powder was at last ignited. Contrary to the usual expectation, the noise and roar of the concussion is not the first thing to break on the senses, but comes a few seconds later. My first perception was that of seeing the earth commencing to rise on a line a hundred yards in length; then to split open by fissures, from which emerged a dense volume of smoke, dirt and dust; followed by sulphurous flames, as if the whole center of the globe was belching forth some monstrous volcanic masses. The smoke and flames rose perpendicularly at first; then spread out into a great sheet; and commenced slowly to fall in the form of a great water spout. This was soon followed by the detonation of the combustibles. The sound of the explosion did not equal my expectations, and came so late that those whose eyes were not turned that way missed much of its sublimity. As in all such cases, a large proportion of the upheaved material fell back near to the place from which it was hoisted upward. The crater formed was probably one hundred and fifty yards long, and of course deepest in the center.

Then commenced a furious cannonading from the Union line for a mile to the right and left, under cover of which the assault was to be made. It is believed that no such thunder of cannon was ever heard on the American continent, and probably not in the world, as on that occasion. . . .

In the free off-hand conversations on military affairs which often occurred in the Adjutant's tent, and elsewhere about headquarters, I had been declaring for weeks that it would be a comparatively easy thing to storm the rebel works at any one of a half dozen points named. Very few coincided. I said if one division of my selection was assigned to this duty I would cheerfully head it, and stake my life on its accomplishment. The question of supporting the storming column would rest on the Army of the Potomac. This offer was often called to my recollection for a few days after the mine failure; and I was asked what I thought of it then. My conclusive and sufficient reply was, that it was unchanged—that the storming party without any authorized leader, had penetrated the enemy's lines, advanced to the crest of the ridge beyond them, and could, and would, have remained there, had the main army put forth a tithe of its strength in well-directed support.

One good result followed not long after. Gen. Burnside ceased to command the Ninth Corps, which was placed under Gen. [John G.] Parke.

Towards the close of August some one of a gang of men unloading a transport of ammunition at the City Point wharf, dropped something which exploded. This fired all the cargo

in an instant, destroying a large number of vessels near at
hand, killing many men, and destroying over a million dollars' worth of property. Fragments of flesh, hands, feet and
other parts of human bodies, were literally gathered by the
basketful, one-fourth of a mile distant. Showers of shot, shell,
grape and canister, minnie balls and other missiles were rained
down in every direction. The ridge pole of my tent was
snapped in two by a solid shot, many holes cut and torn in
the canvas, and several hundreds of pounds in fragments lay
within a circle two rods in diameter. Singularly, no one connected with headquarters was injured. . . .

By the end of October, or middle of November, everything
in front of Richmond also settled down in a monotonous procedure which showed that active hostilities in any extended
sense were over for that year. Skirmishing along the lines;
some demonstrations against exposed rebel positions, enliv-
ened by an occasional iron-clad or gunboat collision on the
James, occupied the fall and winter.

This period of inactivity was checkered with a class of incidents peculiar to such phases of camp life. Disobedience
to orders, insubordination and desertion, rarely occur in the
midst of active operations. The soldier who will lead a forlorn hope, face instant and almost certain death, when ordered
to do so, under the excitement of battle, becomes the most
restless mortal in existence when confined to the daily routine,
of eating, sleeping, performing a little fatigue duty and clean-
ing his arms equipments and clothing, without any apparent
compensations. He becomes morbidly discontented and homesick, commencing perhaps with laziness, sulkiness, and ending in desertion.

During the fall and winter desertions became alarming in
frequency. Some of these went boldly over to the enemy,

thinking no doubt, that escape from there to their homes in the north would be easier than from the rear of our own armies. But the Confederates induced or compelled some of them to enter the rebel service, and several were captured in the rebel ranks, bearing arms against the United States. On one occasion three such were court-martialed, sentenced to be shot, and were formally executed in the presence of as many of our own troops as could be conveniently assembled to witness it. It was hoped this would end desertions for awhile. The impotence of the measure was shown by the fact of seven desertions taking place the first night after this military execution, every one of whom had seen their comrades shot to death, only the day before, for the same offense. This form of punishment was not repeated.

For my own convenience in passing the headquarter guard-line by day or night, I had my tent pitched squarely on it, so that the front door of the tent opened inside the line, and the back door outside. One bright forenoon on returning to my tent a woman with an infant in arms was sitting at the back door waiting to see me. She was deeply veiled, poorly dressed, and evidently in great distress. She wanted to see Gen. Grant. I directed her to the proper headquarter entrance, told her to send her name to Gen. Grant by one of the guards, and perhaps she would be admitted. She said she had been told to come to me, and to no one else. I questioned her as to her business with the general, her name, her residence, by what means she had reached the front at a time when so few women were given this permission, and especially as to who had sent her to me. To all this her only reply was that she wanted to see Gen. Grant, and that she could only hope to do this through my friendly mediation. She was downcast, tearful and importunate.

I spent considerable time in explaining the unreasonableness of such a request to me, tried to have her go away and send some acquaintance who could and would intercede for her. But all to no purpose. "Wanted to see Gen. Grant." "Wanted to see Gen. Grant" was her continual refrain, interrupted only by fits of weeping. I next essayed some rougher talk—told her I could not have her sitting there all day—that I hoped she would not compel me to have her forcibly taken away by a file of soldiers, &c. But she would neither go, nor enter into explanations. Somewhat provoked I left for awhile, expecting she would leave when she found I was obdurate. On returning an hour afterwards she was still there. Her dumb grief mastered my resolutions. So bringing her through my tent to the inside of the guard line, I pointed out the Adjutant's tent, and told her to ask for Col. Bowers.

I mounted my horse and rode away for several hours to avoid explanations with Col. Bowers. On my return she was sitting at Col. Bowers' tent precisely as she had been at mine. I then learned that she had followed the same tactics with him, as with me. He could learn nothing from her, nor concerning her, excepting that she wanted to see Gen. Grant.

Bowers tried to make her understand that Gen. Grant was too busy to give personal attention to business matters—that his staff officers attended to most of it—that if she did see Gen. Grant she would probably be sent back to him at once —begged of her to state her errand, and if possible he would attend to it promptly. To all this she had but the one answer, she "Wanted to see Gen. Grant." Bowers finally gave up the attempt of getting information from her, and went about his office duties, after telling her that Gen. Grant had ridden away and would not return till night. His efforts to get her to leave had been as futile as mine.

As soon as he knew I was in camp Bowers sent for me, and with as much severity as he could assume, inquired who this woman was? I didn't know. "Who sent her to headquarters?" I couldn't tell. "What did she want?" I had no idea. "Why had I sent her to him?" I was obliged to tell him: "To get rid of her myself."

Poor Bowers didn't quite know what reply to make at first, but finally commenced: "It was a most outrageous liberty I had taken. I was as bad as everyone else around headquarters. Whenever there was extra hard work and annoyance for somebody, all seemed to unite in throwing it on him. His time, and his feelings, were always disregarded. He should have to do what I should have done at first—send her away under guard. He had already lost nearly two hours on the case for nothing," &c.

I said: "Col. Bowers, you are the kindliest, truest man living. I could not send this woman away. My whole nature was so stirred by her sorrow, that I could not do it. I would rather leave myself." We looked each other in the face a moment with not very dry eyes.

At noon Bowers had provided her a good dinner. At three or four o'clock in the afternoon Grant returned. After a lunch he lighted a cigar and seated himself under his marquee for a smoke. Bowers pointed him out to the woman and said: "Madam, that is Gen. Grant." I witnessed the performance, and asked him why he sent that woman to Gen. Grant? He replied: "To get rid of her myself." His good humor was restored.

We soon learned that she was the wife of a federal soldier who had deserted to the enemy, been captured armed and in rebel uniform, had been court-martialed and sentenced to be shot; and was then at the front awaiting execution. She came to plead for his life. Gen. Grant spent an hour in trying to show her how impossible it was to grant her request. Desertion was an unpardonable military offense; but when it was aggravated by taking up arms in the enemy's ranks, every civilized country in the world inflicted the death penalty. He expressed his sympathy for her, and urged her to return to her home and friends, and try to forget the man who had shown himself to be so unworthy of the affection and love of any good woman—that a man who could so far forget his wife, child and country, would never prove a good husband and father. She listened stolidly; but said over and over again that he had always been a good husband to her. She made no apologies for his conduct, but kept on repeating he had always been a good husband, and begging him to spare his life.

The General left her sitting at his tent door, strolled around headquarters awhile in silence, chewing and pulling at his cigar abstractedly, interviewed Bowers, and again endeavored to get her away from camp without violence. She absolutely refused to leave. Supper time came on, but there she sat. He then ordered a servant to provide her with a supper. By this time Grant was reduced to about the same extremity as Bowers and myself had been. He finally telegraphed Gen. Meade to review the court-martial proceedings and see if there were any technical informalities in them which would justify a review, or a commutation or suspension of sentence. Meade replied that he could find no errors or informalities of any kind. Grant then telegraphed to the President, and received full authority to do as he pleased in the matter. His next order was to Gen. Meade to send the man to his headquarters under guard. He arrived in an ambulance, strongly guarded, about daylight in the morning. The husband and wife were brought together. The former made no attempt to justify

his conduct; but was greatly affected at meeting his wife under such circumstances. It was a total surprise to him, as he
had not been informed of her presence, and broke him down
completely.

Grant gave him a lecture of unusual severity—scored him
unmercifully—told him he richly deserved a thousand deaths,
for one such act often led to the deaths of thousands of innocent men—told him he could stand by and witness his execution without a single emotion of pity for him—but concluded
it all by telling him that out of sorrow for his wife, who had
proven herself so true and so good a woman, he would give
him one chance for his life. He would not pardon him, nor
in any way release him from the verdict pronounced against
him, except to delay the day of his execution. He would order
him to be restored to the ranks of the company from which
he had deserted, subject to further orders in the matter.
He told him plainly he would be under daily and hourly sur-
veillance, and upon the first dereliction of duty in any way,
he would order him to be shot within twenty-four hours. After
breakfast the husband was returned to the front, and the wife
placed on the ten o'clock forenoon mailboat for Washington
City. I made inquiries about the soldier for awhile afterwards;
then lost all track of him. He probably served out his enlist-
ment; and may be drawing a fat pension.

It was a matter of pride with Gen. Grant, and one to which
he sometimes alluded complacently, that he had never signed
a death-warrant while commanding in the west. To which
Gen. Sherman replied: "No he didn't, no he didn't; but he
left the prisons full of miserable devils, deserving death, whom
I had to execute, or turn loose." To which I may as well add,
in passing, that he generally turned them loose!

During the fall and winter the prohibitory regulations were

somewhat relaxed at Washington and there was a great influx of visitors to the Army. *Herald* headquarters had become widely known for its hospitality, and I was constantly besieged by sight-seers from northern cities and villages, some in quest of information as to the location of friends and relatives; others asking for temporary accommodations in the way of mess and lodging; and still others seeking through me to obtain an introduction to Grant.

The last request was the most perplexing. Nearly all of them were strangers of whom I knew nothing beyond a letter of introduction to me from some former visitor. I was compelled to exercise great caution in presenting anyone to the general, as I became to some extent responsible for the standing and respectability of every one to whom he accorded this privilege. A man from Boston hung around my tent for several days importuning me to take him to see Gen. Grant. He was presentable in dress and address, but I scarcely felt warranted in complying with his wishes, and referred him to others. He would take no polite intimations of my unwillingness, and I was obliged to plainly and flatly refuse him.

A few days after this I was sitting in the cabin of the Washington mail boat reading a file of northern newspapers I had just received, when I overheard some one using my name in conversation. A group of officers, soldiers and civilians were talking freely and loudly about the military situation, military commanders, &c., and in the middle of the crowd stood my man from Boston. He was entertaining the company by repeating a conversation he had held with Gen. Grant a few days before at City Point. From his statements the company supposed him to be an old acquaintance, but in answer to a direct question he said it was the first time he ever saw him.

Some one asked who introduced him to the general when he unblushingly replied: "Cadwallader of the New York *Herald*."

I waited for a lull in the conversation and then confronting him said: "I do not often meddle in what does not concern me. But you have made an unwarrantable use of my name, by saying to these people that I introduced you to Gen. Grant. I am Cadwallader of the New York *Herald*. I not only did not give you such an introduction; but expressly refused to do so. I try to present none but respectable people to him. I now find you to be a disreputable fellow, as I all along suspected, and I want you to apologize to me, and to this assemblage." To say that he was "thunderstruck" expresses it mildly. He undertook to slip out of the crowd and get away, but I collared him, and made him confess that his whole story was a fabrication and lie. He came near being thrown into the river by his listeners.

September and October of 1864 were very busy months, east and west, in perfecting arrangements for the campaign subsequently made famous by "Sherman's march to the sea" and Thomas' victory over Hood at Nashville. Much correspondence was required with Washington City and other places to effect the necessary consolidation of troops already in the field, and to hasten the organizing, equipping and forwarding of new recruits from the north. . . .

Many contradictory opinions existed at that time, and for years afterward, as to who originated Sherman's movement on Savannah. So far as most of the details were concerned, and the particular time of starting, I have no doubt Sherman deserves the credit. But the advisability of just such an undertaking had been discussed at headquarters for more than a year preceding the fall of Atlanta. . . . In giving Gen. Sherman credit for the whole scheme, Gen. Grant went far beyond what the facts warrant. He says on page 376, 2d volume of his Memoirs: "I was in favor of Sherman's plan from the time it was first submitted to me. My chief-of-staff, however, was very bitterly opposed to it, and, as I learned subsequently, finding that he could not move me, he appealed to the authorities at Washington to stop it."

This charge against Gen. Rawlins must not go uncontradicted. It was certainly made by Gen. Grant (if he in fact ever made it) under grievous misapprehension and misinformation. He admits, by implication, that he did not know at the time that Rawlins was opposed to the plan; but "subsequently learned" it. This, of itself, will be a sufficient refutation of this charge to all who knew Rawlins' character, and his personal relations to Grant. Rawlins had no concealments as chief of staff. Gen Grant might sometimes attempt some minor concealments from Rawlins, not affecting public or official duties; but it was not in the nature of the latter to do so. Scores of cases can be cited in which Rawlins took strong pronounced ground against contemplated operations; but not one in which he concealed his opposition. His fault, if it were a fault, was in being too open and outspoken in all his intercourse with his chief. Scores of incidents of this class could also be enumerated if it were necessary.

In addition to this I know that Rawlins approved this, as he substantially did, every offensive operation which Grant was ever engaged in. He was an enthusiastic believer in it from the outset, and rejoiced at its consummation as unreservedly as Grant himself. But Rawlins did object to Sherman's stripping Thomas to the extent of leaving him but few really available troops in front of the advancing triumphant rebel host under Gen. Hood. He wanted the line of the Ten-

nessee river absolutely secured before Sherman left Atlanta. . . . I assert that beyond this limitation, this charge
against Gen. Rawlins is unjust and untrue. I go beyond this,
and assert that I shall never believe that Gen. Grant wrote
the paragraph alluded to, until I have seen the original manuscript in his own handwriting; [2] nor will I believe that Gen.
Rawlins ever appealed to the War Department to put a stop
to it, unconditionally, except upon the same evidence. . . .

As previously mentioned, after the "Crapsey" affair at Cold
Harbor all newspaper correspondents with the army (excepting myself) and those in Washington City united in ignoring
Gen. Meade's official existence. His name never appeared in
print if they could prevent it. At the end of three or four
months of such treatment Gen. Meade became very restive,
I was informed, and admitted that his treatment of Crapsey
had probably been too severe.

I wrote to Mr. Hudson concerning it to which he replied
that Gen. Meade's official position entitled him to better treatment. I thereupon directed all *Herald* correspondents to gradually change their bearing towards him. The public presentation

---

[2] In the original manuscript of Grant's *Memoirs,* now in the Library
of Congress, I have been unable to find any assertion by Grant of opposition to Sherman's movement on the part of Rawlins. The latter part of
the manuscript, though lucidly written, lacks continuity and unity; and
it would seem that Grant, with death from cancer overtaking him,
hastened to put down his recollections in whatever order thoughts happened to come to him. Adam Badeau, who was appointed Grant's military secretary in March 1864, served on his staff until March 1869, and
later accompanied him on a tour around the world, claimed after Grant's
death that he wrote the Memoirs, and demanded $10,000 compensation
from Grant's family. His claim to authorship is obviously absurd, but
the nature of the original manuscript, and the fact that his demand for
payment seems to have been met, indicate that he did at least revise
the latter part of Grant's work in order to make it suitable for publication.

of some honorary medals to several soldiers in his command, by Gen. Meade in person, gave me an excellent opportunity to break the existing blockade against him. I sent a short-hand reporter to the front on that occasion who brought me a verbatim report of Meade's address, and a good description of the whole affair. I also sent Meade a note calling his attention to what I had done, and that so far as the *Herald* was concerned, he might depend upon fair treatment in the future. To this I received the following autographic acknowledgement which lies before me as I write:

> *Head-Quarters Army of the Potomac.*
> *October 28th 1864.*

Dear Sir:—

I have to acknowledge receipt of your note of the 26th instant, and to thank you for the same. I noticed the publication of the dispatches referred to in the Herald *but presumed as you infer, the omission of my name was accidental; and as they were not written by me with any expectation of publication (in the newspapers) I attached no importance to the name being left out.*

I am obliged to you for the trouble you have taken about the matter, and feel quite assured you would not intentionally do injustice to any officer.

> *Respectfully yours.*
> *Geo. G. Meade, Major-General*

Soon after this I needed some special passes for Mr. Hannam, one of our correspondents, and called upon Gen. Seth Williams (Adjutant-General of the Army of the Potomac under every commander which it ever had) [3] to obtain them,

---

[3] Williams served as adjutant general until November 1864, when, owing to ill health, he was appointed inspector general.

leaving with him my written request for the same. During this interview he invited me to step into Gen. Meade's tent, as he would be pleased to see me. To this I replied that I had never been formally presented to him, and did not feel warranted in doing so.

Gen. Williams was greatly surprised. I explained that whilst I knew Gen. Meade by sight as perfectly as any one in his army, and that he knew me in the same way quite as well, and saluted whenever we met, yet I had never exchanged a word with him since I came to the department. I explained further that Gen. Meade had the reputation of feeling unfriendly towards army correspondents, as a class, and I had purposely avoided him for that reason.

Williams rose from his seat hastily, and asking me to wait a moment, rushed into Meade's tent, and came back in a few minutes beaming with delight, and said Gen. Meade asked me as a personal favor to come to his tent for a short time. I was not much inclined to do so; but Williams took me by the arm and marched me into Meade's presence. The latter threw aside all reserve at once, and commenced on the subject in both our minds. He declared that all charges of unfriendliness to correspondents as a class, were absolutely and wholly untrue, no matter from what source they emanated. A few individuals had incurred his displeasure, one of whom he had punished perhaps too severely. He said Mr. Crapsey richly deserved some form of exemplary punishment for the falsehoods he had written from the army, but he was now satisfied that one of the greatest mistakes of his life, was degrading him in the manner he did. He then went on to say that he had the utmost charity for the unavoidable mistakes of correspondents, because he sat down to write an official report of the battle of Gettysburg, with full reports before him from every command engaged in it, and felt himself competent to give a true and just account of it. Yet when it was finished and published he found that he had made many mistakes. Ever since then he had always felt like overlooking unintentional mistakes of army correspondents who were compelled to write hurriedly, often from the field while battle was raging, from the best information then obtainable. His wonder was that more mistakes were not made under such circumstances.

His confession was so full, free and spontaneous, that I was disarmed at once. At the end of a rather lengthy conversation I left him; but the acquaintance which began there lasted till the day of his death. I think he never came to Washington in post-bellum days without calling at my office, and sometimes spending hours in what was always to me a pleasant, delightful and charming strain of conversation. He was distinguished in appearance, polished in manners, and one of the finest types of a conventional gentleman that I ever met.

CHAPTER

Eighteen

THE SIEGE of Petersburg and Richmond, the operations in the Shenandoah Valley and Sherman's campaign in Georgia were matters of absorbing interest in the fall of 1864. Southern newspapers were in demand, and I was requested to obtain them as regularly as possible. To this end I conferred with Gen. Godfrey Weitzel, commanding the 18th corps, on Butler's front, to make some permanent arrangement for passing through his lines daily, and exchanging files of New York City papers for those from Richmond and other southern cities. My authority for doing so was satisfactory to him, and I had him select a brigade from the front of which these exchanges should be made. I explained to him that my multifarious duties made it impossible for me to do this work in person; and that I wished to delegate Mr. John A. Brady, *Herald* correspondent with that corps, to attend to it in my behalf; and pledged myself to be personally responsible for Mr. Brady's faithful performance of that specific duty. He was to exchange nothing else—do nothing else—hold no conversations on other subjects—and to neither convey, nor seek to obtain, any other kind or form of information.

Gen. Weitzel knew Brady quite well and was willing to

trust him. He sent a staff officer with me to the brigade commander to introduce Brady and myself, and fix the time and place for this exchange. It was carried on successfully for some time, and the *Herald* was filled with southern editorials, showing the animus of the writers and the state of southern opinion in the Confederacy.

To prevent the possibility of a single copy of any southern newspaper brought to our front, falling into other hands, or of being found on any rebel prisoner that might be captured by our troops, Brady was instructed to get possession of every copy he possibly could. On extraordinary occasions I often paid five dollars per copy, in Confederate money for a large number of extra papers. After selecting such as were wanted for my own use, I burned the others at once. I usually mailed one copy to New York, and one to the *Herald* correspondent in Washington, to provide against delays or accidents in transmitting my own dispatches.

Gen. Butler's provost-marshal had been making frequent exchanges of papers, for the general's information. When my regular daily exchange commenced, Butler was no longer able to obtain any, and set his officer at work to learn the reason for the sudden embargo. He finally traced it out and reported the facts to Butler. It raised quite a commotion at the latter's headquarters, and a telegram was sent to Gen. Grant requesting him to send me there under arrest.

Col. Bowers read the telegram to me with a smile, and said Butler was evidently on the warpath. I stated my intention of going to him at once, but was seriously cautioned against doing so. His hot temper and arbitrary procedures were no secret, and the general belief was that he would make life a burden to me if I fell in his power. Knowing the matter would have to be faced sooner or later, I decided to settle it at once.

Bowers was informed that if I was not back and in his tent by five o'clock p.m., it would be because of forcible detention; and was also requested to order my immediate return to headquarters by Gen. Butler.

On arriving at Butler's headquarters I walked into his tent with as much unconcern as I could assume. His countenance was glowering and angry, and he began at once: "You have reported under arrest I suppose."

I informed him that I had not.

"Consider yourself under arrest sir, from this instant."

I began mildly to expostulate and make explanations.

He wouldn't listen for a minute but burst out in great rage at what he considered the enormity of my offense and asked if I realized that he could have me shot by drum-head court-martial in about fifteen minutes? Without waiting for my reply he went on, swaggering and towering in speech and behavior; said affairs had come to a pretty pass when a civilian could assume to pass through the lines of his army in broad daylight, and hold communication with the enemy; and he intended to make short shrift of all such work.

I had managed to say that I was exercising my rights and ingenuity as a correspondent, in the service of an employer, and was doing this legitimately.

"How do I know," said he, "but what you are a paid Confederate spy, carrying maps and drawings of all my fortifications to the enemy, daily?"

Feeling that he had some grounds for indignation in the outset, I had been very moderate and careful in speech; but this implication raised my temper, and I said: "Gen. Butler, fortunately for myself, my loyalty to my government stands high above all suspicion, which is more than can be said of many of our major-generals. I will not allow it to be questioned by you or any one else," &c., &c. Other hot tempered expressions followed, when he directed a file of soldiers to be brought to his tent door, presumably for my arrest and imprisonment.

I then exhibited my written authority from Gen. Grant, previously mentioned, ordering "all guards, and all picket guards, in all the armies of the United States, to pass me by day or night, with horses or vehicles"; and said to him that I would only submit to a forcible arrest; and if so arrested would leave Gen. Grant to vindicate his own authority.

After his first ebullition of anger Butler toned down considerably in speech, and tried to convince me of its impropriety. Without directly asking me to do so, he intimated that in view of all the circumstances if I would promise to do so no more, it would go far in mitigating my offense. I refused all compromises; stood on the written privilege accorded to me by Gen. Grant; and at the first lull in the conversation, saluted and started out, not knowing whether I would be permitted to go or not. No one stopped me. I mounted and returned to City Point.

Butler disliked me after that, but probably felt more angry at Gen. Grant. In our after intercourse, which was very stormy for a year or two, no allusion was ever made by either of us to this episode.[1]

---

[1] After the war, good relations between Butler and Cadwallader were restored and Butler evidently hoped for Cadwallader's support in furthering his political ambitions. On October 8, 1865 W. M. Merriam wrote to Butler from Richmond: ". . . I hear with profound pleasure that Mr. Cadwallader has done himself the honor and credit of meeting you, I trust that he will remain sound to our cause for he has both great talents and wide influence. With the *Herald* he is potent, and with his aid or rather countenance I can do so much more for the common good of the Butlerian equation, never absent from my mind or heart. . . ." Butler Papers, Library of Congress.

During the battle for the possession of Ream's Station,[2] Lieut. Charles S. Sholes, of the 36th Wisconsin regiment, was taken prisoner, with hundreds of others, and conveyed to Andersonville prison. I had known him from boyhood and his father, C. Latham Sholes, had been my intimate friend for years. I was importuned to do all in my power to secure his release. His father sent me one hundred dollars in gold, to send to him, if an opportunity offered, to relieve the distress of his prison life.

There was no difficulty in doing this so far as our regulations and authority extended, for flags of truce were frequently interchanged. I commenced by transmitting an installment of twenty dollars gold coin, then some greenbacks, and at last a large sum in Confederate money, none of which ever reached him. I also tried to send him a supply of clothing, with no better success; but during the winter of 1864-5, I did manage to get him returned to our commissioner of exchange, Gen. John E. Mulford, who telegraphed about noon one day that Sholes had been delivered to him between the lines on the James river, and that he would start down the river with exchanged prisoners before night.

I took a government tug and steamed up stream till I met the exchange boat, New York. As I rounded alongside, the first person I saw was Sholes, standing at the gangway on the lower deck, fat, sleek and jolly-visaged, clad in a tattered cotton shirt, a pair of tow-linen pants with the legs torn off half way from the knees to the ankles, and the crown of an old straw hat. He had been detailed as cook for a mess of prisoners, and had looked out for his own share of the rations.

---

[2] Actions occurred at Ream's Station on June 22, June 29, July 12, and August 25, 1864.

Before reaching City Point I supplied him with money, and soon heard of his safe arrival at his home in Milwaukee.

These negotiations and conferences with Gen. Mulford for the release of Sholes commenced an acquaintance with him which ripened into intimacy and gave me an insight into the matter of exchange which I had hitherto lacked. Exchanges had been substantially stopped for many months on various pretexts; but the underlying reason for it was the belief among federal officials that the Confederates were receiving all the benefits of the system. They returned to us sick, half-starved, emaciated, dying men, a large proportion of whom did die on the way home, and the residue were so broken down as to almost never be fit for further service; whilst we returned to them healthy, well-fed men, most of whom could be sent directly to their regiments. It was also believed that Confederate conscriptions had about exhausted all the men in the south, and if we held on to these prisoners the rebel army would be permanently reduced to that extent. This last condition did not apply to the north, for it was still possible to fill every draft, and meet every requirement of our government, by a liberal system of bounties. It was quietly argued that the war could be sooner ended, by refusing further exchanges; and that the loss of life in southern prisons, would be far less than by future battles, if exchanging continued.

It was a peculiar feature of the times and state of opinion, that so far as my observation extended, officers divided on this subject again, as on many other questions, upon the line of West Point and Volunteer military education. I do not remember ever hearing a West Point graduate openly advocate a free exchange of prisoners. Many maintained an ominous silence, and a few openly opposed it. Officers and men in the volunteer service, were a unit for exchange.

It soon became known at headquarters that I was uncompromisingly in favor of exchanging as fast as equivalents could be received and delivered, at all hazards, upon any and all terms ever proposed; and favored the policy of yielding many minor details which had hitherto been given as excuses for not doing so, and of giving two or three men for one, if it could not otherwise be accomplished. My indignation rose to fever heat at the heart-breaking delays which lasted month after month, and I was by no means careful in expressing my feelings. . . .

Gen. Mulford was an ardent friend of exchange, and in the absence of many sympathizers at Gen. Grant's headquarters, was naturally drawn closer to me. His trips to the front, near Richmond, to meet Col. Robert Ould, the Confederate commissioner of exchanges, were frequent, and he rarely passed up or down the river without spending some time with me. Col. Ould was urgent and clamorous for exchanging; and would request Mulford to meet him again and again to see if some agreement could not be reached fairly satisfactory to both sides, if not entirely equitable and just. It is due to him to say that he went fully to the extent of his authority in that direction, and I have no doubt often transcended it. But so far as I know his agreements with Mulford were always carried out by his government.

From one of these trips to meet Ould, Mulford returned greatly depressed. He said our government had given him no authority to exchange another man, nor any reasons which he could communicate to Ould, for not exchanging. He said Ould had made so many offers which he was obliged to refuse for lack of instructions, that he was discouraged and humiliated. He said "our government don't want to exchange another man till the war ends; but I dare not say so to Col.

Ould. Secretary Stanton will never, in my opinion, exchange another soldier unless driven into it by superior authority. I am ashamed of the paltry excuses I am obliged to make."

He reported Col. Ould as saying: "My government instructs me to waive all formalities, and what it considers some of the equities, in this matter of exchange. I need not try to conceal from you that we cannot feed and provide for the prisoners in our hands. We cannot half feed or clothe them. You have closed our ports till we cannot get medical stores for them. You will not send us quinine, and other needed medicines, even for their exclusive use. They are suffering greatly and the mortality is excessive. I tell you all this plainly, and still you refuse to exchange. What does your government demand? Name your own conditions and I will show you my authority to accept them. You are silent! Great God!, can it be that your people are monsters? If you will not exchange, I will give you your men for nothing. I will deliver ten thousand Union prisoners at Wilmington any day that you will receive them. I will deliver five thousand here on the same terms. Come and get them. If your government is so damnably dishonest as to want them for nothing, you shall have them. You can at least feed them, and we cannot. You can give us what you please in return for them."

Mulford represented Col. Ould as being especially stormy at many of these interviews; but his wrath was leveled at the federal government. The personal relations of the two commissioners were not seriously disturbed at any time. Ould was usually cold and self-possessed in manners, but always courteous to Mulford. I am sure Gen. Mulford's account of these interviews was correct, for I had it corroborated in many ways afterwards. Ould repeated to me the substance of his communications to Mulford (after the war) in almost the identical language used by Mulford.

Of course such offers as these could no longer be disregarded, and tardy exchanging began in the winter and spring of 1864–5. The George Leary, Ocean Wave, New York, and perhaps other steamers, were used on the James river in February, 1865, to receive and transport our men north.

Nothing in the foregoing is intended to (or can possibly) excuse the bad treatment which thousands of Union prisoners received. Nor is it possible to overstate the sufferings of those men, nor their miserable pitiable condition when exchanges delivered them to us. . . .

I do not know, (or think) that Gen. Grant always favored a liberal system of exchanges. The matter was often discussed in his presence, on purpose to draw him out, but always failed to do so, in any public manner. He had a habit of sitting and smoking quietly under such circumstances, and rather encouraging the discussion that otherwise, by an occasional smile and a twinkle of the eye peculiarly his own, when pleased or interested; but without saying a word for an hour, that could be absolutely construed into assent or dissent. I always believed him to be indifferent, since he could easily have changed governmental action by taking positive grounds in favor of exchange. At a later period, when he realized the frenzied state of public opinion in the north, he trimmed his sails to the popular breeze. . . .

During the last campaign in the Shenandoah Valley under Gen. Sheridan I made several flying visits to that locality to locate correspondents, and provide for a better transmission of their dispatches. My last one was between the 15th and 20th of November, 1864. I made a short visit to New York for a conference with Mr. Bennett and Mr. Hudson. On the evening of November 19th the whole city was electrified by the news that Gen. Grant would arrive on the evening train. He had slipped away from the army for a few days to visit his family at Burlington, New Jersey, where his boys were at school, and came on to New York with his wife and children, accompanied by a single staff officer, hoping to be unannounced and unknown, and to enjoy the privileges of a humble citizen. But he was thwarted at every step. The news of his coming preceded him several hours. The Astor House had private carriages and policemen at the ferry landing, who whisked him speedily from there to his room in the hotel, but crowds jammed the corridors and entrances to the house, and finally forced their way to his presence.

Reuben E. Fenton, governor-elect of New York; Lieut. Gov. [William] Bross, elect of Illinois; ex-Lieutenant-Governor [Butler G.] Noble, of Wisconsin; Gen. Dan. E. Sickles; Lieut. [William Barker] Cushing, of Albemarle fame; [3] and many other notables were stopping there. It devolved on me to present most of them to Gen. Grant, for the first time.

The dining room of the immense hostelry was cleared for speech making and serenading at night, and when Gen. Grant and Governor Fenton entered, locked arm, no one ever witnessed more excitement and enthusiasm. Men and women mounted chairs and tables, and cheers and huzzahs were kept up at intervals the whole evening, to the great interruption of speakers and the orderly program prepared. It was all Grant, all the time.

---

[3] On the night of October 27, 1864 Cushing ascended the Roanoke River in a steam launch with a volunteer crew and rammed and torpedoed the Confederate ironclad *Albemarle;* then escaped by swimming downstream.

By the general's request I stopped all mention of his being there in the different papers (I think none of them mentioned it); or from being telegraphed abroad, till the second morning afterwards, so the enemy might not attempt to take advantage of his absence from the front. He returned with his family to Burlington, Monday, November 21st. The staff officer who came with Grant was given a short furlough, and I took his place. I left Grant with his family at Burlington on the evening of the 21st, and rode on to Philadelphia, where I was to await the General's arrival next morning, for breakfast, at the Continental Hotel.

By some management the public was kept from knowing the train by which he would come. This success emboldened him somewhat. After breakfast he donned an old, faded blue army overcoat which completely hid all insignia of rank, and we sauntered from the private entrance of the hotel and strolled through a few streets without attracting attention. He was finally recognized by some one, and beset in a few minutes by a crowd that became impenetrable. People came running by hundreds from all directions, shouting, "Gen. Grant; Gen. Grant," at the top of their lungs. Policemen crowded into his presence for his protection by dozens, but still the mass increased.

A carriage was procured, into which Grant and myself were thrust, and an attempt made to force a way through the street. The effort was futile. The carriage windows were shivered into fragments by the good-natured throngs which surrounded it, that all might at least have a chance to see him. The situation became so serious that we were at length drawn out of the carriage and by the aid of a strong cordon of policemen, hustled through an office, out of that through a back way into an alley, and from there driven hurriedly to the Continental hotel. But the hundreds and thousands by this time assembled reached the hotel nearly as soon as we did, filled the lobbies and hallways as densely as they could be crammed, and were with great difficulty prevented from ascending the stairs and carrying him to the street on their shoulders.

He came to the head of the stairs, bowed his acknowledgments, and retreated in great haste by the back stairs to a court yard where a carriage was waiting, and escaped across the Schuylkill river to where a special train stood waiting to carry him to Washington City. This pulled out before the crowd could reassemble there, and we obtained a breathing spell. The spectacle on Chestnut street was ludicrous, embarrassing, awful; and at times the presence of the crowd became actually dangerous.

Soon after starting from Philadelphia we were served with an elegant dinner in the palace dining car, and reached the capital at 7:00 p.m. on the 22d, and drove to Willard's without interruption. The next day we started for City Point on the general's private dispatch boat.

Early in the evening of the night spent at Willard's Hotel, I missed the general from the crowd in the public reception or sitting room assigned him, and commenced an instant search to learn where he had gone. I soon found him in the bar-room, surrounded by many old army friends and West Point acquaintances. Wine was passing freely, and I was greatly alarmed. At the first chance afforded me without attracting too much attention, I took him by the arm, said that our time was up, that we had some engagements to keep, that our carriage was waiting for us, and quietly walked him out of the room and away from his associates without provoking any comment. The crowd insisted on another bottle of champagne at parting, but I got him away without it.

On the way to City Point, a card-party was arranged for the night. I only remember Grant and Ingalls as seated at the table, but towards midnight, a basket of champagne was opened, and I expected some bad results to follow.

The general had come before this, to recognize my authority to act in such cases, and my presence kept him in the bounds of reasonable restraint. I could not always prevent his taking a glass of wine; but I could, and did, always prevent much excess. He never resented my interference, after my first experience with him on the Yazoo River; but would leave a room-full of his old cronies and go with me whenever he thought I considered him in danger. I may have mentioned before this that on going to the Army of the Potomac, he was scarcely ever allowed to leave headquarters on a trip to Washington, or elsewhere, without Rawlins, Bowers or myself accompanying him, for the reason that we were the only persons whose control he would recognize or permit.

In December 1864, preparations began for the first expedition against Fort Fisher. It lay within the territorial limits of Gen. Butler's command, and he was therefore entitled to the privilege of fitting it out, and personally directing and superintending all its operations from start to finish, unless otherwise specifically ordered by Gen. Grant or the Department of War. Gen. Grant always said he had no intention of intrusting the matter to Gen. Butler, and that he supposed his order to the latter to send Gen. Weitzel to do that work was sufficient. Butler thought differently, and did not think himself forbidden to go with the troops sent for the reduction of the place. Unfortunately for all, as it turned out, Butler did go, assumed command of all the land forces sent there, failed ignominiously in the undertaking, and laid the foundation for much acrimonius correspondence and recrimination, which ended in his removal from the command of the Army of the James on January 8th, 1865. . . .

When detailed reports of all the operations at Fort Fisher, under Butler, first came to hand, Grant determined to have him removed. Some letters and telegrams were interchanged between City Point and Washington, in which Grant sought to have the removal made by the president or secretary of war. It ended in his receiving authority to remove him if in his opinion the good of the service demanded it. . . .

When this last dispatch was received from Washington, Gen. Rawlins repeated it to me, but cautioned me against saying anything about it, till Grant spoke of it himself. I met him several times in the afternoon but he said nothing of what was uppermost in my mind. After supper he came into the Adjutant's tent and lighted his cigar. While doing so he looked me in the face quizzically and remarked that one of my friends had come to grief. I expressed my regrets of course, but inquired who it was. He answered: "Gen. Butler." I wanted to know what had befallen my friend Butler, and was told that the president had removed him from command. I said interrogatively: "The president has removed him?" He replied: "He has authorized me to remove him." I then said: "That is a different matter." Grant said it would make no difference so far as Butler was concerned; and that the order of removal was already written.

This was on Saturday evening, and it was decided to wait till morning to dispatch a staff officer to Butler conveying the order for his removal. Sunday mornings are lazy ones with army officers as well as other mortals. Col. Horace Porter, who was to serve the order on Butler, had a late breakfast; the men on the boat which was to take him to Aiken's Landing were slow in getting up steam and starting; and it was just twelve o'clock, noon, of Sunday, January 8th, the anniversary of Gen. Jackson's victory at New Orleans, when Col. Porter delivered the order to Gen. Butler.

Without thought as to possible delays, and the importance that subsequently attached itself to the question of an hour or two in time, I sent a dispatch to the New York *Herald* by ten o'clock forenoon mail boat from City Point, announcing Butler's removal from command of the Army of the James, as follows: "The news of the President's order, No. 1, series of 1865, removing Major General Benjamin F. Butler from the command of the Department of Virginia and North Carolina, is causing much comment; but so far as I can learn little or no animadversion. Whether rightfully or not, Gen. Butler has for months past been losing the confidence of the officers of the army, until very few will regret his departure outside of those who swarm around, and attach themselves to those in power. It has been Gen. Butler's misfortune to appoint too many of these selfish and irresponsible persons to official positions of trust and responsibility. The ostensible grounds for depriving him of command are undoubtedly his recent fiascos of Wilmington and Dutch Gap," etc. It was a very short dispatch, intended mainly to state a consummated fact. It would have been much longer had I not supposed his removal would be telegraphed to every hamlet in the north one or two days before it could appear in the *Herald*. Mr. Stanton refused to allow the fact to be telegraphed from Washington until the *Herald* reached that city containing my dispatch.

The sporting fraternity of several cities staked thousands of dollars on the truth or falsity of this small newspaper paragraph; some because it was not promulgated from the War Department, and others because of my known standing and facilities for obtaining information.

Gen. Butler soon seized on the facts. He found that I had not telegraphed it; that it must have been transmitted by mail or messenger; that it could not have reached the *Herald* in time for publication Tuesday morning, except by leaving on the Sunday forenoon mailboat; and that Gen. Grant must therefore have committed the military discourtesy of publishing it to the world at least two hours before the order was officially served on him at his own headquarters by Col. Porter.[4] The points were shrewdly and truly transmitted to the committee on the Conduct of the War . . . with a request that Gen. Grant and myself be summoned before it for examination.

I don't know that this disturbed anyone but myself. I dreaded this proposed examination for many reasons. I feared that I should be asked a string of questions upon this, as well as other equally important subjects, about which I could not state the facts without a breach of confidence. But summons were not immediately issued, and I was soon in a position to ward off danger from that quarter. . . .

When Gen. Butler was brought before the Committee on the Conduct of the War to testify in relation to the Wilmington and Fort Fisher affair he was a swift witness for himself, and against General Grant and Admiral Porter. He charged the former with great bitterness, with indecision, if not prevarication; and by indirection at least, accused him of keeping me at his headquarters, as his special correspondent. He kept repeating and reiterating the charge at every opportunity during his examination until the committee was in a measure, obliged to summon Gen. Grant to appear before it, to offer such defenses or explanations as he might deem necessary.

---

[4] For correspondence relating to this imbroglio, see *O. R.*, Series I, Vol. XLVI, pt. II, pp. 120, 186.

Admiral Porter came in for a large share of his censure, inter-
larded with contemptuous suggestions and innuendoes affecting his judgment and lack of personal courage. Butler's testimony was drawn out to a great length, and was filled with
sarcasm and incrimination of others from beginning to end.

Among other things he said that he (Butler) had appointed
"Cadwallader a Second Lieutenant of the 2d United States
Volunteers, to save him from the liability of being drafted,"
by Gen. Grant's request as he supposed, and as communicated
to him (Butler) by me (Cadwallader).

There was one small element of truth in this, purposely intended by Butler to cover much extended falsehood, for he
knew the falsity of all his allegations. Gen. Grant never asked
Butler, or anyone else, to appoint me to this, or any other position, from the beginning of our acquaintance, to the day of his
death. I never asked Gen. Grant for this, or any other appointment, during the war. On the contrary I was invited by Gen.
Grant to accept more than one honorable appointment which
other engagements prevented my accepting.

The single streak of truth in Butler's statement was, that in
the fall of 1864, without any solicitation from me, or from
any of my friends, he did give me an appointment by the
following order:

Headquarters Department of Virginia and North Carolina.
Army of the James.
In the Field, October 7th 1864.
Special Orders, No. 278.
Extract.
*3. The following appointments are hereby made in the 2d
Regiment, United States Volunteers, subject to the approval
of the President of the United States.*

Sylvanus Cadwallader to be Second Lieutenant.
He will report for duty at these Headquarters. . . .

By command of Major General Butler.
Ed. W. Smith,
Asst. Adjt. Gen'l.

Inclosed with the appointment was the following in Gen. Butler's own handwriting: *Lieutenant Colonel Smith. Let Lieutenant's Commission be made in the 2d U. S. Volunteers for Mr. Cadwallader. He will be unattached for the present.*
B. F. B.

I never knew the reasons, or circumstances, which induced this appointment, although I made many inquiries concerning it. My own participation in it was this: I received a letter from Col. J. Wilson Schaffer [Shaffer], Gen. Butler's chief-of-staff, inclosing a closely sealed letter addressed to Gen. Butler, which he requested me to deliver in person. Supposing it to be in relation to some matter which Gen. Butler wished to question me about, I did so deliver it. Butler read it through and handed me my appointment. It surprised me very much. He would give no names, nor explanations, and never did afterward. I thanked him for the compliment; but spoke of my engagements to the *Herald* and the difficulties in the way of my entering the service—and especially at that late date, in the history of the rebellion. He may have thought that I hesitated because I was ordered to report to him for duty, and said if I preferred it, he would order me to report to Gen. Grant for assignment. This was probably because I had told him that the place of Quartermaster at Grant's headquarters had been offered me, and still remained open for me, if I chose to accept it. We parted on good terms, apparently, without my having positively refused his appointment.

I always thought Gen. Butler's object in giving me this commission was a selfish one, and two-fold in what he hoped to accomplish by it. My position on the *Herald* gave me many opportunities for unfavorable criticism on him as an officer. He knew I lacked but little of being openly hostile to him. He also knew that I had the confidence and esteem of Gen. Grant and staff. He intended this mark of his favor to at least partly silence my dreaded strictures; and perhaps hoped it would be viewed by Gen. Grant as a gracious, friendly act to one who had sustained such intimate relations at his headquarters in all his chief commands. He also felt the coils tightening around himself, and suspected that Gen. Grant was only awaiting a suitable time and excuse for his removal. These are the only reasons which I could ever think of, for his giving me this appointment.

But he overlooked, or was ignorant of, important facts. As said before, the Quartermaster's place at headquarters was held subject to my approval for several weeks, if not months. I had one or two other positions offered me of honor and profit. A place on Gen. Hancock's staff, with rank above my expectations was tendered me. At the time of this Butler appointment I was exempt from draft. So there was no reason why I should have made any such request as he alleges I did make. . . .

When Gen. Grant was brought before the same committee, he emphatically denied every charge made by Butler against me, as well as those against himself in that connection. To the question as to whether he had requested my military appointment, he replied: "Never." He was then asked: "Do you know anything about his appointment?" He answered: "I do not know anything about it except what I have since heard from Cadwallader himself." This ended the examination of Gen. Grant, so far as I was interested. . . .[5]

---

[5] After Butler's removal, Cadwallader began collecting instances of his arbitrary and unlawful acts while commanding the Army of the James, with the idea of using them if Butler should attempt to persecute him.

CHAPTER

Nineteen

. . . On Christmas eve, 1864, I was restless, discontented and homesick. On going to my tent about ten o'clock p.m., I sat for an hour brooding over the pleasures of past anniversaries, and the gloominess of the present. Filling my pocket with cigars I walked to the Adjutant's tent, where a light was still burning, and found Col. Bowers stretched out in a large camp-chair in front of the fire, and wearing a subdued, downcast countenance. To my inquiries as to what was the matter, he replied that he had been thinking of his mother, his home, and the difference between his present cheerless surroundings, and those of happier times.

We had chatted but a few minutes when Gen. Rawlins entered and wanted to know if we had not heard the bugle blow "taps," and "lights out," and whether he should be obliged to put us under arrest for such flagrant violation of army regulations? We turned the tables on him by inquiring why he was wandering about camp at that time of night? He made his excuses similar to those of Col. Bowers. Within five minutes we heard the tread of some one else approaching, and Gen. Grant walked in. We all greeted him with a burst of laughter, and requested honest confession. He went over the same string of sentimental expressions. But conversation soon took a wide and pleasant range, and we talked for more than an hour about everything uppermost in our minds, excepting war; and until all my cigars had been consumed.

Asking us to keep our seats a few minutes, Grant went to his tent and returned with an unopened box of large, excellent cigars which some one had just sent him from New York. We smoked one or two, each, from this box, when it was agreed that we ought to be in bed. The general insisted on our taking one more smoke before breaking up. Instead of lighting mine I put it in my pocket, and said I would smoke it the next Christmas Eve in memory of that one. I had to take another, however, and smoke then.

One year from that night we were all in Washington City. Remembering my promise I drove out to Gen. Grant's home, and timed my arrival so exactly that I met him in the hall, on his way from the dining-room to the library. I was ushered into the latter, where the general commenced pushing papers about on the table, set cigars and matches within reach, and invited me to take a cigar. I pulled one slowly and deliberately out of my pocket as if to light it.

He stared at me a moment and asked me if I was afraid of the quality of his. I replied by asking if he remembered where we were one year ago that night. "Yes, at City Point." "Don't you remember that I pocketed one of your cigars then, promising to smoke it *in memoriam?*" A smile lighted up his face. "Yes, but you have not saved that cigar till now?" "This is the identical cigar, general, and I am here to fulfill my promise." "Oh well, if you have kept it so long, smoke out of the box tonight, and save it another year." I complied, saved it another

year, and all the succeeding years, from that to this. It lays in
my house, safely incased in glass, a sentimental reminder of
those days so long past, and where I hope it will continue to
lie, till I too have joined "the bivouac of the dead." Bowers,
Rawlins and Grant have gone to "fame's eternal camping
ground."

The months of January, February and March were devoid
of much public interest till towards the close of the latter when
a few exciting things took place. Generals Grant and Rawlins
sent for their wives to spend a few weeks at City Point, and I
thereupon sent for mine to visit me at the same time. They all
arrived early in January, and passed an enjoyable time till a
start was made on our final campaign against Gen. Lee the
last of March. Mrs. Grant went on the headquarter boat,
anchored in the river, and remained there a week or two
longer. But having no gunboats or iron clads for my wife's
protection, I started her home the day before we broke camp
at City Point. . . .

During the last six months of the war, Mr. Lincoln and
family made several short visits to City Point on a small steamboat, the River Queen, which he was in the habit of taking for
such purposes. On one of these visits, their youngest son,
familiarly called "Tad," came with them. The boat always anchored out in the river, and Mrs. Lincoln rarely came ashore.
But the President, and "Tad," landed in a tug regularly every
morning, soon after breakfast.

Mr. Lincoln would go directly to the Adjutant's Office to
hear all the news from the front which had been received during the night; and would often have long conferences with
Gen. Grant and others concerning prospective operations.
When these subjects had been exhausted the chat would take
another turn, and Mr. Lincoln's propensity for story telling

would be given free-play, and be encouraged to the utmost. His faculty in this way was absolutely marvelous. It has never been exaggerated, and never can be. He abounded in apt illustrations, and his stories were side-splitting. He would occasionally join as heartily as any one else in the laughter his stories provoked; and enjoyed these seasons of relaxations in a way that was charming to all who were present.

Mrs. Lincoln seemed insanely jealous of every person, and everything, which drew him away from her and monopolized his attention for an hour. She would send "Tad" with a message to come to the boat, nearly every day. At one time "Tad" found his father enjoying himself in animated conversation, and a little oblivious it may have been to his wife's message. "Tad" went back to the boat but soon returned with a more urgent command, which he kept repeating loud enough for all to hear. He finally burst out: "Come, come, come now, mama says you must come instantly." Mr. Lincoln's countenance fell from unconstrained good-humor and gayety, to the sober, careworn, lugubrious expression so common to him in those days. After a moment's silence he rose, saying: "My God, will that woman never understand me"; and departed meekly, and sadly, convoyed by "Tad."

On another occasion—the first one of her visits after Mrs. Grant's arrival in January—Mrs. Grant, Mrs. Rawlins and Mrs. Cadwallader had a conference as to the propriety of their making a joint call on her aboard the River Queen anchored in the river. It was finally decided that as none of them had ever met her, and in view of the exalted opinions she was known to hold as to what was due to her as wife of the president of the United States, it might be better for Mrs. Grant to make her first call a very formal and semi-official one. She would go as the wife of the Lieut. Gen., and present her respects to the wife of the President. This would be a safe and warranted procedure, and the after presentation of the other two, should be left to Mrs. Lincoln's wishes.

Mrs. Grant accordingly made what I suspect to have been as near a "state call," as any in her life. She was received coldly, rather haughtily, and in a manner and spirit which convinced her that Mrs. Lincoln felt it a condescension to receive her. Mrs. Grant returned displeased. It was her first and only call on the Lady of the White House, so far as I ever knew. Mrs. Rawlins and Mrs. Cadwallader never ran the risk of being snubbed, and kept away.

But during that visit Gen. Ord had a grand review of the Army of the James, and some of the staff found an old Virginia carriage and harness, in which they gallantly escorted Mrs. Lincoln, Mrs. Grant, Mrs. Rawlins and Mrs. Cadwallader to the review ground, that they might see the grandeur of a great army. The four women were thus thrown together perforce.

Nothing unusual occurred until they arrived on the ground. By some means, Mrs. Gen. [Charles] Griffin (*nee* Carroll, of the famous "Charles Carroll, of Carrolton [Carrollton]" family) obtained permission to come from Washington to see the review. She was an accomplished equestrienne; was handsomely mounted and dressed; and being the only woman on the field, so mounted, was invited by Mr. Lincoln to ride at his side.

As soon as Mrs. Lincoln came in sight of them she burst out with all manner of violent imprecations—wanted to know "what good-for-nothing hussy that was riding by the president's side, and trying to make the people believe that she was Mrs. Lincoln." She could neither be quieted nor restrained, and her conduct was so shameful that the other ladies in the carriage would have left it and walked to City Point, had it been possible, rather than remain longer in her company. . . .[1]

A year or two after Mr. Lincoln's death Col. Geo. Senter of Cleveland, Ohio, a member of the Republican National Executive Committee for the campaign of 1864 (and probably its chairman) [2] told me that he was compelled by official position to tender the hospitalities of his house and home to Mrs. Lincoln, when she once visited his city. His whole establishment was placed at her disposal as long as she remained. She gave parties and suppers, invited who she pleased, and entertained them at his expense. Throughout her stay, from first to last, she exacted everything as her right, and never expressed the slightest gratitude for these favors. . . . Col. Senter was clearly of the opinion that she was then insane. All these opinions and suspicions were verified in the last year or two of her life. No woman ever lived with grander opportunities for gaining the undying affection of the American people; yet she died "unwept, unhonored and unsung." Her mental infirmity was not sufficiently known, to draw out the pity, and the charity, of the Nation. . . .

Mrs. Grant brought with her on this visit to City Point their youngest child, a sober seven year old little gentleman in knicker-bockers, named Jesse, for his paternal grandfather Grant. He made daily visits to Mrs. Cadwallader to listen to "bible-stories" she was in the habit of relating to him. When she once was speaking of God, he asked who God was. She tried to answer the question in words adapted to childish

---

[1] For an account of this incident which is more sympathetic to Mrs. Lincoln, see Ruth Painter Randall: *Mary Lincoln, Biography of a Marriage* (New York, 1953), pp. 372–4.

[2] George B. Senter was an alternate delegate to the National Republican Convention of 1864 and was appointed a member of the National Committee at that convention.

comprehension. After a little silence he said with the open eyed, wondering look of innocent childhood: "Well, I guess my mother and God are older than anybody!" I hope his childish faith as to God, and his love for his mother, have never forsaken him.

In the after part of the night of January 24th, a little episode broke the quiet at headquarters. In consequence of the known absence of Admiral Porter's fleet at Wilmington, the rebels concluded to make a naval demonstration on the Upper James. Arrangements were also made to make a formidable attack by land, if the Confederate iron clads accomplished enough to warrant it. We received, through deserters, sufficient information to put us on the alert. Three rebel iron clads, resembling our Atlanta in size and appearance, dropped down from their anchorage just below Fort Darling, succeeded in running past Fort Brady uninjured in the darkness and fog, and at three o'clock in the morning, were reported lying under cover of their fortifications at Howlett's below the upper end of Dutch Gap, and were busily engaged in removing the obstructions we had placed in the channel between there and Aiken's Landing. They came prepared with torpedoes to blow up all our sunken hulks, and did destroy one of them about daylight. One rebel gunboat got past by the assistance of lighters, and acted as a cover to their working parties which were trying to clear the channel.

Comparatively few guns could be brought upon them from the north bank of the James, but Gen. Ferrero's [3] negro troops on the south side of the river engaged them furiously. At nine o'clock A.M. Ferrero reported that his guns at Fort Parsons had exploded and sunk one of the enemy's iron clads and had

---

[3] Edward Ferrero commanded the colored division of the 9th corps.

disabled another. The two remaining vessels—there being four of them instead of three as first reported—appeared to be aground, considerably upstream from where he was in position. The shots from his batteries struck them fairly at every discharge, but seemed to be shed off without much damage. They remained there all day, floated off on the high tide, and returned to their old moorings.

Great astonishment prevailed, and much dissatisfaction was expressed, at the impotent conduct of our double-turreted monitor Onondaga, the only Union iron clad in that vicinity. Instead of resisting the enemy's advance she dropped down the river through our ponton bridge, and was not within gun shot of the rebels until a staff officer was sent aboard requesting her to cooperate with Gen. Ferrero in capturing the grounded rams. Her arrival was too late to be of any service. Her commander was soon retired.

The first report telegraphed to Washington created more alarm there than it did at City Point. The Navy Department was about to send Farragut to assume command when it received more assuring dispatches.

The sound of heavy artillery came thundering down the river not long after midnight, and soon after telegrams were received giving an account of the attack of the rebel rams and iron clads having passed all our shore batteries above Howlett's, and of their being engaged in blowing up and removing our sunken obstructions in the channel below Howlett's, which had been placed there in the summer as a protection against just such a descent as had been made upon us.

A staff officer was sent to every headquarter tent to waken the inmates and tell them of the situation. It was barely possible that the rebel fleet might force its way down as far as City Point, where if not promptly arrested or destroyed, immense destruction of property would inevitably ensue. The river was filled for a mile, with transports, sutlers' boats, and all manner of water craft. The masters of these vessels were ordered to be in readiness to drop down the river if safety should require it; but as a half day would be consumed by the rebel gunboats in getting to City Point, if there were no hindrances in the way, no haste nor hurry was enjoined on them. The land forces were also informed of the facts, and the troops were practically under arms and breakfasted by daylight.

Should the rebel gunboats approach near to City Point, it was intended to send all women, children, civilians, and noncombatants out of harm's way, down the river. It was curious to see the way in which this summons was received at the various tents in the night. The ladies and civilians were all more or less excited, and there was no more sleep for them that night. All who had seen service in this, or other campaigns, heard the announcement with apparent indifference. It was not wholly unexpected, and was considered in a matter of course sort of manner. Such officers as were not summoned to duty upbraided the messenger for disturbing them for nothing at that time in the night, and many of them returned to their cots for a "little more sleep, and a little more slumber," and remained there till called to breakfast. By nine o'clock in the morning all danger was past, if any had existed, and the question then was how to severely punish the bold marauders. This was ineffectually done, all must admit; but they were repulsed and driven back with the total loss of one vessel, serious damage to others, and a considerable loss in killed and wounded.

The Confederate loss of prestige was a heavy blow to that government. Admiral [Raphael] Semmes of great fame in the south, directed the movement, and his failure was a keen disappointment to the rebels. Some sailors escaped from the rebel boats on their way down, and many more on the return trip up the river, all bringing the same information.

Januaiy 31st 1865, some stir was created at headquarters, which extended all over the north, by the arrival of a Peace Commission, under a flag of truce, consisting of Alexander H. Stephens, vice-president of the Southern Confederacy; Judge [John A.] Campbell, Assistant Secretary of War; and R. M. T. Hunter, formerly United States Senator from Virginia, and then a member of the Confederate Senate. They arrived about night, and after a short interview with Gen. Grant, were quartered aboard the Mollie Martin, till the Washington authorities could be informed and instructions received as to what should be done with them.

On the second of February they were sent to Fortress Monroe, when Mr. Lincoln and Secretary Seward met them unofficially, but nothing resulted from the conference except Mr. Lincoln's declaration that the only terms of peace which the U.S. government would entertain for a moment, were: A recognition of the abolition of slavery by the Confederate government—an immediate laying down of its arms and cessation of hostilities; and a return to the Federal Union. These conditions the gentlemen were not prepared to accept, so they returned to Richmond in a few days.

Gen. Grant's magnanimity at Appomattox Court House to Lee's defeated, starving army, was foreshadowed at City Point by his treatment of these Peace Commissioners. They were given the best accommodations which could be provided; no guards were placed over them, or around them; no restraints prevented their wandering about as they pleased on shore though the day; no promises, nor paroles, of any kind,

were exacted from them; and they came freely to the general's
headquarters every day for conversations and conferences.

Gen. Grant mentions Mr. Stephens's immense overcoat,
which gave him the appearance of being much stouter than
he really was, tells an anecdote of Mr. Lincoln's repeated to
him by the President at their next meeting. He asked Grant
if he noticed Stephens's overcoat, and if he saw him take it off?
Grant replied that he did. Mr. Lincoln then said: "Well, didn't
you think it was the biggest shuck, and the littlest ear, that
ever you did see?" I would venture a hundred to one that Gen.
Grant did not report it exactly. It should have been "biggest
shuck and littlest nubbin." The word "ear," applied to corn,
was not common in the south nor with those of southern
descent, as was Mr. Lincoln. "Nubbin" was the word for a
dwarfed ear of corn, and was the word Mr. Lincoln used, I
suspect.

About the tenth of March, 1865, it was given out that the
Confederate Congress had finished all business brought before it, and was ready to adjourn. Jefferson Davis requested a
few days' delay, that he might prepare and transmit to it a
message on public affairs. It was generally believed, north and
south, that that Congress would never re-assemble—as it never
did—and that this message would be the last public one Mr.
Davis would ever transmit to any Congress, as it also proved
to be. Unusual interest was consequently manifested to hear
what the Confederate President should say on such an occasion. I took every precaution to secure early copies of it, and
to transmit them with the utmost dispatch for publication in
the *Herald*.

My plans worked well, but I could not get hold of the document in time for the Wednesday (March 15th) forenoon mail-

boat to Washington. All I could do was to send it by a special, fast dispatch boat to Fortress Monroe, and have the mailboat held there, till my dispatches arrived. This was done by Gen. Ingalls, at my request, and the mailboat reached Washington, March 16th (or 17th) a few hours behind time, but in ample time for my dispatches to be telegraphed from there to the *Herald* for publication March 18th. I also arranged with Capt. Blakeman, of the fast boat George Leary, to run from City Point to New York, and to deliver duplicate copies, with his own hands at the *Herald* counter. This last scheme was also successful, as the following letter from managing editor Fred. Hudson to me attests:

New York, March 18th, 1865.
  My Dear Sir:—Our arrangements are working splendidly. The George Leary came in about five o'clock in the afternoon, and Capt. Blakeman delivered the parcel in person. This morning we published Jeff. Davis' message exclusively. We received copy direct, and a telegram from Col. Whitely, that he also had received the Richmond Whig, from you. . . .
                                        Very truly yours
                                          Frederic Hudson.

The reader will probably inquire if all these arrangements did not cost a large sum of money; and if the cost was not far beyond the value of the dispatches? To this there is but one reply: The cost was indeed great, but in Mr. Bennett's opinion the character of the news justified the expense. The world depended on the *Herald* for the latest and fullest accounts from the seat of war. Its circulation became enormous.

Immediately after this I was requested by Mr. Hudson to send him the best statement I could obtain, of the comparative circulation of the *Herald* and other newspapers, in the Army of the Potomac, for publication, if it should prove to be a good advertising card. This led to the accumulation of a mass of information which may be interesting to all readers by throwing light on the spirit and history of those times.

In 1861 [1862] when the army lay in front of Yorktown under Gen. McClellan, a number of newsdealers were engaged in supplying daily papers. These were all sent from the offices of publication to Fortress Monroe, and thence conveyed by transient boats and government vessels, to Cheeseman's Landing, which was at that time the base of supplies in rear of the army. But government transports were soon found to be too slow and uncertain to be trusted where success depended on minutes. The rivalry was too keen between competitors to allow hours, or days, to slip away between shipments. So notwithstanding the facts that the roads were bad and obscure, the country swarming with bands of desperadoes, and every thicket an ambush, the fearless men having the matter in charge organized a line of wagons and pack-mules and transported their papers across the country to the flank of the army, in face of all these dangers and difficulties. At that time Messrs. [J.M.] Lamb, Bohn, Thayer, Kinney, and perhaps others, were in the business.

Several metropolitan, and not a few provincial, papers finding army orders for their respective sheets declining from day to day, adopted the plan of sending out special agents for the sale of their own publications. Among these was Mr. Kinney, who came charged with the heavy responsibility of bolstering up the waning fortunes of the New York *Tribune*. He struggled awhile with manfulness deserving a better fate. With the death of his agency was buried that paper's last hope of army circulation.

When the army lay in Maryland, beyond Frederick, pack-mules were again the mode of conveyance from the nearest railroad station. About the time of Sandy Hook being made the base, Clark and Hull established an army newspaper agency and followed the troops back to Aquia Creek. At this point Dan. O'Neill, of New York, and Gregory of Alexandria, came to the front. In addition to these, Mr. Jackson of Philadelphia, came as special agent for the *Inquirer* of that city.

Until Gen. Hooker assumed command permits had been granted to all unobjectionable applicants who desired to engage in the business. Rivalry naturally engendered ill-feeling. Complaints of sharp practice and abuse of privileges began to accumulate against some of the dealers. Mr. George Wilkes of the *Spirit of the Times,* who was there ostensibly as correspondent for his paper, used his personal influence with Gen. Hooker to such purpose that he secured the exclusive privilege of supplying the army with papers. He enjoyed this exclusive franchise, with the single exception of Stewart and Bro., special agents for the Washington *Chronicle,* which was understood to be the administration organ, and to maintain its footing by the direct interposition of the Secretary of War. Mr. Wilkes was believed, by those familiar with his business, to have made about ten thousand dollars, before the combination broke down his monopoly.

Previous to May 1863, all leading dailies had been sold in the army at ten cents per copy. In June the Provost Marshal General gave notice that the exclusive privilege of supplying the army with newspapers would be given to the highest bidder therefor, and solicited applications for the same. On June 13th the contract was awarded to J. M. Lamb, who agreed to supply the demand at the uniform rate of five cents per copy for each newspaper, and give fifty-three dollars and twenty cents per day for the privilege, payable monthly in advance. This bonus was paid by Mr. Lamb to the Medical Director of the Army of the Potomac, to be expended by him in procuring such delicacies for the sick as were not furnished by the government.

The concurrent testimony of all engaged in the business is that 1862 was the year of the greatest sales of army newspapers. Our soldiers were then a different and better class of men. No conscripts, no bounty-jumpers, and but few "shoulder hitters," were then in the service. All were intelligent intellectual reading patriots. Early in the war every soldier was a newspaper reader. At its close thousands could not read, and other thousands did not care to. In the outset the papers published nearest the seat of war was supposed to contain the latest war news. At a later period it was seen that enterprise annihilated time and space in the transmission of army news; and that the Washington and Baltimore papers, almost at the door of the army, were indebted to reprints from the New York papers for all that gave them value.

At Brandy Station the circulation of the Washington *Chronicle* ran up from almost nothing to fully five thousand daily, because it contained [more] one-day-later telegrams than any other. The *Herald* increased greatly because it had established a reputation for full reports, so accurate as to be well nigh official.

From that time on till the end of the war the discrepancy in the circulation of papers grew continually wider. By the last of March, 1865, the *Herald* had attained a circulation of eleven thousand every day in the army of the Potomac; the Washington *Chronicle* varied from a thousand to twelve hundred; the Philadelphia *Inquirer*, fifteen hundred; the *Staats-Zeitung*, two hundred; the Baltimore *American*, five hundred;

the New York *Tribune,* and New York *Times,* from one hundred to one hundred and fifty each; the New York *World,* about sixty; Harper's *Weekly,* two thousand; Leslie's, two thousand; New York *Ledger,* fifteen hundred; Waverly twelve hundred; Harper's Magazine six to eight hundred; Atlantic, one hundred and fifty to two hundred; Service Magazine, one hundred; and others smaller numbers. The *Herald* had established a complete supremacy. It was demanded everywhere, sold everywhere, read everywhere.

On arrival of the mailboat from Fortress Monroe bringing Washington and Baltimore mails and New York City papers, the newspaper stand situated at the foot of the hill, about one hundred yards from the wharf, became the prominent and animated feature of City Point. There all congregated who were masters of their own time. Sutlers from their tents, tradesmen from their places of business, staff officers from different headquarters, soldiers furloughed and on their way home, conscripts on their way to the front, officers on pleasure or duty, convalescents from hospitals, stevedores from the wharves, drivers from scores of teams, civilians and idlers, black and white, men from every rank and walk in life, assembled daily in quest of the latest papers, and elbowed, struggled, and jammed their way to the counter for fear they would be too late.

A curious feature of the scene was that as long as the supply of *Heralds* held out, every countenance wore an eager, expectant amiable expression. An observer would say that the world evidently went well with the whole crowd. Laughing, joking, and struggling, those in front would seize their papers and endeavor good-naturedly to give place to those in the rear. But the instant "No more *Heralds,*" is heard, smiles disappear, jokes are abandoned, faces elongate, the struggling becomes vicious, humanity is darkened, and as with Dickens' Jarndyce,[4] the wind becomes "due east."

But observe the blandishments of the salesmen: "Plenty of *Inquirers* and *Chronicles*—have a *Times* or a *Tribune,* just as good." Blankety-blank the *Times* and *Tribune,* was the certain rejoinder, as the angry men would push and punch their way out of the crowd. When the announcement fairly spread that the *Heralds* were all sold, the struggling was at an end, muscles relaxed, sales fell off, and salesmen had time to breathe. Then such as could neither buy, beg nor borrow a *Herald,* nor get a chance to read it over some one's shoulder, might return to the stand, hand out a nickel, and take whatever was thrust in their hand without so much as looking at it. . . .

The activity at the City Point newsstand had counterparts elsewhere. Mr. Lamb was obliged to avail himself of the intermediate agency of Henry Taylor of Baltimore, to have his packages put up on the trains before their arrival at the latter city, and then conveyed quickly to the steamboat for Fortress Monroe, and to employ many subordinates who took the business of supplying particular divisions off his hands.

Before the railroad was built around the rear of our lines the papers were carried out by boys on mules. It was a ludicrous sight to see them seize their respective bundles of papers, mount in hot haste and set off to the front, whipping and spurring, whooping and yelling, like a legion of imps in infernal hurdle-chase. When the roads were dusty they made a formidable cavalcade. Unable to see ten feet ahead of their mules they nevertheless urged them to the top of their speed, and rode down all obstructions. Wise people gave them a wide roadway, and fools paid dearly for the folly of not clearing the track when they approached.

---

[4] The allusion is to a character in *Bleak House.*

Arriving at the outskirts of camp the boys would soon be surrounded by officers and privates, and hundreds of bronzed, weather-beaten veterans could be seen sitting on stumps and logs, studying *Herald* war maps, discussing the "military situation," and forgetting for the time, cold and hunger, home and friends, war and its realities.

Some deep-lunged comrade was generally selected to read aloud, and few more picturesque groups were ever found than these brawny, stalwart fellows, standing, lounging and reclining in all attitudes with upturned faces and breathless interest. Perhaps it was an account of Schofield's gallant stand at Franklin—or Thomas' destruction of Hood at Nashville—or Sherman's march to the sea—or Wilson sweeping like a besom of vengeance through the south, defeating, capturing and annihilating everything in his course. Shouting, huzzahing and patriotic sing-song followed till the echoes were waked for a mile. The sickly convalescent would be transfigured; the lazy man of the squad stretched on the ground would come to a half erect position; a wiry little fellow would spring to his feet like the click of a jack-knife; the jolly fellow standing on a pine-knot, looking over the reader's shoulder; the abstracted man of the crowd who had been trying to balance an old tobacco quid on the point of a minnie ball; all would break into fresh roars, till neighboring regiments caught the infection, and answered cheer for cheer.

Or, perhaps the papers were received after dark and read by the lights of hundreds of campfires, the lurid flames of which brought into plain view the faces of all, outlined their forms in the shadowy darkness, and furnished a picture that would have delighted a modern Rembrandt, with its rich coloring, sombre background, and its infinite suggestion of farm and forest, plains, woodlands, and mountains. . . .

March 27th, Gen. Sherman arrived at City Point for a conference with Gen. Grant, and found the President there also.
His march from Atlanta to Savannah, and subsequent progress northward, had made him the favorite of the hour, and
every one was glad to meet him. I cannot better describe his
visit perhaps than I did to Mr. A. D. Richardson in the winter
of 1867–8, for use in his Personal history of U. S. Grant, pages
455–7: "Several general officers met him at the wharf and escorted him to headquarters where many more awaited him.
'How are you Grant?' 'How are you Sherman,' with cheery
smiles on the face of each, comprised about all formal salutations. Sherman said: 'I didn't expect to find all you fellows
here. You don't travel as fast as we do.'

"No time was spent in compliments. Sherman sat down in
Grant's stockade cabin with the general and his staff, and
asked for a map. He was given to poring over maps. . . . A
large one was brought, and Sherman began to point out what
he proposed to do. His plan was to bring his army up to
Weldon, where it would be within supporting distance and
could either join Grant, or go west to Burke's Station to intercept Lee. When Sherman was through Grant said: 'Well Sherman, I am going to move up to Dinwiddie on the 29th, and
think that will force Lee out of his lines to give me battle there,
which will be all I want; or so weaken his lines that I can
attack him.'

"'A big banter! A big banter,' said Sherman, 'but we *can*
make things perfectly sure.'

"'Well," said Grant, 'if we don't succeed here, probably I
can keep him from drawing back till you come up.'

"Sherman remained two days. Grant's fear was that Lee
might escape and join Johnston. He was anxious that the army
of the Potomac, which had fought so many battles for such

slight compensations, should win a final triumph. To every suggestion from Sherman, or others, that the western army should be brought to cooperate in defeating Lee, he invariably replied, in substance as follows: 'No. Some western men, or commands, would taunt this army with: "We had to come to your assistance before you could whip Lee, or end the war." It will be better for the future peace of the country that the Army of the Potomac should finish the job.' Mr. Lincoln, who at first favored Sherman's joining Grant, was greatly impressed by the latter's reasoning, and heartily approved it."

C H A P T E R

Twenty

BEFORE it was fairly light on the morning of March 29th 1865, Meade, Ord and Sheridan had all broken camp, and the army was once more in motion. Sheridan's cavalry, nine thousand strong reached Dinwiddie before dark, and camped for the night. On the morning of the 31st he held Five Forks, but was obliged to fall back temporarily.

After breakfast on the 29th, Grant and most of the staff left for the front, distant about twenty miles. I remained behind till the middle of the afternoon, and then accompanied by George Alfred Townsend ("Gath") rode to Gen. Meade's headquarters for the night. On the 30th, Meade's and Grant's headquarters were within a half mile of each other on Gravelly Run, and remained there till Richmond and Petersburg were evacuated on the night of May 2d.

Warren's Fifth Corps advanced on White Oak road, [Samuel W.] Crawford's Division leading the attack. It was severely repulsed in the forenoon and driven back in great confusion. While Crawford was attempting to reform and renew the fighting, Gen. Warren rode up white with rage, and without

THE PETERSBURG AND APPOMATTOX CAMPAIGNS

waiting for explanations, commenced the most abusive tirade on Crawford that mortal ever listened to. He called him every vile name at his command, in the presence of officers and privates, and totally forgot what was due to his self-respect as an officer and gentleman. Crawford sat on his horse, stolid as a block of marble, and so far as I can remember, did not utter a syllable in reply. When he had emptied his last vial of abuse on Crawford, Warren rode away, and I never saw him afterwards.

That afternoon Sheridan rode to Grant's headquarters to see about the infantry reinforcements which had been promised him, to retake Five Forks, destroy [George E.] Pickett's command, and thus completely turn the enemy's right flank. He had asked for Wright's Sixth Corps to be sent to his assistance. But Grant had other work laid out for Wright and notified Sheridan that Warren would be sent to him. To this Sheridan had strong objections and came to headquarters to express them.

His plea was that the Sixth Corps had been with his cavalry in the Shenandoah Campaign; officers and men knew and trusted each other; that the Fifth Corps were strangers; and when hard pressed said he had no confidence in Warren, under such circumstances. He would not like to be subordinated to him (Sheridan) and he expected nothing but trouble. Grant explained to him the impossibility of moving Wright so far within the time required, whereas Warren was on our extreme left but a few miles from Five Forks, and was, on every account the suitable one to be detached for that service. Noting Sheridan's dissatisfied countenance, Grant said: "Gen. Warren will be ordered to report to you for duty," speaking slowly and emphasizing every word.

Gen. Grant says in his Memoirs that he sent a staff officer to

Sheridan to say to him that as much as he liked Gen. Warren, "now was not a time when we could let our personal feelings for any one stand in the way of success; and if his removal was necessary to success, not to hesitate. It was upon that authorization that Sheridan removed Warren." All this is no doubt true, but Sheridan did not need this specific authority. It was conveyed by the strongest possible implication, in his previous conversation with him, and was fully understood by Sheridan, as he told me at Appomattox.

Warren was ordered to move to Sheridan's support on the night of March 31st, so as to cooperate with Sheridan by nine o'clock next morning, at the latest. He reported to Sheridan about eleven o'clock in the forenoon of April 1st, but his corps did not arrive on the field, so as to go into battle, till late in the afternoon. All this time Sheridan was waiting, fuming, and fighting. The chances of success were growing fainter hourly. The enemy was changing his position, and might escape unhurt.

To add to this Sheridan's aids who had been sent to hurry up Warren's infantry, and lead them into position, claimed to have received scant courtesy on delivering their orders; and when Warren's Corps finally arrived, instead of moving forward into line as ordered by Sheridan, it was halted until Warren actually rode over the ground to inspect it personally, as if distrusting Sheridan's judgment, and rebelling against his authority. Warren's tardy arrival, his apparent unwillingness to render cheerful obedience so incensed Sheridan that he removed him from command on the spot, sent him to the rear to await orders and placed Gen. Griffin, next in rank, in command. The whole corps was rushed into battle and nothing but the lateness of the attack prevented the capture of the entire rebel force.

Warren's reasons for his late arrival at Five Forks were never satisfactory to Grant or Sheridan. He claimed that high waters, broken bridges, deep mud, and the worn out condition of his men, made it impossible for him to get there sooner. There was undoubtedly an element of truth in all this, but his constitutional temperament had more to do with it than anything else. Had conditions been reversed, and Sheridan ordered to Warren's support, no imaginable hindrances could have kept him away for so long a time. He would have borne down and surmounted every obstacle. . . .

There is no doubt but his removal from command of the corps with which he had been so long identified, came like a clap of thunder to Gen. Warren. I have reason to know that such a possibility had never entered his mind. He had a good opinion of himself, and so far as such thoughts ever projected themselves into his reflections, considered his position as secure as that of Meade, Sheridan, or even Grant. And for a while afterward, he never seemed to doubt that he would be vindicated, restored to command, and Sheridan be in some manner reprimanded for his action. It was a pitiful chapter in the war; and Gen. Warren was driven to a premature grave, as his friends always believed, by what he felt to be an undeserved punishment. The close of the war turned public attention away from individual cases. Grant, Sheridan, Sherman and others were the popular idols, and many deserving officers and men were overlooked and forgotten. . . .

To this chapter I wish here to record that Sheridan always spoke of the matter in a subdued sorrowful tone of voice in the many conversations I had with him in relation to it. He justified the act by protesting that it was a positive military necessity, the wisdom of which he never doubted, then or since. With Warren left in command, the battle of Five Forks would have been a Confederate victory, followed by more desperate fighting, possibly by further temporary Confederate successes lasting for days or weeks, would have caused delay in the surrender of Lee's army, and caused much additional bloodshed. I have tried to state such facts as came within my knowledge without setting down aught in malice.

The morning of April 2d I wrote the New York *Herald*: "The most unexpected event of the day (April 1st) or of the season, was the removal from command, in the presence of the troops, and in the face of the enemy, by General Sheridan, of Major-General Warren, so long commanding the Fifth army corps. His corps was turned over to General Griffin, as the ranking officer. But little has transpired as to the immediate provocation, or justification, but it is understood to have been because of Gen. Warren's tardiness or refusal to obey orders, by charging the rebel lines. From a tolerably thorough acquaintance with Gen. Warren's usual behavior in somewhat similar circumstances, I have not a particle of doubt that his removal was right and proper."

This moderate statement provoked a fierce quarrel with a few of Warren's real and pretended friends. . . .[1]

Gen. Sheridan's conduct during the battle of Five Forks attracted wide attention and comment. It was the impersonation of everything soldierly, blended with instances of personal daring and exposure scarcely to be justified in the commander of an army. He rode up and down the lines under fire for hours, encouraging his men by waving his hat and sword, and exhorting them to seize the opportunity now within their grasp, and sweep their enemies to destruction. To an officer

---

[1] As late as September 2, 1888, a letter of Cadwallader's in the *Milwaukee Sunday Telegram* induced Col. John A. Watrous to write in Warren's defense.

he would say: "Take your men in—make your men fight—
push on your column." "Go in boys, go in." "Ha! the d—d
rascals are running." "The cowardly scoundrels can't fight
such brave men as mine." "Kill that infernal skulker." "Shoot
every man down like a dog, that tries to skulk from duty,"
were yelled in tones of thunder as he dashed along where the
fight was hottest, and the result a trifle uncertain.

Or, as he encountered a slightly wounded soldier making
for the rear, he would say: "They've hit you have they? Don't
give it up just yet. Give the bloody rebels a round or two more
to remember you by. Down three or four of the rascals before
you go to the hospital." In scores of cases such men resumed
their arms and fought on to the end. His presence was a consuming fire to his enemies and a tower of strength to his men.

Probably no living soldier was ever more terrible in battle
than Sheridan. With the first smell of powder he became a
blazing meteor, a pillar of fire to guide his own hosts. The
rather small short, heavily built man rose to surpassing stature
in his stirrups, to the sublimity of heroism in action; and in-
fused a like spirit in his troops. I think it no exaggeration to say
that America never produced his equal, for inspiring an army
with courage and leading them into battle. Absolutely fearless
himself, with unwavering faith in his cause and his plans, he
always raised the courage and faith of others, to the level of
his own; passed from rank to rank in action, flaming, fiery,
omnipresent, and well-nigh omnipotent.

It has often been said that such conduct is no proof of great
generalship; that his position was properly in the rear; that
his duty was to overlook and direct the fighting of others; and
that the commander of an army should never needlessly expose
his own person. Sheridan's answer to such criticisms was that
the outlines of his battles had been previously planned and

matured, subject only to exigencies and surprises that always
occur—the execution of these plans often demanded the utmost
stretch of human endurance—the issue of a battle or campaign
might at some critical moment turn upon the conduct of a
single soldier, who stood and fought, or sought safety in flight
—his own highest duty in that event was to keep that man at
the post of duty, &c., &c.

But Sheridan's claim to great generalship does not rest on
his admitted courage. He gave abundant proof of extraordinary
military ability on every field to which he was assigned, and
in every official position he ever held. It was well-known to
Gen. Grant's intimates, that he considered Sheridan incom-
parably the greatest general our civil war produced. Other
generals might be equally good under ordinary circumstances,
under the eyes of an able superior commander, and up to the
point of a given or limited number of men. Sheridan he believed could be more safely trusted with an independent army
than any of them; and he often said in private confidential
conversation, that no army would ever be raised on this continent so large that Sheridan could not competently command
it. In this last respect, Grant had unbounded confidence in,
and admiration for Sheridan.

Late in the afternoon of April 1st, I returned from the Union
front, tired, muddy and hungry. Gen. Grant said his staff were
all away on duty, scattered in all directions, and asked me if
I felt equal to a ride to City Point. I answered in the affirma-
tive, as a matter of course. He said Sheridan had just sent him
a number of regimental and Confederate battle flags, captured
during the day at Five Forks, which he wished me to carry
to the President, with his compliments, as an evidence of the
good work which had been done in that quarter. I swallowed
a hasty lunch, changed my saddle to the back of my favorite

horse which had been held in reserve for any unexpected emergency, and soon mounted and started, with a heavy armful of captured colors. The roads were execrable, filled with moving troops and trains, and the ride a distressing one to myself and horse.

Reaching the City Point landing between sundown and dark, Mr. Lincoln (who had been notified of my coming by telegraph) sent his tug to the shore, and on its return met me at the hatchway of the lower deck with a beaming countenance and outstretched arms. As soon as I could convey my orders, he seized the flags, unfurled them one by one, and burst out: "Here is something material—something I can see, feel, and understand. This means victory. This *is* victory."

Taking me up into the after cabin of the River Queen, he had me repeat over and over, my message from Gen. Grant—what I knew about affairs at the front—what I had personally witnessed—and manifested the joy of a schoolboy, as I narrated each bit of good news. Turning to some large maps spread out on the tables, where he had marked the lines of Union and Confederate forces with red-headed and black-headed pins, with such changes as our rapid movements had made to the date of his last dispatch from the front, he asked me to go over them with him, and correct them, wherever I knew them to be faulty. An hour or two was spent with him, when I went ashore; saw my horse attended to; stretched myself on a cot for rest, and sleep if possible; gave strict orders to be called at a certain hour; and was at headquarters again on Gravelly Run soon after daylight, April 2d. . . .

It will be remembered that one of Gen. Grant's excuses for not sending Wright's corps instead of Warren's to assist Sheridan at Five Forks, was that: "he had other work for Wright to do." That work was to assault the rebel intrenchments on his front on the night of April 1st, and if successful, to attack their troops at that point on flank and rear; effect a secure lodgement for himself; and open a way for other columns to press through.

I had intended riding to the Sixth Corps headquarters, to see, and share in, a project I had so long believed a safe one. When Gen. Rawlins informed [me] that Wright had received such orders, he remarked jocularly, that the General had decided to try my plan! But Rawlins objected seriously to my incurring such unnecessary risks. There would be broken heads and disabled men, beyond question, and it was not in the line of my duty to possibly swell the number of such, by rushing in where I was not obliged to go.

I declared the head of Wright's column would be found the safest place in the Army of the Potomac. It proved to be so. Very few men were killed in the first attack. The heavy fighting came later, after daylight, when Wright took them in reverse, and rolled them back along their own intrenchments until they became formidable by numbers, and by the cover of two or three forts into which they were driven. The attack proved successful beyond the expectations of most general officers, and was the first substantial break in the defenses of Petersburg.

On the evening of April 2d, I was sent to our extreme left to learn the name of a plantation house standing there, which proved to be Dabney's. As I returned in the dusk of approaching night, at full speed along White Oak Road, I noticed a regiment of Union troops forming into line a few rods from the road to my right. Supposing that the officers knew me, I never slackened my gait, but rode on furiously. I was supposed by the officer in command to be an escaping Confederate, and ordered to halt. This order was not distinctly heard by me at first; nor at all understood, until it was repeated in stentorian tones once or twice, and the click of musket locks ran along the line with orders to fire. I stopped barely in time to escape a volley of musketry which must have been instantly fatal. A single minute of explanation and recognition satisfied the watchful federal officer; but I rode back to headquarters at a slower pace, and with greater care to my surroundings.

Sometime during the day of April 2d, headquarters were moved up to within four or five miles of the Petersburg public square. By night of that day, the entire outer line of the city's intrenchments, had [been] carried by our troops, and the Union army lay strongly posted from the Appomattox river below Petersburg, to the river above it. Sheridan had cut off large detachments of rebel troops, as he followed up his victory at Five Forks, which had been driven up the river towards Burkesville Junction, or across it to join Lee towards Richmond. Our troops went into camp at night, with orders to assault everywhere as soon after daylight next morning, as they could be put in motion.

I followed Wright and Ord, through the day of April 2d, alternately, riding from point to point, across the open fields, sometimes in rear of our troops, often in advance of them, and frequently coming unexpectedly under fire from both sides, and running the risk of being shot or captured. I was within less than a half mile of the Confederate General A. P. Hill, when he was killed, but did not witness it. In the afternoon a spent minnie ball struck me on the inside of the left knee joint, passed under the skin between the inner tuberosity of the tibia and patella for an inch and a half, and glanced off, and out through my pants without penetrating the capsular ligament of the joint. It felt at first like a severe blow from a club, or piece of iron, and was followed in an instant by excruciating pain. I dismounted with the assistance of an orderly, called a passing surgeon to examine it, and was able to proceed in less than a half hour. The surgeon was not sure on first examination, but what the knee joint was permanently injured; but twenty-four hours removed all apprehension, and beyond the soreness which lasted a few weeks, I suffered no further inconvenience from it.

The noise and commotion in Petersburg that night, gave positive assurance that Gen. Lee was evacuating. I started into the city alone, on the morning of April 3d, at daylight. When I reached the head of the main street leading to the center of the city from that side, I saw a procession of old men, in homespun, butternut clothing, coming towards me on the sidewalk, bearing an improvised flag of truce that looked suspiciously like a dirty linen table cloth. They came along at a sober gait, as if attending a funeral. Seeing me approaching, with staff equipments on my horse, they faced to the curbstone, made an awkward attempt to give me a military salute, when their spokesman began a pompous official address, stating: "That on behalf of the municipal government, and the people of the City of Petersburg, he had the honor of tendering the formal surrender of the place, &c., &c."

The hour, the place, the simple ignorance of these town councilmen—for such they declared themselves to be—the apparent honesty of their intentions—their mistake in supposing such an humble individual as myself to be in position to receive the surrender of a city—conspired to make it the most ridiculous event of my life. They were very slow to believe that so jaunty and self-possessed a horseman as I evidently was that morning, was not clothed with a large measure of military and civil authority.

With more impatience of manner, perhaps, than their simplicity deserved, I told them I should have been glad to have met them on that errand at any time for many months last past; but it was now too late—that we were already in possession of the city—no surrender had been asked for, nor would be formally received by Gen. Grant, or anyone else—and advised them to hurry to their respective domiciles—to remain closely in their own premises—and there await future events. "But," they enquired, "was property not to be respected and the rights of unarmed citizens observed?" I was obliged to ride away from their questionings and protests. By the time I reached Jarratt's Hotel, Union cavalry were swarming through the streets, soon followed by infantry, and thus I have always jestingly claimed, this celebrated rebel stronghold was officially surrendered to me. . . .

Without a minute's delay, I sat down at the first table I could find in Jarratt's hostelry and commenced writing, as for life. Owing to the hurry and confusion of the morning, my messengers failed to find me that morning. At a few minutes before nine o'clock I started for City Point with all *Herald* dispatches at hand, caught the ten o'clock mailboat for Fortress Monroe, and was back in the public square of Petersburg before eleven o'clock Monday, April 3rd.

On my return I found most of the corps commanders assembled there. Mr. Lincoln, Admirals Porter and [David G.] Farragut, Gen. Grant, Gen. Meade and other distinguished men were sitting on the Court House steps. The president and the two admirals had ridden from City Point immediately after breakfast for a conference with General Grant. This lasted till about noon, when the visiting officials returned to City Point, went to Richmond that afternoon by steamboat, and left next day for Washington. This was the last time I ever saw, and spoke to, Abraham Lincoln.

Early in the afternoon, Grant and staff rode westward following Ord's line of march, and camped for the night at Sutherland Station west of Petersburg. . . .

[*Accompanying Grant and his escort as they sought to keep pace with the flying Union columns, Cadwallader sent dispatches to the* Herald *at every opportunity. On the morning of April 5 the party entered the dilapidated village of Nottaway Court House.*]

While Grant was viewing the place a staff officer arrived with dispatches from Sheridan, stating that he had captured a large number of prisoners, artillery, part of a wagon train, had driven the enemy's advances back with considerable loss.

Soon after receiving this dispatch two trusty scouts arrived from Sheridan with additional news, and urging Gen. Grant to come to that place and capture Lee's whole army. The general sent a staff officer to read this news from Sheridan at the head of every brigade in the line of march. Although the men had already tramped over twenty miles that day and were hoping to camp for the night, this news encouraged them to make several miles before stopping.

About sundown the general and staff had a short halt by the side of the road, saddles were changed to fresh horses, when Grant, Rawlins, the staff surgeon, myself, and I think Lieut. Col. (afterwards General) Horace Porter, and four orderlies, started for Jetersville, perhaps twenty miles distant, preceded by the scouts who brought the last dispatches. The ride was lonely, somewhat hazardous, and made at a slow pace part of the way. The scouts, or couriers, acted as guides, riding from one to two hundred yards in advance, in perfect silence. At all forks or crossings of roads, one remained till we caught up, when he spurred forward and joined his companion. Occasionally our gait was quickened on a good stretch of road; but farm houses, possible places of ambush, junctions and crossings of roads, were approached with caution.

We reached Sheridan's headquarters between eleven and twelve at night and found them in a small log cabin in the middle of a tobacco patch. Some of his staff were at work by candlelight, the general was trying to sleep in a loft above on a clapboard floor, and came scrambling down a ladder as soon as we were announced with no clothing but a shirt, pants and boots. He commenced by pointing out on the maps the position of the enemy at nightfall, the positions held by his own troops, the lines of retreat which Lee was now compelled to adopt along different roads, the combinations and marches which could be made to cut him off, and ended by declaring this to be the final battle ground. Meade's troops must be forced to certain positions during the night, and then not a man of Lee's army could escape. He was enthusiastic, positive and not a little profane in expressing his opinions.

Grant was all this time brimming over with quiet enjoyment of Sheridan's impetuosity, but finally said the Confederate army was certainly in a bad predicament; it would be compelled to abandon its intended line of retreat; that it would unquestionably be further demoralized by this; but if he was in Gen. Lee's place he thought he could get away with a part of his army, and he supposed Gen. Lee would. Sheridan didn't believe a single regiment could escape and reiterated the opinion many times. Grant said in his quiet, pleasant way that we were doing splendidly; everything was now in our favor; but we must not expect too much. We would do all in our power, but it was too much to expect to capture the whole Confederate army just then, &c., &c. . . .

CHAPTER

Twenty-One

. . . Grant, and such of the staff as had accompanied him remained all through Thursday, April 6th, at Jetersville, from which place the general thought he could best direct affairs. In the morning the Union army lay in line of battle, stretching across about four miles of country, facing northward, with [George A.] Custer's cavalry division on the right flank, and McKenzie's [Ranald S. Mackenzie's] on the left. The infantry line was formed with the Sixth Corps on the right, and the Fifth in the center and the Second on the left. The first movement of the day was to transfer the Sixth Corps from the right (where it was likely to be left squarely in Lee's rear) clear around to the left, where, if it could arrive in time, it would be nearly in front of Lee on the new line of march he would be obliged to pursue.

The transfer of this corps was the only direct command which I ever knew Gen. Grant to give to any body of troops after assuming command as Lieutenant-General. He paid the utmost deference to Gen. Meade's official position as commander of the Army of the Potomac, and his own tactics were executed through Meade, on the latter's orders. On this occasion Gen. Meade was several miles in the rear, too sick to sit on horseback. He had been obliged to ride in an ambulance, most of the way from Petersburg. Feeling that too much valuable time would be lost by any other procedure, he ordered this movement, and dispatched an officer to notify Meade of the fact, and the reasons for its urgency.

Jetersville, like many other southern places first introduced to northern readers by the movements of armies, was an insignificant station on the railroad, comprising a half-dozen buildings all told, with nothing to boast of but an old revolutionary church, built at some remote period in the history of the state. This had withstood the ravages of time until two seasons before, when the old roof and weather-boarding gave place to new. The inhabitants absconded on the approach of the "Yankees," and no one was left familiar with its old traditions.

In the forenoon the Second and Fifth corps overtook and fell upon [John B.] Gordon's Corps, which was acting as rearguard to Lee's army, in the vicinity of Deatonville, and captured some prisoners and a wagon train. . . .

Gen. Grant left Jetersville at five o'clock p.m. of April 6th, and rode to Burkeville Junction, where his headquarter train had orders to await him at night. Soon after reaching that place a staff officer arrived from Sheridan with the glorious news of the day's work at Sayler's Creek, and the taking of thirteen thousand prisoners, and several hundred wagons.

Gen. Ord's infantry reached Burkeville during the night of April 5th and the forenoon of the 6th. Sheridan's and Meade's occupation of the railroad north of that place made it of no value now that the tracks of the crossing railroads were destroyed, and with the instincts of a soldier, Ord pushed ahead as fast as his wearied men could march, hoping to head Lee off at some place west of Burkeville. . . .

The morning of Saturday, April 8th found the Union troops in the following positions: Sheridan's cavalry was at, and beyond, Chickentown, five or six miles south of the Lynchburg railroad, and fifteen miles southwest of Farmville; the Fifth and Twenty-fourth Corps were moving rapidly in rear of the cavalry on different roads, directly westward; the Second Corp was on our extreme right and squarely in rear of the main rebel column; the Sixth Corps was somewhat in rear of the Second, but rather to its left, closing the gap between the Second corps and the Appomattox river; the Ninth corps was at Burkeville Junction. Very little fighting took place that day, but every nerve was strained to cut Lee off completely from Lynchburg, and the army had full confidence in its ability to do this.

A careful study of Gen. Lee's last dispatch [1] to Grant confirmed Gen. Rawlins in the belief that it had been very carefully prepared after a consultation with the Confederate corps commanders, and one or two of his ablest and confidential Staff officers. Rawlins expressed the opinion very confidently that its apparent refusal to surrender his army just then, was solely to obtain the best possible terms for many of his officers, who had made themselves liable to severe punishment by the Federal government; and the natural dread Lee would have,

---

[1] On April 7 Grant had sent a note to Lee suggesting that further resistance was useless and declaring that he felt it his duty to shift from himself the responsibility for further bloodshed by asking Lee to surrender the Army of Northern Virginia. After consulting Longstreet, who said: "Not yet," Lee wrote to Grant: "I have recd your note of this date. Though not entertaining the opinion you express of the hopelessness of further resistance on the part of the Army of N. Va.—I reciprocate your desire to avoid useless effusion of blood, & therefore before considering your proposition, ask the terms you will offer on condition of its surrender."

that Gen. Grant would take the utmost advantage that circumstances permitted. Grant soon coincided with this interpretation of the note, and made his arrangements accordingly. The
headquarter train was sent off on the Chickentown road towards Appomattox Court House early in the morning, and the
general and staff started for Meade's headquarters which were
known to be near the head of his troops in Lee's rear.

We moved leisurely along all day, expecting every hour to
hear something further from Gen. Lee. Nothing came but
night, which found us twenty-five miles from the headquarter
train; and without any accommodations for ourselves or horses.
Gen. Meade established his headquarters for the night near
an old country homestead known as the Clifton House, and
invited us all to supper. The Clifton House had been deserted
on our approach and most of the household effects hauled
away. Some old house servants were left behind to look after
the premises as well as they could, and from them it was
learned that one bed remained standing in good condition in
an upper chamber. After supper with Gen. Meade, we all
went to the Clifton House. Grant and Rawlins took possession
of the one bed, upstairs, and the staff threw themselves on the
parlor floor for rest and sleep. I "retired" early and selected the
best place on the floor for my own occupancy.

It has often been asked if one spot on the parlor floor was
not as good as another. But such questioners never had any experiences of the kind. The best place was in the corner of the
room farthest from the door, where there would be the least
likelihood of being stepped on, or stumbled over, by those
coming in and going out. With my field-glasses for a pillow I
slept soundly till towards midnight, when the challenge of
the guard outside awoke us all. The sound of jingling spurs
and clanking saber was next heard, and then the announce-

ment: "Dispatches for General Grant." We were instantly on
the alert. When the dispatch had been carried upstairs to
Gen. Grant, we threw the parlor door wide open at the foot
of the stairway, and it must be confessed, played the part of
privileged eavesdroppers.

A light was soon struck upstairs when Rawlins opened and
read the dispatch in so loud a tone that we heard the most of
it. It ran as follows:

April 8th 1865.

*General:—I received at a late hour your note of today. I did
not intend to propose the surrender of the Army of Northern
Virginia, but to ask the terms of your proposition. To be frank,
I do not think the emergency has arisen to call for the surrender. But as the restoration of peace should be the sole object of all, I desire to know whether your proposals would
tend to that end. I cannot, therefore meet you with a view to
the surrender of the Army of Northern Virginia; but as far as
your proposition may affect the Confederate state forces under my command, and tend to the restoration of peace, I
should be pleased to meet you at ten A.M. tomorrow, on the
old stage road to Richmond, between the picket lines of the
two armies.*

Very Respectfully Your Obedient Servant.
R. E. Lee, General C.S.A.

To Lieutenant-General Grant;
Commanding Armies of the United States.[2]

The reading of this cool disingenuous dispatch threw Gen.
Rawlins into unusually bad temper, and he began at once:
"He did not propose to surrender," he says. "Diplomatic but

---

[2] The text of this note given by Cadwallader is essentially though not
absolutely correct. See Douglas Southall Freeman: *R. E. Lee* (New
York, 1947, 1949), IV, 133, for the exact text.

not true. He did propose, in his heart, to surrender. He now tries to take advantage of a single word used by you, as a reason for extending such easy terms. He now wants to entrap us into making a treaty of peace. You said nothing about that. You asked him to surrender. He replied by asking what terms you would give if he surrendered. You answered, by stating the terms. Now he wants to arrange for peace—something beyond and above the surrender of his army—something to embrace the whole Confederacy, if possible. No Sir! No Sir. Why it is a positive insult; and an attempt in an underhanded way, to change the whole terms of the correspondence."

To this outburst Grant replied: "that it amounted to the same thing. Lee was only trying to be let down easily. That he could meet him, as requested, in the morning, and settle the whole business in an hour."

But Rawlins was inexorable; said it: "would be presumptuous to undertake to teach Gen. Lee the force of words, or the use of the English language. That he had purposely proposed to arrange terms of peace to gain time, and better terms. That the dispatch was cunningly worded to that end, and deserved no reply whatever. 'He don't think the emergency has arisen!' That's cool, but another falsehood. That emergency has been staring him in the face for forty-eight hours. If he hasn't seen it yet, we will soon bring it to his comprehension! He has to surrender. He shall surrender. By the eternal, it shall be surrender, and nothing else."

Then came Grant's soft, moderate, persuasive, and apologetic voice: "Some allowance must be made for the trying position in which Gen. Lee is placed. He is compelled to defer somewhat to the wishes of his government, and his military associates. But it all means precisely the same thing. If I meet Lee, he will surrender before I leave."

Then Rawlins took another stand: "You have no right to meet Gen. Lee, or any one else, to arrange terms of peace. That is the prerogative of the President, or the Senate. Your business is to capture, or destroy Lee's army."

Rawlins' knowledge of constitutional law enabled him to add legal arguments to common sense in discussing this phase of the subject, and he reminded Grant that when the Peace Commission arrived at City Point, and he had telegraphed the fact to Washington and asked for instructions, Secretary Stanton had gone to the verge of giving him a "snubbing" as follows: "The president directs me to say to you that he wishes you to have no conference with Gen. Lee, unless it be for the capitulation of Lee's Army, or on solely minor and purely military matters. He instructs me to say that you are not to decide, discuss, or confer upon any political question. Such questions the president holds in his own hands, and will submit them to no military conferences or conventions. . . ." [3]

Grant felt at the time that Stanton's dispatch was an open rebuke. Finding that Gen. Rawlins was irreconcilably opposed to the proposed meeting, Grant abandoned the project, and Rawlins carried his point, as he always did, when resolutely set. But Grant said it was a duty to give respectful attention and answer to all official communications—that Lee was entitled to that much—and Rawlins yielded this minor objection of his. . . .

By previous invitation we all breakfasted with Gen. Meade, before daylight, Sunday morning, April 9th, 1865. We started

---

[3] This letter of March 3, 1865, which Cadwallader quotes with some slight inaccuracies, was actually written by Lincoln though signed by Stanton. It had no connection with the Hampton Roads conference, but resulted from an effort by Lee to draw Grant into a military agreement that would end hostilities.

as soon as it was light enough to do so safely, to ride around
the left flank of the rebel army to join Sheridan, whom we
knew to be squarely in Lee's front, somewhere near Appomattox Court House. We had to make a wide detour, to avoid
running into Confederate pickets, flankers and bummers. It
proved to be a long rough ride, much of the way without
any well-defined road; often through fields and across farms;
over hills, ravines and "turned out" plantations; across muddy
brooks and bogs of quicksand. About eleven o'clock A.M. we
halted for a few minutes to breathe our horses, in a new
"clearing" where a number of log heaps were on fire. At one
of these the party mainly dismounted, and lighted cigars from
the blazing logs. While there some one chanced to look back
the way we had come, and saw a horseman coming at full
speed, waving his hat above his head, and shouting at every
jump of his steed. As he neared us we recognized him as
Major [Lieutenant Charles E.] Pease, of Gen. Meade's staff,
mounted on a coal black stallion, white with foam, from his
long and rapid pursuit of us.

It seemed that when Lee received Grant's dispatch written
in the early morning hours of that day, declining to meet him
to arrange terms of peace, that he immediately decided to
accept the terms of surrender offered by Grant, and sent a
dispatch to that effect to Clifton House, where he supposed
him still to be. This reached Gen. Meade's headquarters an
hour or two after we left there, and Major Pease was sent with
the dispatch to overtake us if possible.

Major Pease rode up to Gen. Rawlins, saluted, and handed
him the sealed envelope. Rawlins tore one end open slowly,
withdrew the inclosure, and read it deliberately. He then
handed it to Gen. Grant, without a word of comment. The
staff were all expecting Lee to surrender, and searched the

countenance of Gen. Rawlins eagerly for some clue to the contents of the package. There was no exultation manifested —no sign of joy—and instead of flushing from excitement, he clinched his teeth, compressed his lips, and became very pale. Grant read it through mechanically, and handed it back to Rawlins, saying in a common tone of voice: "You had better read it aloud General." The immovable expression of countenance in these two prominent actors in the great drama drawing to a close, was rather discouraging to the onlookers. Rawlins showed nothing but extra paleness. There was no more expression in Grant's countenance than in a last year's bird's nest. It was that of a Sphinx.

Rawlins drew a long breath, and in his deep sepulchral voice, a little tremulous by this time, read the following dispatch from Lee:

9th April, 1865.

General:—I received your note of this morning on the picket line, whither I had come to meet you, and ascertain definitely what terms were embraced in your proposal of yesterday with reference to the surrender of this army. I now ask an interview, in accordance with the offer contained in your letter of yesterday, for that purpose.

R. E. Lee, General.

Lieut. Gen. U. S. Grant.[4]

A blank silence fell on everybody for a minute. No one looked his comrade in the face. Finally Col. Duff, chief of Artillery, sprang upon a log, waved his hat, and proposed three cheers. A feeble hurrah came from a few throats, when all broke down in tears, and but little was said for several

---

[4] Except for punctuation, the text of this letter is correct. See Freeman: *R. E. Lee,* IV, 127.

minutes. All felt that the war was over. Every heart was thinking of friends—family—home.

Presently Grant turned to Rawlins with a smile and said: "How will that do Rawlins?" to which the latter replied: "I think *that* will do" laying strong emphasis on the word "that."

Gen. Ely S. Parker, Chief of the Six Nations, then military Secretary to Gen. Grant, was directed to write the following note to Gen. Lee:

April 9th 1865.

Gen. R. E. Lee:—Yours of this date is but this moment (fifty minutes past eleven) received, in consequence of my having passed from Richmond and Lynchburg to the Farmville and Richmond road. Am at this writing about four miles west of Wallace Church, and will push forward to the front for the purpose of meeting you. Notice sent to me on this road where you wish the interview to take place will meet me here.[5]

This was carried to Gen. Lee (under flag of truce) by Lieutenant Colonel Orville E. Babcock and Lieutenant William McKee Dunn. . . . They found Gen. Lee sitting under

---

[5] The correct text of the note is:

Headquarters Armies of the U. S.
April 9, 1865

General R. E. Lee,
  Commanding C. S. Army:
Your note of this date is but this moment (11:50 A.M.) received. In consequence of my having passed from the Richmond and Lynchburg road to the Farmville and Lynchburg road I am at this writing about four miles west of Walker's church, and will push forward to the front for the purpose of meeting you. Notice sent on this road where you wish the interview to take place will meet me.

Very respectfully, your obedient servant
U. S. Grant,
Lieutenant-General

O. R., Series I, Vol. XLVI, pt. III, p. 665.

an apple tree on the bank of a narrow road the track of which had been cut down or washed away a couple of feet. He received the package, opened one end of the envelope, and started to endorse on this, the day, hour and minute of its receipt. He fumbled in his pockets a minute, and finding that he had no pencil, borrowed a stub of a cedar pencil about three inches long, from one of his staff. After using this he handed it back over his shoulder mechanically to the person from whom he borrowed it, as he supposed. Babcock reached out, took the pencil, and I now have its point, an inch long, in my possession. It has never made a mark on a piece of paper since then.

Babcock was pompously parading and exhibiting that stub of pencil at headquarters all the afternoon; and pronounced it his only valuable trophy of the war. The staff were badgering him about it till night, wanting to buy it, to trade for it, and making him all manner of extravagant offers for it, and proposing every ludicrous exchange for it their waggish propensities could think of, ranging from broken jack knives to a fine-tooth comb. He finally consented that I might have a piece of it, not to exceed an inch in length, and after exacting the most sacred promises from me to not cut off more than that, handed it over. I deliberately cut off the point, with less than an inch of wood, and handed the butt end back to him. The laughter became uproarious at my sharp practice, and Babcock had to stand treat for more oysters in after times than a load of pencils were worth.

From this incident sprang the story of Lee's surrender to Grant under an apple tree. Gaudy lithographs were printed by hundreds of thousands, representing these two eminent military men as meeting under the umbrageous boughs of a large apple tree, both hat in hand, Grant rather erect, with

one hand extended to receive Lee's sword, and Lee rather
bowed and in the act of presenting his sword, hilt forward, to
Grant, whilst staff officers, lines of battle, squadrons of cavalry,
batteries of artillery, and all the paraphernalia of war, were
pictured in the background. No such meeting between Grant
and Lee ever occurred. They never met under an apple tree
at any time or place. I was present at both meetings of Grant
and Lee, one on April 9th and the other the next forenoon,
April 10th. These were the only times they ever met.[6] Yet not
less than a car load of charms, trinkets and keepsakes have
been sold which were manufactured from that famous apple
tree under which it was pretended Lee surrendered to Grant.

I have probably been asked one hundred times by intelligent men to describe minutely what each said and did, and
how they looked and acted when Lee surrendered his sword
to Grant. These otherwise intelligent men seemed to have
never known, or to have forgotten, that by the terms of the
surrender each Confederate officer was to retain his sidearms;
and as a consequence no surrender of them was offered or
accepted. Gen. Lee never offered his sword to Gen. Grant—
never thought of doing so—as any reader of the terms of surrender should know. I contradicted the fable, in print, for
years. So much for some pretended history, and historical
paintings. . . .

After dispatching this last note to Lee, Grant and staff rode
on towards the Court House. The firing, which had been heavy
through the early forenoon gradually died away, until it wholly
ceased. The news of the pending negotiations for the surrender
spread rapidly through both armies. As we came out on the

---

[6] Cadwallader undoubtedly refers to meetings during the Civil War.
They had, of course, met in the old army during the Mexican War.

open ground near the village [Appomattox], both armies were in plain view. The soldiers of each were in line of battle, and ready to renew the contest on short notice. Officers were galloping in all directions, colors were flying, and it had more the appearance of a grand review of troops, than of two contending hosts. A nearer view, however, disclosed dirty, tattered, ranks of soldiers, none of them well clad, and nearly all officers in fatigue dress.

We struck the upper or south end of the principal street of the village, and turned northward to the Court House. Lee's army still lay north and east of the town. A close lookout was kept for Gen. Lee. When nearly in front of a two-story brick house on the right, or east side of the street, an orderly in rebel uniform was seen holding a couple of horses near the north end of the building. One was a dapple-gray, with a Grimsley saddle and plain single-reined bridle on him, without anything to denote rank.

A staff officer dashed across the open blue grass yard and inquired whose horses they were. The orderly said they belonged to Gen. Lee, who was in the house. The house stood back several rods from the street. The front fence was wholly down, and mostly carried away. So Gen. Grant rode across the yard to the front entrance to a long porch which extended the whole length of the house, dismounted, ascended a half dozen steps onto the porch, and was about to enter the half-open door of a wide hall which separated the ground floor into two suites of rooms, when Gen. Lee met him, exchanged salutations, and conducted him into the front room on the left side of the hall. The staff all remained on their horses. In a few minutes Gen. Grant came to the front, and beckoned to us to come in. All were formally presented to Gen. Lee, and

Colonel Lewis Marshall of Baltimore,[7] one of his Aides, and who was the only member of his staff that came with him.

The conversation was short and commonplace from necessity. After the ordinary civilities were exchanged, the military secretaries were set to work to reduce the terms of the capitulation into proper form. This did not take long. The terms being fully understood and agreed to, were written out in duplicate by Col. Ely S. Parker, in whose possession I saw the original, written on yellow manifold paper, in 1890. . . .[8]

The time occupied in making duplicates of the foregoing letters gave an excellent opportunity for studying the two principal actors in the great drama. Gen. Grant had been separated from his headquarter train about forty-eight hours. He was compelled to meet Gen. Lee in the ordinary fatigue blouse, a hat somewhat the worse for wear, without a sword of any kind (as he seldom wore one on a march) and with no insignia of rank excepting the Lieutenant-General's shoulder straps on the outside of his blouse to designate him to his own troops. His appearance, never imposing, contrasted strongly with that of Gen. Lee. But his quiet, unassuming deportment rarely failed to impress everyone with his force of character, no matter what his surroundings might chance to be.

Gen. Lee was much older in appearance, but soldierly in every way. He was over six feet in height, rather heavily built in these later years of his life, neatly dressed in the full uniform of his rank, and wearing an elegant costly sword by far too valuable for field service, or for any but ceremonious occasions. I afterwards learned it was one presented to him

---

[7] Lee was accompanied by Colonel Charles Marshall.

[8] Cadwallader's account of this celebrated meeting differs in some minor details from that of Freeman: *R. E. Lee*, IV, 134–43.

by the State of Virginia. He wore his hair and whiskers cut short, both of which were iron gray in color. He was rather stout and fleshy than otherwise; with bronzed face from exposure to storm and sun; but showing a remarkably fine white skin above the line of his hatband when uncovered. His manners and bearing were perfect, and stamped him a thoroughbred gentleman in the estimation of all who saw him. His position was a difficult and mortifying one to a proud and sensitive man; yet he comforted himself with that happy blending of dignity and courtesy so difficult to describe, but so befitting to the serious business he had in hand. There was no haughtiness or ill-humor betrayed on the one hand; nor affected cheerfulness, forced politeness, nor flippancy on the other. He was a gentleman—which fully and wholly expresses his behavior.

His deportment was in marked contrast to that of Gen. Pemberton at Vicksburg. The latter was so insufferably ill-natured, peevish, and actually ill-mannered, that nothing but his being a prisoner of war, prevented his personal chastisement. He was held in contempt ever after, by all Union officers with whom he came in contact. Gen. Lee, on the contrary challenged admiration from the outset; and had the lifelong respect and sympathy, of Grant and staff, and such other officers as had the pleasure of meeting him.

Before leaving, Lee made an appointment to meet Grant at ten o'clock next day between the lines of the armies to arrange some further details of the surrender. He also stated that his men were nearly starving; that they had been living on parched corn for several days; and said he should have to ask for rations and forage, both of which were issued to them. Lee and Marshall then bowed themselves out, mounted, saluted, and rode away. . . .

While the writing was going on in the house, I went outside

and made a rough drawing of it on yellow manifold paper in my note book. I have the original yet. Several copies were sent north. One of them, I was told, was published by Harper Brothers of New York, although I never saw it. Another copy was forwarded to F. A. Sydston, an artist friend in Milwaukee. With my consent he photographed several thousand copies of it, and sold them at fifty cents each to aid a Soldier's Home Fair, held in that city. A few of these photographs are also in my possession.

Generals Grant and Lee were scarcely gone from the house when the craze for mementoes of the occasion seemed to spread among officers and privates. Large sums were offered Major [Wilmer S.] McLean [9] for the chairs in which the generals sat during the meeting—for the tables on which the writing was done—for substantially every article of furniture. There were two tables in the room. On one of these the minutes of the meeting were first made out. This table Gen. Custer obtained for twenty-five dollars, and his widow still has it in her possession. The other table was the one at which Grant and Lee sat when they affixed their signatures to the final notes which completed the surrender. This table Gen. Ord purchased for fifty dollars; and it is still in possession of Mrs. Ord. There has been much sharp contention between the families of these distinguished officers, as to which of them owned the celebrated table used on the day of the surrender. [1] . . .

Numerous offers were made for the chairs in which Grant

---

[9] Owner of the house where the terms of surrender were signed.

[1] Sheridan obtained the table at which the surrender terms were drawn up and later presented it to Mrs. Custer. It is now in the Smithsonian Institution. The table at which Lee and Grant signed the terms is now in the Chicago Historical Society. Members of the McLean family have denied that any articles were sold. They claim that Union officers looted the house.

and Lee sat, but Major McLean steadily refused to part with them. It seems that a couple of cavalry officers, finding they could not obtain the chairs by any other means, seized them by force and carried them away. They tried to induce McLean to accept pay for them; but he flung the "greenbacks" on the floor indignantly. Sometime after the chairs were carried off a cavalryman rode up, thrust a ten dollar "greenback" into McLean's hands, and exclaimed as he rode away: "This is for the Major's chair." Search was made for the chairs, and the officers who confiscated them, but neither could be found.

Cane bottomed chairs were ruthlessly cut to pieces; the cane splits broken into pieces a few inches long, and parceled out among those who swarmed around. Haircloth upholstery was cut from chairs, and sofas was also cut into strips and patches and carried away.

In the afternoon I rode to the headquarters of the Fifth Corps to put its *Herald* correspondent, Mr. John A. Brady, in possession of all the facts I had gathered concerning the events of the day that he might commence his dispatches, and get them off at the earliest possible minute. Mr. Brady was lying on the grass, so I dismounted and stretched myself on the ground by his side, and commenced my narration. Gen. Griffin, who succeeded Warren, was standing with a group of Warren's old staff officers, on the other side of a railfire, conversing among themselves, and I supposed out of hearing. But I had not been talking long to Brady till I overheard some one remark: "D—d unlikely." I thought nothing of it, and kept on with my account of the terms of the surrender. Griffin turned round with his face towards me, and said: "I should like to have some better authority for all this."

As I had not been speaking to him, I was slow to believe

that his insulting remarks were addressed to me, but began to feel rather uncomfortable. Seeing that I made no reply, Griffin then broke into a violent tirade, and became very abusive to me. He said in substance that I seemed to know a great deal about the surrender—more than the general officers knew—that he didn't believe a word of it, &c., &c. I rose from the grass and said: "Gen. Griffin, I do know a great deal about this business. It is no fault of mine if the generals in the army are ignorant of its conditions. They will probably be informed officially in due season. But I have stated the facts, and nothing else; and will not allow you, nor any one else, to dispute what I assert to be a fact."

Griffin was greatly enraged, and said he supposed I wrote the *Herald* account of Gen. Warren's removal. I answered that I did. He said "if he were in Gen. Warren's place, one of us would soon leave the army." I replied that Gen. Warren had been *sent* out of it. By this time he was in a towering passion, and said: "Things had come to a h—ll of a pass when civilians and outsiders presumed to criticise the military conduct of Major-Generals commanding army corps; and that he proposed to stop it so far as his corps was concerned by putting me under arrest."

I said that: "I had occasionally criticised general officers and might do so again—that I was entirely competent to teach most of them many things about their business, which was more than any of them could do for me, about mine—that I had great respect for the privates and subordinate officers of the Army, and very little for some of the Major-Generals commanding army corps—that as to my arrest, no Major-General in the Army of the Potomac could safely undertake that job—that I should ride in and out of his corps whenever I pleased, by day or night—would ride over him if he didn't get out of my way—and if he attempted my arrest, he would join Gen. Warren in less than twenty-four hours."

The staff fearing a personal encounter between us, led Griffin aside, when I mounted and rode away.

Being thoroughly angry I went directly to Gen. Sheridan's tent to get the circumstances of Warren's removal directly from him. He said there was no alternative left to him. He was obliged to remove Warren. That my information and statement was correct. That Griffin was a fool, &c., &c.

As I was leaving the front of Sheridan's tent I encountered Gen. Griffin, who had followed me there, as I supposed at first, to finish our quarrel. But an earthquake could not have surprised me more than he did by coming squarely to me in smiles, and reaching out to shake hands with me. I said, "No sir, you can't shake hands with me"; and attempted to pass on. He detained me, however; said he had spoken in anger and was sorry for it; that he was provoked at Warren's removal; had been inconsiderate in speech, and hoped I would forgive him. After a few moments' silence I said that he had outraged my feelings in a public manner and that I was not disposed to drop it there; but one man could not carry on a quarrel very long alone. If he absolutely refused to continue it further I supposed that I would be compelled to let it end as it then was. He repeated several times that he didn't want a quarrel— wouldn't have one if he could help it—and begged me to overlook his hasty speech, and forget the whole affair.

Griffin's conduct was from the first, studiedly insulting. I was not addressing him, and had not said a word reflecting on our officers or men. He was insufferably impertinent, and determined to provoke a quarrel. He may have been trying to "show off" in the presence of Warren's old staff, at my expense. It may also have been that he was honestly and sincerely angry, and thought he could vent his ill nature by abusing me as much as he pleased. His after conduct admitted of several explanations. He may have been sorry for giving away to his temper, and apologized for it from a sense of duty. Or, he may have thought, on cooler reflection, that he was likely to have quarrels enough as a new Corps Commander, without rushing into such as could be avoided. Or, he may have taken a cowardly view of possible consequences to his own interests, should he array the *Herald* against him, and incur the active hostility of any one at Gen. Grant's headquarters. I could not understand his motives then, never have since; and simply record the facts.

The belief seemed widespread among Confederate officers that the United States government had pledged itself to grant no amnesties for treason, and that "they must all hang together, or hang separately." On learning that Gen. Grant had taken no advantage of their desperate situation, but had voluntarily extended to them the same magnanimous terms offered two days before, and refused by Gen. Lee, they expressed their extreme gratitude. Discussion among themselves strengthened this feeling. All admitted that their army had no further power of resistance, and that it was obliged to surrender on our own terms. They seemed surprised to find no appearance of vindictiveness on our part. Judging from their hearty confessions of generous treatment, one would conclude that they had expected to be chained together as felons, to grace the triumphal march of our victorious army. No one who witnessed the behavior of the rebel officers and listened to their conversation, could long doubt the wisdom of Grant's policy. Their first questions had been: "Well, what are you going to do with us?" showing extreme anxiety. The feeling of relief from all suspense was universal. Half the "regulars" on both sides found some old acquaintance, or West Point classmate, in the other army, and in many instances their greetings were warm and unaffected. . . .

The appointment of officers to carry out the details of the surrender were made during the night by Grant and Lee, respectively. On our part, Gen. John Gibbon was the ranking officer.

At ten o'clock A.M., Monday, April 10th, 1865, the two generals met by appointment on the brow of a hill north of the Court House. Grant and staff had barely arrived when Lee, accompanied by an orderly came galloping up the slope, and wheeled to the side of the Lieutenant-General who sat on his horse a few rods in advance of the line of the staff. Their conversation lasted nearly an hour, in a drizzling rain which had just set in. During this conference Lee stated that if Grant had assented to a meeting which he had proposed some weeks before, peace would undoubtedly have resulted therefrom. The conversation between them was unheard by others; but enough was gleaned from Gen. Grant to know that Lee acknowledged his army to be completely beaten; the Confederacy about destroyed; and further prolongation of the war impossible. Johnston was expected to surrender to Sherman without firing another gun.

While this interview was carried on, a study of the surroundings interested me. Meade and staff, Sheridan and staff, Ord and staff, and a large concourse of general officers were ranged in semi-circular line in the background, presenting a tableau not often witnessed. Back of us lay the Federal troops compactly massed, and many of them in view. In front of us across a ravine which separated the two armies, lay the shattered remnants of Lee's grand army of invasion, which had carried consternation to the north until Antietam and Gettysburg had driven them from our borders. Grant's staff, whilst nominally the ranking one, was by no means the most pretentious in appearance. . . .

About eleven o'clock, Lee saluted, rode down the hill, crossed the ravine, entered his tent, packed his traveling portmanteau, and left the same day, attended by a single servant, to join his family in Richmond.

Gen. Grant turned the head of his thoroughbred horse "Cincinnatus" towards the Court House; gave directions to the staff quartermaster to take the headquarter train to Prospect Station for that night; to move it from there back to City Point by easy marches; and started with some of his staff for Washington to stop the draft then progressing.

We had some delays along the road in the afternoon, and did not reach Prospect Station till dark. The headquarter train arrived soon after, when tents were pitched, supper prepared and eaten; and all assembled in front of a roaring log fire; ankle deep in mud, but exalted above most earthly discomforts by the crowning success of the campaign.

Before retiring that night we were surprised and gladdened by the arrival of Hon. E. B. Washburne, on his way to the front to witness the surrender of Lee's army, as he supposed. He was a day too late, and returned with headquarters to City Point and Washington. . . .

Grant and staff reached Burkeville Junction about 2:00 o'clock p.m., Tuesday April 11th, and started at 4:00 p.m., by special train for City Point. The road was in a frightful condition, and in spite of slow locomotion and the utmost care, the cars frequently jumped the track, and had to be got on again at great disadvantage. One locomotive lay hopelessly wrecked and imbedded in mud near Wilson's Station, and de-

railed cars and trains, stopped us every few miles. Twelve
hours were consumed in running the sixty-one miles between
Burkeville and City Point.

In anticipation of what actually occurred, I took the precaution before leaving City Point the last week in March, to have
forwarded to me from Baltimore a stock of supplies for use on
my return. At the risk of incurring the censure of temperance
reformers I confess that these supplies embraced one five gal-
lon keg of whiskey, one barrel of bottled Glasgow Ale, and
one large pork Tierce filled with bottled champagne. In the
forenoon of April 12th, I turned over the whiskey (by military permission) to the Cavalry and Infantry escort commanders to be carefully issued to their men. The barrel of Ten-
nant's Glasgow Ale, was opened and drank among ourselves in
less than thirty minutes! The champagne was used at dinner
in drinking confusion to the enemies of the republic; and to
the memory of fallen comrades in the Great Rebellion. The
occasion was one of mingled joy and exultation, of sorrow
and sadness, that can never be fully understood by any except
those who have gone through the experiences.

In the afternoon of April 12th Gen. Grant left City Point
for Washington. I was obliged to remain behind to ship
horses, tents and camp equipage, and did not reach the capital till some days after Mr. Lincoln's assassination.

On Saturday morning, April 15th, 1865, I rose between daylight and sunrise, and stepped out of my tent to give some
directions for the day's work. The telegraph operator had his
instruments in a tent on the opposite side of the main driveway which led into the grounds, and as soon as he could do
so without attracting the attention of others he beckoned me
to come to his tent. He was the cipher operator in charge of
the office, was alone, and in a great state of excitement. He

informed me that the President had been shot at Ford's Theater the night before, and was fatally wounded. I had heard such reports before, and was incredulous. But he assured me it was true—said cipher dispatches from Secretary Stanton to Gen. Meade, at Appomattox, had been passing at intervals all night, giving many details—and then cautioned me against whispering a syllable concerning it, until I was officially informed from some other source.

A few minutes after my return to my own tent, a long-nosed lean cadaverous man from Maine, whom I had formerly employed as messenger, came striding across the campus in great haste and inquired if I had heard from Washington that morning? I answered indifferently that I had; but betrayed no surprise at, nor interest in, the question. After a minute's silence he asked again if I had heard any bad news? Determined to not give away a secret which was not my own, I replied that what was good, or what bad, news depended on the person receiving it. To one, a piece of news would be esteemed good. To another the same news would be pronounced very bad. He then stepped in front of me, looked me in the eye, and wanted to know if I had heard the very worst news ever sent from that city? I answered that in my own opinion, I had. My questioner turned on his heel like a flash and started for the steamboat weeping and moaning aloud, and wiping his eyes till he passed out of sight.

I hurried back to the telegraph tent and told the operator the secret was out. He declared this was impossible. The only telegraphic connection with Washington was our military wire, over which nothing could be transmitted without the written approval of the Secretary of War—that the dispatches were all in a difficult cipher that no one could read or translate between City Point and Washington—that he had not breathed a word of it to any one but myself, &c. After discussing the strange behavior of my visitor, we were both uneasy. It was plain that a few persons knew of the tragedy soon after it took place. We tried to ascertain how this man got his information, but never succeeded. He belonged to a fleet of sutlers' vessels waiting for permission to go to Richmond. Some cipher operator was probably corrupted by a large sum of money to give the "key" to the dispatches, where by tapping the wires, they could take off and translate everything passing. There seemed to be no other explanation.

About noon the Post Commandant received official notice of the President's death, and announced it in orders, after taking precautions to prevent an outbreak. Confederate prisoners were arriving daily by thousands, and the situation was grave. A foolish scuffle or fight—the accidental discharge of a gun— might have precipitated a massacre. It was easily within the power of any reckless stump-speaker to mount a pile of cracker boxes, or a wagon, and have so maddened the Union soldiers as to cause the sudden murder of every man wearing a gray coat. Happily the afternoon and night passed without violence, and the soldiers were amenable to reason by the next day. . . .

CHAPTER

Twenty-Two

[*Cadwallader arrived in Washington amid intense excitement. Soon afterward he was made head of the* Herald's *Washington news bureau. In that capacity he witnessed the execution of George Atzerodt, Davy Herold, Lewis Paine, and Mrs. Mary E. Surratt as accomplices in Lincoln's murder.*

In June 1865 he "scooped" all other reporters in obtaining a copy of the indictment of Jefferson Davis for treason. He held frequent interviews with Davis's lawyers at Willard's Hotel. Later he persuaded Secretary Stanton to allow him to interview Henry Wirz, commander of the Andersonville Prison, who had been condemned to death by a military court for mistreatment of Union prisoners.

Cadwallader was soon on intimate terms with President Andrew Johnson. He carefully reported the widening rift between Johnson and the radical Republicans over the reconstruction of the South, and warned Johnson that "neither of the old parties trust you. Between these two stools you are liable to get a fall."

In August 1865 James Gordon Bennett sent Cadwallader on a tour of the Northeastern states to appraise popular opinion on reconstruction policies. Later that month and during early September, Cadwallader accompanied President Johnson on his "swing around the circle," a speaking tour designed to gain popular support for Johnson's lenient reconstruction policies; and one of the most competent students of this period is of the opinion that Cadwallader's reports furnish the only trustworthy newspaper accounts of this trip, all the others having been highly colored by political bias.[1]

Cadwallader recalled that "the Cleveland Reception Committee on the train had a refreshment car loaded with eatables and potables, and waiters passed constantly through the cars, plying everybody to eat and drink. Gen. Grant had to be taken into a baggage car; compelled to lie down on a pile of empty sacks and rubbish; and remain there . . . till we reached Cleveland. Gen. Rawlins and myself stood guard over him, alternately, every mile of the way; locked out all callers for him; and protected him from observation as far as possible."

Toward the end Cadwallader's reminiscences take on the garrulousness of old age, and he seems to fumble for a stopping point. But interspersed with his ramblings are interesting sidelights on Grant, and on Grant's opinions of other generals, which, together with Cadwallader's own appraisals of those generals, make a significant commentary.

Cadwallader, for example, could never agree with those who regarded Sherman as a greater general than Grant. "Each gravitated to the position he was best qualified to fill," he thought.]

As a corps and department commander, Sherman had no superior when all the then circumstances and environments were taken into account. He was pre-eminently a man of ac-

---

[1] Howard K. Beale: *The Critical Year* (New York, 1930), p. 363, footnote.

tion, and exhibited his greatest qualities in aggressive movements and campaigns. The impetuosity of his character was exemplified wherever he was in supreme command.

In the famous Atlanta campaign he waged offensive warfare to the extreme limit of daring bravery, and often came close to the verge of rushing headlong into needless danger. But the greater strength of his army in men and material and his sagacious estimate of his opponent's weakness enabled him to retrieve such errors as were occasionally made, without the carnage and delay which might otherwise have ensued. But it is a matter of grave doubt whether he could ever have brought any Fabian policy to final success. His temperament forbade a "waiting race."

He was never subjected to the test of a defensive campaign; but it is not probable that he could have equaled Gen. Joseph E. Johnston, had their positions been reversed.

He would have chafed like a caged wild beast, would have rushed into hopeless battle, would have risked too much upon the decision of one day's fighting. He was thoroughly subordinate and obedient to higher military authority, and enforced his favorite maxim, that "the first duty of a soldier was obedience," by obeying all orders in letter and spirit. This quality, perhaps above all others, endeared him to Gen. Grant.

But he lacked Grant's superb equipoise. He often failed to control his temper. Had he been made Lieut. General in 1864, instead of Grant, it is morally certain he never could have tranquilized the jealousies and animosities existing in the Army of the Potomac; and doubly certain that he would have quarreled with half of the corps commanders in less than six weeks.

Grant always exhibited marvelous self-control and was thereby enabled to control others. There was scarcely ground

for comparing the two men. Grant was immeasurably above
Sherman in many essential elements of true military great-
ness. . . .

[*Cadwallader thought Grant loved Sherman like a brother,
but that he had greater trust in Sheridan.*]

His attachment for Sheridan sprang from his unbounded
belief in his abilities as a great commander. He thought Sheridan free from many of Sherman's infirmities of temper, and
cooler in judgment. It was well known to Grant's intimates that
he considered Sheridan the ablest general of the war on either
side.

[*Looking back after the lapse of years, Cadwallader thought
that, of all the Union generals, Meade had fallen farthest short
of the appreciation he had earned.*]

. . . Unavoidable circumstances growing out of the emer-
gencies of war, often made him the military "football" of these
days: but the sober second thought of the American people
ought to have corrected, long before this, much injustice
there done him. That he was a great soldier, is scarcely denied by any one. But Grant, Sherman, Sheridan, Wilson and
even Logan became for a time the popular idols, and made it
difficult to give Gen. Meade the place in the list that his services deserved. . . .

Gen. Meade's military and classical education was at least
equal to that of any officer in the Union army. His integrity
was never questioned. His capacity to command great armies
is no longer disputed. His comprehension of strategy was
rarely at fault. His tactics were those of the best schools,
broadened by experience in the field, and modified by the
ever-changing conditions constantly confronting him. For a
few months after assuming command of the Army of the

Potomac he allowed the opinions of his corps commanders, and the decisions of two or three councils of war, to over-ride his own judgment; and in every recorded instance it was afterwards proven that his own instincts and convictions were the wisest. Had he acted on these, independent of advice, and in disregard of the opinions of his less competent subordinates, it would have placed several splendid achievements to his credit, and greatly enhanced his reputation in public opinion. . . .

My acquaintance with Gen. Meade began on the Wilderness battle field, extended to Appomattox, and became intimate after the war. Gen. Grant's estimate of Meade's character was no doubt sincere; but I think it magnified the infirmities of his temper. I never witnessed the slightest exhibition of it.[2] He was uniformly dignified, polite, attentive and generally quite affable in demeanor, under all the conditions I ever saw surrounding him. His health was greatly impaired by the strain and anxiety of the opening campaign of 1865. He was obliged to make the march from Petersburg through Jetersville to Appomattox in an ambulance, and should have been in the hospital instead of camp. Some petulance and irritability is almost inseparable from such a bodily condition; and if it was sometimes manifested, deserved pity and compassion instead of the mildest criticism. I was with him nearly all of April 6th; all the afternoon of May [April] 8th; took supper with him that night; breakfasted with him at daylight on the morning of May [April] 9th, made memorable by Lee's surrender—and found him remarkably cheerful and pleasant in manners at all times. In all our after meetings

[2] Cadwallader has evidently forgotten the Crapsey incident. See pp. 206–10.

for years, he proved to be an accomplished gentleman. He was as free from personal or professional vanity as Gen. Grant himself. . . .

In my own opinion Gen. Meade combined in larger measure than Sherman the requisites for successfully commanding all the armies of the United States. He had better command of himself, and was therefore better fitted to command others. Sherman was often beside himself with anger and wrath. Meade was always a conventional gentleman in manners. Sherman was never polished in bearing and deportment; but was often brusque and insulting. Meade rarely gave offense to subordinates, or superiors. Sherman's impulsive temperament frequently made enemies. Meade was correct in speech and act. Sherman was often very profane. Meade was a man of deliberate conservative judgment; whilst Sherman was preeminently a man of swift executive tendencies. . . .

[*Cadwallader had little respect for Halleck and believed that Halleck, in his relations with Grant, had played a two-faced role. This opinion was confirmed by the discovery of certain papers that Halleck inadvertently left behind him when, shortly after the close of the war, he was put in command of the Department of Virginia and moved his headquarters to Richmond.*]

The large building which he had occupied nearly opposite and a little south of the old War Department on Eighteenth street, was assigned to Gen. Grant for his headquarter accommodation. Halleck had gone through the records and papers of his office rather carelessly; had transferred such as seemed of value to the War and Executive officers; and destroyed, as he supposed, all the others. Among the articles of office furniture left by him was a case of "pigeon-holes" (half filled with apparent rubbish and waste paper) which Col. Bowers concluded to empty and use himself. Before consigning its contents to the flames he examined some of them mechanically, and came upon a bundle of telegrams to the president and secretary of war, from Gen. Halleck, while the latter was in command at St. Louis. These he considered might be worth reading.

That Halleck had been insincere and treacherous to Grant was firmly believed by nearly every member of the latter's staff while in the west. Although professing the warmest friendship for him in personal unofficial intercourse, Halleck was Grant's insidious enemy from Cairo to Vicksburg. To a careful reader of Halleck's official correspondence, this is everywhere apparent. The occupation of Paducah drew but faint praise—the capture of Fort Henry was largely credited to others—the siege and reduction of Fort Donelson was barely acknowledged to his credit—Grant's trip to Nashville immediately afterward, was sharply rebuked—the battle of Shiloh was pronounced an unpardonable blunder—the credit for our final victory there was given to Buell, so far as Halleck could bestow it, and all the losses charged to Grant—and nothing but his own ignominious failure in front of Corinth decided him to return to St. Louis and leave Grant in command. . . .

During all the time covered by the foregoing events, Halleck was profuse in expressions of friendship to Grant when face to face; but was secretly telegraphing to Washington that he was incompetent, insubordinate, drunken, and unfit to command. These telegrams found by Col. Bowers were filled with such complaints and charges. I read many of them, and have not overstated the case. But Grant's faith in Halleck's friendship remained unshaken through all this troublous period down to that day.

Gen. Rawlins, Col. Bowers and myself discussed at great

. . . length what should be done with these tell-tale proofs of Halleck's duplicity?

It was decided to inclose several of them in a closely sealed envelope, addressed to Gen. Grant "personally," and leave them upon his desk. He thus first acquired indubitable evidence of Halleck's false friendship. The nobleness of Grant's character was never more strikingly revealed than by this mischanced disclosure. He never allowed it to embitter him against Halleck, but spoke of the matter forgivingly and tenderly, as an instance of his infirmity having overcome his other admirable qualities. He was sorry the telegrams had been shown to him, and said that he would have greatly preferred remaining in ignorance concerning them, and been left to believe in Halleck's friendship. His own good fortune had greatly exceeded his highest hopes—and was still in the ascendant—whilst Halleck's was on the wane, and certain to leave him a disappointed man. . . .[3]

[*Cadwallader believed that the grinding poverty of Grant's early married life left a permanent impression on his character, and that it largely explains his later financial indiscretions.*]

---

[3] General McClellan states in *My Own Story* (New York, 1886), p. 217: "In the latter part of 1866, while I was in Europe, Gen. Grant, through one of his staff, communicated with Gen. [R. B.] Marcy [McClellan's father-in-law and also his former chief of staff] in regard to papers missing from the files of the office of general-in-chief during my tenure of the place.

"In searching my papers Gen. Marcy found my retained copy of the dispatch of March 2 [1862] from Halleck in which he reports Grant's unauthorized absence, etc. This he forwarded to Gen. Grant, who was thus for the first time informed of the truth. This dispatch and my reply had, with many others, disappeared from the files in the office. So with regard to my correspondence as general-in-chief."

Thus McClellan confirms Cadwallader's assertions as to the disappearance of the files, but if Cadwallader's recollection is correct, Grant had already learned of Halleck's double-dealing.

. . . He had been driven into avocations which, to him, were humiliating, to obtain a bare support for his family. His army habits of undue conviviality unfitted him for close application to any business pursuit, and made him untrustworthy in the estimation of his father and brothers, and of his father-in-law, W. Dent. They were at length compelled to throw him more upon his own resources.

The stories of his hauling and selling wood for a living in the streets of St. Louis are known to all, and are true. When he moved his family to Galena, Illinois, he entered his father's leather store at that place on the footing of a common clerk and traveling salesman, with no interest in the business. His brother Orville was the head of the concern, and general manager. U. S. Grant drew a monthly salary only. When made colonel of a regiment he borrowed from outsiders the money to pay for horse and equipments. His own relations were slow to believe in his future success. As he rose through rapid promotions to command the department of the Tennessee, his increased pay enabled him to save some money, and it stands to his credit that the lessons of adversity were not lost in his case; and that he commenced a careful investment of his surplus earnings, mainly I think under the advice and direction of J. Russell Jones of Chicago. At the end of the war he had accumulated thousands of dollars.

Then followed generous gifts and benefactions of houses, lands and money, from municipalities and grateful citizens. His large salary as Lieutenant-General soon made him a rich man. There was a strong element of Scotch thrift developed, which he retained to the end of his life. He was accused of undue readiness to accept gifts, even after his election as President, and it cannot be denied that he often swerved close to the line of impropriety. His behavior contrasted glaringly in that particular with the conduct of all his predecessors in office; and with none more than that of Thomas Jefferson and Andrew Johnson, both of whom studiously avoided this apparent evil.

No man is wholly impervious to such environments, and it was universally felt that his nomination of Alexander Stewart, of New York, for Secretary of the Treasury, was one unfit to be made for this reason.[4] Mr. Stewart had the good sense to decline the doubtful honor; but Grant never quite outgrew the odium. Gen. Grant was incorruptibly honest, as he interpreted the term. No doubt he believed sincerely that Stewart would fill the office with signal ability (as he probably would have done); he was not conscious of being influenced by the millionaire's gifts; and he saw no reason why he should not appoint him to office.

There are reasons for believing that the days of Gen. Grant's Galena clerkship, under the direction and control of his brother, were sometimes trying and exasperating. The latter was of coarser fibre, and not very considerate in his exactions. He thought only of the "shop," was vain of his position, and asserted a superiority that must have been difficult to bear with. He handled leather, thought only of leather, measured all things by leather, until by the natural law of assimilation he grew to be leathery, and leather-headed. He held the purse strings of the concern, and doubtless doled out his brother's salary in a disagreeable manner. The general was driven to every available method of earning a few dollars outside the store, as opportunities offered.

One circumstance which came to my knowledge shows the extremity to which he was reduced. A few nights after Grant's

---

[4] Stewart was the millionaire owner of the country's largest drygoods business and of other large concerns.

first election to the Presidency was certainly known, a great crowd of politicians and public men of the state were assembled at the Newhall House, Milwaukee, Wisconsin. Among them was Mr. James H. Earnest, who was for years a state senator from the Mineral Point district, and closely identified with the railroad legislation of Wisconsin. When the Milwaukee & Prairie du Chien railroad was first projected Mr. Earnest was actively interested in the struggle to have the line located from Waukesha (then called Prairieville) through Janesville and Monroe, and thence on to Galena, instead of to Prairie du Chien.

Mr. Earnest took me into a secluded corner of the hotel corridor, and said he wished to give me a scrap of unwritten history, which would not bear publication at that time. After enjoining me to secrecy he proceeded (with bated breath) to narrate one of his experiences. He was one of a committee from Galena and south-western Wisconsin selected to attend a meeting at Janesville, to formulate plans for obtaining a right of way, and cash subscriptions, to secure the desired railroad. When this committee was ready to leave Galena, in carriages, for Janesville, it was found that for some reason the driver of one of the carriages had failed to put in his appearance.

The committee was impatient, and the person having the transportation in charge, was making ineffectual efforts to get another driver. Some one said: "Send for Grant, he'll go." Grant was sent for—came promptly—mounted the box—and drove the carriage in which Earnest and three others were seated. None of them knew Grant; but supposed him to be some hanger-on of the livery stable waiting for a job. The party was generously supplied with sandwiches and spiritus frumenti. The driver was invited to join them whenever the bottle was passed around; and they were not long in discovering that he was companionable, intelligent, and for some reason, out of place as a common hack driver. But no troublesome questions were asked on their part, and no information proffered on the other.

At the end of a two or three days' journey the party arrived at Janesville, and the committee quartered at the best hotel in the place. They voted the driver a good fellow, and directed him to put up his team where he pleased, and come back to the hotel and remain with them, at their charge during their stay. But he declined the invitation, sought cheaper accommodations, and they saw but little of him till ready for the return trip.

His behavior provoked some curiosity, and when back at Galena they were informed that he was a West Point graduate who had been mustered out of the United States service for some cause which no one seemed to know or care much about. "That man Grant is President of the United States," said Mr. Earnest; and "I will never doubt the truth of scriptural miracles hereafter." Experiences, such as these, brought Gen. Grant to a greater appreciation of money than he otherwise would have had.

[*Cadwallader was not satisfied with any of the photographs or portraits of Grant. None of them showed the general to advantage, he thought, nor were they true to life.*]

. . . He seemed constrained and unnatural when sitting for pictures, and was too stiff and austere in appearance to do himself justice. In his every day life he was inclined to carelessness in dress and attitude. His clothing was unexceptionable in quality and condition, but his manner of wearing it was scarcely up to military requirements. It is safe to say that no one ever saw him with his coat buttoned up to his chin except on ceremonial occasions. Three or four lower buttons of his vest were all he commonly used. His linen was conspicuous, but immaculate. His overcoat was generally the army blue of regulation pattern no wise differing from those of officers and privates, with nothing on it to distinguish him or denote rank. He had finer and better overcoats for journeys, or state occasions; but never wore them in the field. . . .

In the fall or winter of 1864 or 1865, some New York friends presented him with a new one. The material was as fine as could be purchased, and the workmanship artistic. I was present when it was unpacked, inspected, and tried on. The cut, fit, and finish, was perfect. After a few minutes' silence he remarked: "There have been times in my life when the gift of an overcoat would have been an act of charity. No one gave it to me when I needed it. Now when I am able to pay for all I need, such gifts are continually thrust upon me." He was thinking sorrowfully of the storms and privations of St. Louis and Galena.

When standing, his ordinary attitude was that of having his head and shoulders thrown forward till he had the appearance of being a trifle round-shouldered. He also had an inveterate habit of thrusting both hands into the pockets of his pants when walking about headquarters or camp, and usually had a cigar clenched between his teeth, whether smoking, or not. It will be seen he was no military "dude." On horseback, when riding faster than a walk, he threw himself well forward from the hips upward, which gave him a look of eagerness and haste as though he were anxious to forge ahead faster than his horse could go. Because of these peculiarities of figure and habit, any pictorial representing him as standing perfectly erect, with coat buttoned to the throat, posing as a military martinet, would seem unreal to those who saw him oftenest in periods of relaxation. . . .

[*Cadwallader's last meeting with Grant occurred at the Palmer House, in Chicago, sometime after Grant's Presidency. Grant had arrived unannounced on a morning train, breakfasted alone, and retired to his room. A colored boy, who took up Cadwallader's card, returned, bowing and grinning, with the invitation: "Walk up, sir, Gen. Grant will be very glad to see you." Cadwallader found Grant enjoying a cigar, and the two men talked of business and family matters for an hour before Grant's presence became known and a rush of visitors began.*

[*In a final summing up, Cadwallader conceded:*]

There was a vein of carelessness and indolence running through Gen. Grant's character plainly discernible to those who knew him intimately, which seemed at variance with his other qualities of mind, of which I have heretofore said nothing. He disliked the laborious details of office work, and would have been a very inefficient Adjutant General of the United States Army. It was not so much a lack of knowledge and ability in this direction, as lack of application. His plans for marches and campaigns were clearly outlined to his Adjutant, and Chief-of-Staff; and every detail of each quite apt to be thereafter wholly left to them for execution. He was careless, unmethodical, and unbusinesslike, to a remarkable degree in these respects, of which many instances could be given if necessary. . . .

[*But neither these shortcomings nor the vicissitudes of Grant's Presidential years diminished Cadwallader's high opinion of him:*]

. . . He was pure in speech and heart, and came within

one of the "beatitudes." Through all my intercourse with him I never heard an oath (or any substitute for one) escape his lips. He abominated "smutty" stories and would not listen to them. He was honest. His few blemishes of character were incident to our common humanity; and instead of seriously damaging him in the estimation of right-minded men, will tend to emphasize his virtues, which were many and strongly pronounced. I have recorded his principal infirmities plainly, but tenderly. They were the only spots upon his character. The splendor of his achievements will prove amply sufficient to cover all minor imperfections.

Note: Roman numerals refer to the Editor's Introduction, which in the original edition began on page v.

Index